CENTURY OF FAITH

One Hundred Years in the Life of
Las Placitas Presbyterian Church

CENTURY OF FAITH

One Hundred Years in the Life of
Las Placitas Presbyterian Church

by
Suzanne Sims Forrest

Las Placitas Presbyterian Church Placitas, New Mexico

Cover art by Dorothy Bowen

ISBN-10: 172601987X
ISBN-13: 978-1726019873

Century of Faith was originally published in 1995 by Desert Dreams Publishers. This 2016 edition includes updated information and a new Afterword prepared by Las Placitas Presbyterian Church, Placitas, New Mexico, in collaboration with the author. It has been republished in 2016 by Las Placitas Presbyterian Church. All rights reserved.

Printed in the USA by Create Space, An Amazon.com company.

To the People of Placitas
and especially to
the members of
Las Placitas Presbyterian Church

ACKNOWLEDGMENTS

The writing of this history would not have been possible without the help of many, many people who offered information, ideas, help, encouragement and inspiration. First and foremost are those who invited me into their homes or offices and allowed me to record their memories on tape. They are, in alphabetical order, Jim Anderson, Jeanne Army, Carlos Candelaria, Dulcilina Salce Curtis, Rubén Cobos, Florinda and Antonio DeLara, Max DeLara, Tomás Gonzalez, Tony Lucero, Norma Martinez, George Randle, Reynaldo Salazar, Sam and Siria Salazar, Ruthie (Mrs. Howard) Schleeter, Kendall and Wilda Schlenker, David Tafoya, and Harry Willson. Others who gave me information orally or who wrote brief notes are Sally Curro, Kenneth Green, David Hammack, Antonio Jiménez, II, Laurie Macrae, Lynn Montgomery, Floyd Sovereign, and Samuel Torres. Reverend George Jacob Adams wrote a short history of his pastorate especially for this book. Bert DeLara, Willie Escarcida, and Amarante Lucero assisted with the oral histories, the latter two providing me with their own memories and those of Willie's aunt, Celia Longacre. Laurie Macrae, librarian at the Bernalillo Public Library, helped me secure books and provided information on local history. Martha Liebert, former Bernalillo Librarian and present archivist for the Sandoval County Historical Society, supplied me with many photographs from the collection and helped to locate and date other bits of local history. Lauretta Dickey loaned me her unpublished compilation of New Mexico Presbyterian History.

Dr. Carlos Vasquez, Director of the Oral History Program at the Center for Southwest Research at the University of New Mexico, gave me much needed advice and encouragement as I learned to use this marvelous technique for gathering local history. Leland Bowen researched the kinds of materials needed, provided technical assistance, and later made copies of the tapes.

The Historical Library at the Menaul School proved to be an invaluable resource, and I am most grateful to Carolyn Atkins, who began the library some twenty years ago. Carolyn helped locate materials in the library, as did volunteers Marilyn Clark,

Mary Foster, and Mary Buchanan. Nancy Brown, archivist at the Center for Southwest Research in the Zimmerman Library at UNM, was most helpful in locating documents and obscure bits of information about Placitas. Orlando Romero at the Library of the Museum of New Mexico and Al Regensberg and Richard Salazar at the New Mexico State Records Center and Archives in Santa Fe were similarly helpful.

Tony Lucero, of the San Antonio de las Huertas Land Grant Association, provided me with land grant documents and his perspectives of the past history of the Grant. Jim Walker, Southwest Regional Director of the Archaeological Conservancy, sent me valuable information on the San José de Las Huertas site, and Homer Milford, Environmental Coordinator of the Abandoned Mine Bureau of the New Mexico State Department of Energy, Minerals and Natural Resources, sent me information on New Mexico mining history.

This history was immensely enriched by the background information provided by the interviews made by Lou Sage Batchen, Max DeLara, and Christina Gonzales during the 1930s and 1940s. The stories resulting from the interviews are in the W.P.A. files at the Library of the Museum of New Mexico and at the New Mexico State Records Center and Archives. Special thanks go to Mary Sartor who helped me copy and compile them.

I also want to thank those individuals who helped me round up the historical photographs for this book. They are Carlos Candelaria, Bert DeLara, Ephraim DeLara, Vivian DeLara, Frances Escarcida, Martha Liebert, Mia Martinez, Joséphine Ringling and Helen Sanchez. The late Jim Dickey, a retired professional photographer, brought his copy camera out to the Church to make negatives of photographs too precious to be relinquished by their owners for a longer time. I only regret that he did not live to see the results of his efforts.

Jim Army, Max DeLara, Lynn Montgomery, and George Randle helped identify local landmarks, and Sally and Jack Curro, and Ora and Cliff McCathron actually helped me find them. Dorothy Bowen, Sally Curro, Janice Fowler and Denise Raven helped edit the manuscript and prepare it for the printer. Dorothy Bowen, Wilda MacLauchlan and John Miller provided illustrations.

I also owe a debt of gratitude to Wendy Ingram and her husband, Glenn, for their careful and painstaking work of reviewing and revising the layout of this second edition. Also to fellow historian Sherrill Cloud for her eagle-eyed review and editing of the final product. Without their work this volume would never have been printed.

Finally, I must give special thanks and appreciation to my late historian husband, Jim, who listened with great interest to each new tidbit of information, helped me think through historical puzzles, read and commented on each chapter, and put up with the disheveled household that is the inevitable result of a writer at work.

TABLE OF CONTENTS

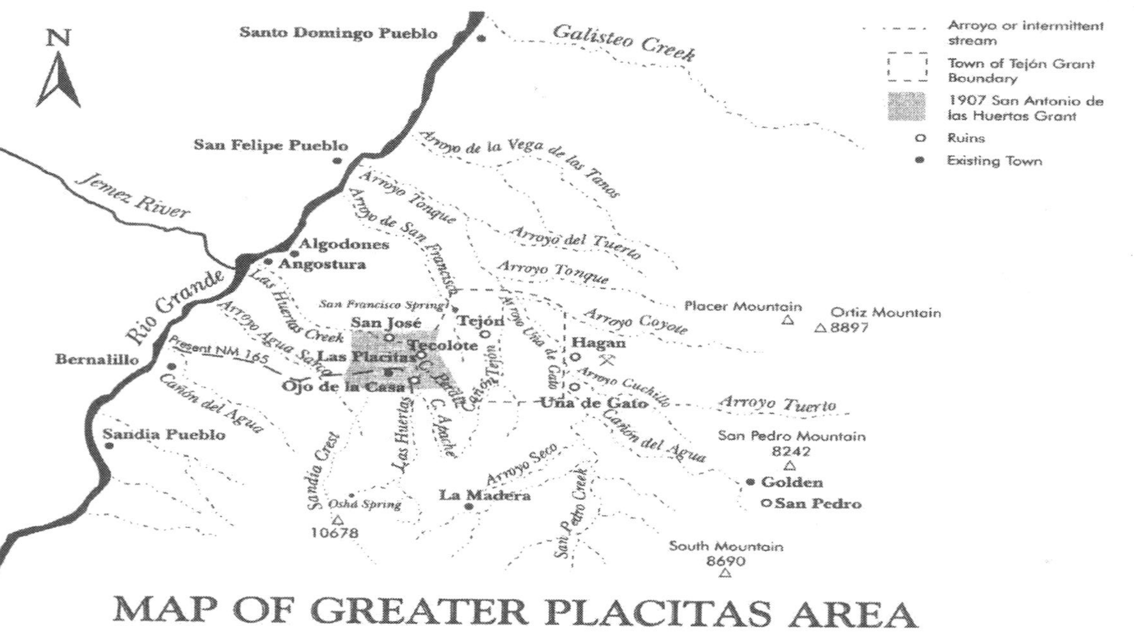

MAP OF GREATER PLACITAS AREA

Most of the displayed map area was included in the original 1768 San Antonio de Las Huertas Land Grant before its eventual reduction to the 1907 boundaries indicated

PROLOGUE

The night was crisp and cold and fragrant with the smoke from piñon wood fires that night in late February 1894. They came from all corners of the village, by twos and threes, trudging down dark streets to the little mission school house. Some fifty souls they were, and as they greeted each other, they whispered in hushed tones of the momentous event to come.

They crowded inside—there was barely room for everyone in the little room lit with kerosene lamps and warmed by a potbelly stove. At the front, where the teacher usually stood, were the principal players in the drama. They had arrived earlier in the day, and would stay the night, as they had many times in the past, at the home of prominent villager *Don* José Librado Aron Gurulé. First of all, there was *Don* José Ynés Perea, son of the wealthy Perea family of Bernalillo and the nation's first ordained Hispanic Presbyterian minister. They respectfully addressed each other according to the Spanish honorific custom of using *Don* or *Doña* before first names. With *Don* Ynés, as he was called, were three friends and associates, the Mexican evangelists *Don* Epifanio Arreola and *Don* Santos Arreola and the Irish-born missionary James Menaul.

All but Menaul were familiar faces. They had been making regular visits to the village for more than a decade, ever since 1882, when *Don* José Gurulé had first invited the Reverend *Don* Ynés to visit the village. Lucas Gurulé, *Don* José's uncle, was a personal friend of Reverend Perea. Lucas, who was then in his eighties and had moved to nearby Algodones, had offered his house for that first meeting with *Don* Ynés.

The 1882 meeting had opened with the hymn "Rock of Ages," the first Protestant hymn to be sung in this area. Reverend Perea preached his message of divine redemption through the Gospel of Jesus Christ to a skeptical audience, that first visit. But his message burst forth as a bright and shining truth. When he finished, the little group of Las Placitas villagers pressed him to tell them more. The hardiest stayed to talk until the wee hours of the morning. Those villagers present at that first meeting, besides *Don* José, were his father Nicolás, his uncle Lucas, Juan Antonio Perez, Preciliano Baros, and Francisco Trujillo.

Twelve years had passed. For a long while *Don* Ynés came every month. The priest in Bernalillo denounced him at Mass as a "corrupt and wicked heretic." He threatened excommunication to those who persisted in going to the services, but the villagers continued to be friendly and defied the priest. When Perea moved south of Albuquerque to establish a church in Pajarito, the Reverend John Menaul, cousin of James, continued the monthly visits. Menaul, who became pastor of the newly established Second Presbyterian Church in Albuquerque in 1889, often came accompanied by Epifanio Arreola, the Mexican evangelist whose impassioned sermons and patient work in the Martineztown community had been responsible for the establishment of that church. Arreola's sermons were just as compelling to the Placitas community as *Don* Ynés's had been.

Then, in August 1893, *Don* José Gurulé brought a Presbyterian schoolteacher to Placitas. Education was something everyone, young and old, wanted. Several years earlier the people of Placitas had sent a petition to the Board of Home Missions asking for a school. They knew that many communities had lost Presbyterian mission schools because of the opposition of the Catholic clergy. In their petition they wrote: "In this part of the country we are not afraid of the Priest or his threats." When word came that a teacher was available, *Don* José lost no time in harnessing his team of oxen and setting out to fetch her.[1]

The teacher, Lavinia Thompson, an Anglo woman from "back East," was prim and neat and warm and loving. Her little classroom was filled right from the beginning with students of all ages. Now just five months later, on that cold night in February 1894, a small but determined number of villagers were ready to take the final step and formally organize The Presbyterian Church at Las Placitas.

The minutes in English of that first organizing session, written by Rev. John Menaul (second Presbyterian pastor at Placitas and cousin of Rev. James Menaul), read as follows:

Organization of The Presbyterian Church at Las Placitas
February 24th – February 25th 1894

Being the earnest wish and petition of a large portion of the inhabitants, and pursuant to a previous call and appointment of our Synodical Missionary, Reverend James A. Menaul, the following persons met on February 24th 1894 at Las Placitas, New Mexico, for the purpose of organizing a church if the way be clear to wit: Reverend James A. Menaul, Reverend J.Y. Perea, and helpers Mr. Epifanio Arreola and Mr. Santos Arreola.

A meeting was called at the Mission School at 7 o'clock P.M.

We met at 7 o'clock P.M. at the Mission school house with some fifty persons in attendance. A sermon was preached by Rev. J.Y. Perea from Deuteronomy 30: 19 "Therefore choose life."

It was a solemn occasion in our lives, as we witnessed thirty-nine persons coming out into the marvelous light and liberty of the "glorious Gospel of the blessed God." The meeting having been prolonged beyond our expectation it was proposed to organize at the morning service at 10 o'clock A.M.

We met at 10 o'clock A.M. at the Mission School house. Present Reverend James A. Menaul, Reverend J.Y. Perea, Mr. Epifanio Arreola and Santos Arreola. After a deeply impressive sermon by Reverend James A. Menaul on Exodus 14: 15 "Speak unto the children of Israel that they go forward" the following persons presented themselves as candidates for admission to the full communion of the Presbyterian Church, a motion having been put to the congregation to ascertain how many persons desired such an organization and wished to become members of such a church. Ninety-five voted for the motion, none against it. The names are as follows, viz: Juan Baros, Francisco Trujillo, Irineo Gurulé, David Trujillo, Preciliano Baros, Daniel Trujillo, Melecia Trujillo, Virginia Trujillo, José Trujillo, Filipita Baros, Virginia Baros, José Baros, Santiago Baros, Agustin Baros (child),

Gabriela Baros (child), Barbara Baros, Placida Lucero, Ana Maria Lucero, Ursula de Lara, Lucianita Lara, Leonor Avela, Eufelia Mora, Antonio Gurulé, Carolina Gurulé, José Teodosio Gurulé (child), Juan Gonzales 1st, Juan Gonzales 2nd, Isabela Gonzales, Natividad Baros, Sipriano Salas, Santiago Martinez, Avelina Trujillo, Juliana Peres, Escelsa García, Floran Trujillo, Francisco Mora, Enrique Mora, Juanita Baros (child), Nicolás Gurulé (child).

These persons were severally examined respecting their experimental acquaintance with the Christian religion and their readiness to submit themselves to the discipline of Christ's house. Their examination being sustained they were received into full communion, after making public profession of their faith in Christ, baptism being administered by Reverend J.Y. Perea, the thirty nine applicants kneeling down as they received the holy sacrament one by one.

Mr. Francisco Trujillo and Mr. Juan Baros were unanimously elected elders, and solemnly ordained to that office by Reverend James A. Menaul. The Lord's supper was then administered by Reverend J.Y. Perea, elders Francisco Trujillo and Juan Baros distributing the elements, forty adult members partaking. The service closed with the Apostolic benediction. A service of Thanksgiving was held at 7 o'clock P.M.

After the service, Elder Juan Baros was appointed to represent the Church at the regular meeting of Presbytery, March 27th 1894.

Three trustees were unanimously elected. On motion the name of the Church is to be "The Presbyterian Church at Las Placitas."

Dismissed with the benediction.

Reverend J.Y. Perea, Clerk

CHAPTER I
San Antonio de Las Huertas

In the beginning was the Las Huertas Valley. Nestled snugly between high ridges on the north end of the Sandia Mountains, it was a verdant and sheltered oasis in the midst of an arid, often harsh and unyielding land. The sparkling spring-fed stream that carved the Valley dropped swiftly from the crest, leaping boulders and pooling in quiet depths, before emerging into a wide and fertile floodplain. Then, dissipating its life-giving moisture into the sands of a broad arroyo, it all but disappeared before surrendering its existence to the mother of waters, the Rio Grande.

From the beginning the Valley was home to all manner of wildlife, from the mighty mastodon and giant ground sloth of the last Ice Age to the rabbits, coyotes, bear, and deer that find food and refuge within its sheltered boundaries today. It has been home for human beings for almost as long as they have lived in North America. No one is quite sure just how long ago—8000 to 24,000 years—a roving band of humans occupied a cave high on the sunny south-facing wall of the canyon. They left some finely flaked tools, along with the bones of animals long extinct, to mark their presence and their passing.[1]

In the years that followed, thousands more left their foot-prints along the stream bed as they searched for piñon nuts and other fruits and berries and hunted and trapped animals for meat and hides. In time some people came to settle permanently. They lived in small villages—pueblos—and planted corn and beans, squash and melons, and they worshipped the spirits of the natural forces that made life in the Valley so abundant and agreeable.

In 1540, the life style that had existed for ages vanished in a flash of steel, the rumble of hoofs, and the acrid smell of gun smoke. New human beings from a different and distant world claimed the land in the name of God and the King of Spain. The Spaniards and their Mexican Indian allies, under their leader, Francisco Vasquez de Coronado, spent the long, harsh winters of 1540-41 and 1541-42 in the Pueblo of Kuaua just west of the Las Huertas Valley, on the far bank of the Rio Grande. The Spaniards had come north in search of gold, but there is no indication that Coronado discovered any signs of the precious metal. Nevertheless, it probably wasn't long before successors to this first party of exploration followed one of the arroyos back into the mountains and found silver and lead, at the entrance to the Las Huertas Valley in what has become known as the Montezuma Mine. At the same time the Spanish discovered the Valley's other source of wealth—its fruitfulness. They named the area Las Huertas, "The Orchards."

Sometime around 1660 one Diego de Trujillo built his home in the Valley. He had arrived in New Mexico about 1632 as a young man of 20 or 22. A second-generation Spaniard, he was born in Mexico City and was a soldier-farmer. By 1661, he had achieved considerable stature in the Spanish colony and was a sergeant major holding the twin posts of Lieutenant General of the Rio Abajo (Lower River) area and *alcalde mayor* (principal official) of the province of Zuni. His ranch, which he called Paraje de las Huertas, was described as being four leagues (approximately twelve miles) from the Pueblo of Sandia. The word *paraje* means stopping place or campground. Its use suggests what later testimony confirms—that Diego built his home on or near a well-known stopping place at the crossing of two ancient trails through the mountains.

Diego and his family farmed and possibly mined silver and lead in the Valley until one frightful day in August 1680, when news reached him that the Pueblo Indians were in rebellion. Exhausted and resentful after two generations of religious persecution, forced labor, and tribute, the Indians ransacked churches, slew priests at the altar, and murdered men, women, and children. Diego fled to refuge in El Paso del Norte, and lived to give his opinions about the causes and problems of the Pueblo Revolt. But he never again saw his old home. He died at Casas Grandes in 1682.[2]

Diego de Trujillo's grandson, Juan de Trujillo, returned with the Reconquest, but instead of reclaiming the family lands at Las Huertas he bought property in the Pojoaque area.[3] Very probably Las Huertas was too vulnerable to attack by the fierce Faraón Apaches, who regularly raided the pueblos and wreaked havoc in the countryside. The Apaches likely entered the Rio Grande Valley from the east by way of one or both of the ancient trails through the mountains that merged at the old Paraje de las Huertas. But like all trails, they went both ways. *Don* Diego de Vargas, who had reconquered New Mexico in 1692, passed through in 1704 with a force of soldiers and Pueblo scouts on a mission of reprisal. He records that he marched his men down river as far as the village of Bernalillo, then followed the Apaches' trail southeastward through the Sandia Mountains.[4] The legacy of this turbulent past remains in the place name Apache Canyon.

Despite the threat of Indian attack, Spanish settlers were soon lured back to the fruitful valley. By mid-century the Hispanic population was rapidly outgrowing the better protected lands along the Rio Grande and the Chihuahua Trail, otherwise known as the Camino Real, the vital lifeline between Santa Fe and New Spain. Settlers were actively looking for new lands to farm, and at first they ventured out only for the day, returning at night to homes along the river. Then, in 1765, a resident of Bernalillo named Juan Gutierres petitioned the King of Spain to grant this land to him and eight other family heads and their heirs in perpetuity.

It was an old Spanish custom, this matter of granting land. Land was granted to individuals for special service to the crown and to communities to provide for a stable, settled population. So it was that Gutierres appeared before Governor Tomás Velez Cachupin to request the San Antonio de las Huertas land grant. His petition, translated from the Spanish, reads as follows:

> To the Governor and Captain General—I, Juan Gutierres, a resident of the place Bernalillo, appear before your Excellency in due form and, Sir, I declare that finding myself with a large family and without any place to live upon, for I am compelled to sell the Pueblo of Santa Ana a ranch from which I have supported myself in order to enable me to pay off some debts. I have therefore registered a tract of vacant public land at the place commonly called Las Huertas, at the foot of the Sandia Mountain, opposite the said place Bernalillo, which tract I petition for, and I beg of your Excellency that in the name of his Majesty, whom may God preserve, you be pleased to grant the same to me for myself and eight families who, owing to the sale of my said ranch, have nowhere to pasture the few livestock they have and nowhere to cultivate. Those families are: Andrés de Aragón (one of his sons called José), Javiel Gutierres, José Antonio Rael, Antonio Archibeque, Miguel Gallegos, Matias Gutierres, and José Gonzales. All of them have like myself large families, for which reason, and as we find ourselves situated as I have set forth, we, collectively and each for himself, make to your Excellency this application, praying that we be treated with your customary justice and as descendants of the pacificators of this country. And should your Excellency make us the said grant its boundaries are: on the East the brow of the mountain on the San Pedro road, on the West some high hills pertaining to Las Huertas aforesaid, on the North the brow of the Casa Colorado Mountain, and on the South a red hill. These boundaries would not injure anyone, and we have ascertained that there will be sufficient water and cultivable land for eight families as in former times the said spot was inhabited. In consideration of all which I request, for myself and in the name of all the parties aforenamed, that your Excellency be pleased to make us

> the grant we have asked, whereby we and our children and successors will receive great benefit and favor. And I declare, for myself and in the name of all the parties aforementioned, that we do not act in dissimulation.[5]

Upon receipt of the petition Governor Velez Cachupin directed Bartolomé Fernández, *alcalde mayor* of the Pueblo of Santo Domingo, to notify the Pueblos of the petition and report to him whether granting it would be to the prejudice of the native Indians. In October 1765, Fernández reported that he had found no impediment to the Governor's making the solicited grant. Two years passed during which time Velez Cachupin left office. In December 1767, the settlers at Las Huertas resubmitted their petition to his successor, Pedro Fermín de Mendinueta. By this time the number of families had grown to twenty-one. The family heads listed their names as Andrés de Aragón, Bisente Sena, Antonio Galban, Matias Gutierres, Pedro Gutierres, Miguel Gallegos, Nicolás Montoya, José Chaves, José Antonio Valencia, Serafin Gurulé, Martín Gurulé, Juan Gurulé, Juan Maese, Francisco Lobera, Antonia Archibeque, Antonio Gurulé, Juan Baldez, Alberto Montoya, Juan García, José García, and Pedro García Jurado. Fermín de Mendinueta acted promptly. He examined the documents submitted to his predecessor and declared that, in the name of His Majesty, the settlers were awarded a grant of land to be known as San Antonio de Las Huertas.

There were some provisions to the land grant. The settlers were instructed to build the settlement in accordance with the royal laws of Spain, in the form of a fortified plaza with houses of adobes in such manner that each house had a corral for livestock. They also had to provide space for additional homes should the settlement increase. For reasons of mutual defense, no settler was to be permitted to build a house outside the plaza. The settlers were ordered to sow wheat, corn, and other vegetables and to set out fruit trees. For the purpose of carrying out these provisions, Mendinueta empowered Alcalde Fernández to mark out the most convenient spot for the plaza, with a lot for each of the families, and to distribute the cultivable land, marking the boundaries with permanent landmarks so as to avoid future controversies. Fermín de Mendinueta also noted a change from the boundaries named in the earlier petition submitted to Cachupin. Because of the increased number of families listed in the second petition as well as their probable increase and because expansion to the north, west, and south would infringe on the Pueblos of San Felipe and Santa Ana and the settlers of Bernalillo, he would extend the eastern boundary. The terms of this extension were to be set forth in the Act of Possession.

The actual granting of the land took place on January 13, 1768. Alcalde Fernández assembled the citizens of the settlement and informed them of the decree. He then led them on a tour of the land, pointing out the boundaries and directing that landmarks be set up so that each might know the extent of his lands. Each settler plucked up weeds and cast stones as a sign of possession. Then all shouted three times, "Long live the King, and may God preserve him." With that ceremony the residents of San Antonio de las Huertas took quiet and peaceable possession of their land.

It is hard for us to comprehend today how very simple and devoid of comforts and conveniences life was at that time in the area we call Placitas. The people had no metal tools or weapons. As late as the 1860s the people of Las Huertas still used bows and arrows with stone points to defend themselves against the Indians and to hunt game. They used ceramic pots, exchanged in trade with the Pueblo Indians, for cooking. Most travel to and from the village was on foot. No one had horses, but there were a few oxen in the village for the heavier farming chores, such as dragging the clumsy wooden plows. Sheep and goats provided milk, cheese, wool, and meat. The women made clothing by hand of leather or wool, the latter spun into yarn and woven on a heavy hand-hewn treadle loom. On their feet they wore the same kind of moccasins as their Indian neighbors. They called them *teguas.*

Houses were typically no more than 30 to 32 feet in length and 15 to 16 feet in width. They commonly had two rooms, one a living-kitchen area with a large bell-shaped fireplace called a *fogón,* the other a room for sleeping. The functions of the rooms could be interchanged. In the winter, the room on the sun-warmed south side of the house became the living-kitchen area. In summer, the kitchen was moved to the cool north side. Doorways usually opened to the east, to the morning sun. Neither room had any beds, tables, or chairs. People sat or hunkered on the floor around the fogón and either ate with their fingers or used a tortilla as a spoon. At night everyone rolled up in blankets and slept either on the floor or on one of the low adobe benches, *bancos*, along the wall. During the day the sleeping blankets were hung on a wooden pole out of the way or were rolled up and used as sitting cushions. The only formal piece of furniture might be a wooden chest to store family valuables.

The houses were built of adobe bricks. With walls 20 to 30 inches thick, and windows tiny and set up high on the walls, they were miniature fortresses. And well they had to be because of the frequency of Indian attack. If it was not the Apaches who raided the settled villages, both Spanish and Pueblo, it was the Comanches or the Navajos. Villagers got accustomed to paying a kind of extortion. The Indians would swoop down on them, carry off their stores of corn and beans and run off with their sheep and goats, and sometimes their children, but they always left enough that, with natural increase, they could expect to find more when they returned the following year. The Navajos even had a saying: "The Spanish are our shepherds."

What the settlers could not produce at home they obtained in trade from their Pueblo neighbors at Sandia, Santa Ana and San Felipe. The villagers not only shared a common life style with their Pueblo neighbors; many had relatives in the Pueblos. Marriages between Spanish villagers and Pueblo Indians, particularly in the early days, were not uncommon. The two peoples assisted each other with defense against the marauding nomadic tribes, and in time of great need, the Spanish settler fortunate enough to claim an Indian kinsman could seek protection within the larger and better fortified Indian community. The Pueblos, left alone to practice their religion as they wished, laid to rest their earlier hatred of the Spanish. Life was hard enough on this frontier. One needed good neighbors. [6]

So it was that life passed in the little village known as San José de las Huertas until 1823. In the meantime Mexico fought and won a war of independence from Spain. But with the Spanish army no longer available to protect the northern province, the Apaches, Navajos, Comanches, and Utes stepped up their raiding. Unable to offer protection to the more isolated villages, the new governor, Antonio Vizcarra, ordered Las Huertas settlers to abandon their homes and fields and take shelter with friends and relatives in the better protected areas along the Rio Grande.

The settlers complied, but only with deep regret and a fierce determination to return as soon as conditions allowed. Calletano Chavez, who died in Placitas in 1913, told his nephew Patricio Chavez the story of how his family left Las Huertas.

> I was fifteen years old. I remember the people putting their things together to leave the place. I went with some other boys to take the goats to the mountains for food. Our fathers told us when we brought the goats in that they would be gone and for us to drive the goats down the canyon to Algodones. They would be there looking for us. When we brought in the goats the houses were all empty and nobody was there, so we drove the goats down to Algodones.[7]

No more than a dozen years passed before the Las Huertas settlers began moving cautiously back to their grant lands, drawn by what they described as "the call of the blood."[8] When they did, they discovered that a severe drought had dried up the springs near the old walled village of San José de Las Huertas. Since they were no longer constrained by Spanish laws to live within a confined area, sixteen families moved a mile south to a place known from ancient times as Las Placitas, because it marked the spot of several small Indian ruins. They named it San Antonio de Padua de Las Placitas.

Several families followed the ancient trail leading east out of San José de Las Huertas to the buffalo country to a spot about four miles distant called Tejón. It was a flat, fertile, well-watered tract that, though it lacked good drinking water, was ideally situated for trade. Not only buffalo hunters passed that way. By 1840, the pass through the mountains had become the southern extension of the Santa Fe Trail. Traders and wagons from Albuquerque, Bernalillo, and places even further south passed by on their way to Las Vegas, the starting point for the annual caravan to "*Los Estados*." Tejón became an important overnight stopping place.

With the discovery of gold in the San Pedro Mountains in 1839, twenty Las Huertas settlers, led by Ramón Gurulé and Jesus Miera, settled on the far east side of the grant at a place they called San Pedro Rancho. A few years later they sold their rights to this land to an attorney named José Serafin Ramirez and moved a short distance away to a place they called La Madera. Although they were several miles distant from Las Placitas, the two villages were connected by a narrow passage through the mountains that made communication relatively easy and kept the families in close association.

Other families settled about a half mile east of old San José de Las Huertas at the spot where the Tejón Road crossed Las Huertas creek. They called this place Tecolote. Later, when water from the springs had become more abundant, families from Algodones and Tejón moved a couple of miles up Las Huertas canyon to a place where a clear cold spring provided water for irrigation. To keep livestock from muddying the water, someone built a little stone house over the spring, and the area became known as Ojo de la Casa. The legendary Montezuma silver and lead mine lay directly above it in the north wall of the canyon.[9] And so, the old village of San José de Las Huertas became five separate communities, all populated by descendants of the original San Antonio de Las Huertas land grant community, together with many newer settlers; and all, they believed, were situated securely within the lands granted to them in perpetuity by the King of Spain in 1768.

José Librado Aron Gurulé (1851-1943) was a visionary who brought a new religion to Las Placitas. In 1882, he arranged a meeting of six prominent villagers with Rev. José Ynés Perea to learn more about Presbyterianism. José L. A. Gurulé's leadership eventually led to the establishment of a Presbyterian Mission School and a Presbyterian Church in Placitas. Living to the age of 92, he continued to support and sustain the Church, as have his descendants.
Photo courtesy Florinda Gurulé DeLara.

Rev. José Ynés Perea, son of the wealthy Catholic Perea family of Bernalillo, sought a different path in life. Ordained to the Presbyterian ministry in September 1880, Rev. Perea was the nation's first ordained Hispanic Presbyterian minister. After meeting with six Placitas villagers led by José L. A. Gurulé in 1882, he and other missionaries came to Placitas often over the next several years. Their visits culminated in Rev. Perea leading an organizational meeting on February 24-25, 1894 that founded The Presbyterian Church at Las Placitas.
Photo courtesy Menaul Historical Library.

CHAPTER II
The Seeds of Presbyterianism

There seems to be no question but that the seeds of Presbyterianism in Las Placitas were sown by the Gurulé family. But events in history don't just happen. To find out how and even more importantly *why* they do, is the problem of the historian.

Too often history is the story of famous men, for famous men have always had a stake in having the history of their deeds, good or evil, recorded as a way of enshrining their memory and achieving a kind of immortality. Nations have also had a stake in enshrining their heroes as a source of national pride. But history is far more than the escapades of famous men.

The history of Las Placitas Presbyterian Church is not, for the most part, a story of famous men. It is a story of ordinary people, men *and* women, living their lives in ordinary and occasionally extraordinary ways. Lives like these are rarely examined in history books. In fact, it is really quite wonderful that we know anything at all of the early history of Las Placitas. That we have such a complete and fascinating record is due to two extraordinary sources of information: the extensive records and testimony relating to the San Antonio de las Huertas land grant in the files of the United States Surveyor-General and the Court of

Private Land Claims, and a collection of stories and oral histories relating to Las Placitas that are on file in the New Mexico State Archives. The stories about Las Placitas were recorded by a woman named Lou Sage Batchen with the assistance of two Las Placitas young people, Max DeLara and Christina Baros (later Gonzales), who did much of the actual interviewing and who translated the stories into English for Batchen.

We don't know exactly when Lou Batchen moved to the area east of Las Placitas known as Ojo de la Casa. She tells us that her husband came in 1897 to work as a mining engineer. He was the first Anglo to put down rather permanent roots. He bought land, and by 1942, Lou tells us, he held the second largest number of water rights on the San Antonio de Las Huertas land grant. Although Lou moved to Las Placitas some time later, she lived in Ojo de la Casa for many years.[1]

Batchen began collecting stories from Las Placitas old-timers in the early 1930s, but the work that she left behind comes to us from her employment by the WPA (Works Progress Administration) Federal Writers Project during the years 1938 to 1942. This Depression era program was created to provide work for unemployed white collar workers. In New Mexico the Project's directors made the gathering of information about the state's Hispanic cultural heritage its first and overriding priority. They specifically wanted their workers to collect folk beliefs, customs, legends, and oral histories.[2] Lou Batchen was ideally based to do this, and she was a born storyteller. Delighted to be paid for what she had previously done for her own amusement, she went to work with gusto and over the next five years sent in sixty-six stories based on interviews with Las Placitas old-timers. One of her principal informants was José Librado Aron Gurulé, the village's most respected senior citizen.

Lou Batchen was physically handicapped and could not get around easily. For that reason, and because she did not speak enough Spanish to carry on the interviews herself, she employed Max DeLara and Christina Baros to help her. Max was an enterprising twelve-year old when he started working with her early in the 1930s. He recalls that she paid him fifty cents an hour, a magnificent wage for the time, to visit with old-timers and get them to tell him stories from their youth. They were delighted to pass on the local wisdom to the eager, bright-eyed young man. Max's favorite story-teller was his grandfather, José Gurulé. Since all the villagers told Max their stories in Spanish, he had to translate them mentally as he retold them to Mrs. Batchen. He made it a point to mimic the way the stories were told to him as closely as possible, so that she could get the right "feel" for each tale. She listened intently, and wrote the stories down on her old typewriter as fast as he told them to her. Max devoted about six hours each week to the project, and the $3.00 weekly wage helped his father buy a lot of groceries.[3] In 1936, Max DeLara left Las Placitas to work in the Civilian Conservation Corps (CCC), and Batchen employed Christina Baros to help her.

Batchen's stories cannot be taken literally. She wrote to her supervisor in Santa Fe that it often took several interviews before she had a complete story. Old minds had to be coaxed to delve deeply into the past and recall almost forgotten people and incidents. When they tired, the interview had to be suspended, to be resumed another day.[4] Perhaps as a consequence, Batchen sometimes related different versions of the same story, with varying names and dates. At other times she probably winnowed out contradictory or apparently irrelevant details to make a better story. Some of her informants may also have embroidered their tales with imaginative details to amuse themselves or to cover up failing memories. Even Lou, we suspect, was not above adding her own literary details and giving an occasional O'Henryesque twist to the ending.

The fact that most of the villagers Batchen talked to on a regular basis were members of the Presbyterian Church at Las Placitas may have added some bias to the stories. Lou also carried many of the common Anglo misconceptions of her time, most notably concerning traditional Hispanic Catholicism. So we have to take these stories with the proverbial grain of salt. But oral testimony, transmitted generation to generation, is a powerful historical tool in a non-literate society. The stories and genealogies that we have been able to check through other sources have turned out to be amazingly accurate.

Despite her association with Presbyterians, Lou Batchen had no particular interest in religion. She regarded it as just one of many interesting activities of the Las Placitas villagers. But religion and the observance of traditional rites and ceremonies are so much a part of Hispanic culture that the subject came up time and time again in the oral histories, especially in those supplied by or about the family patriarch, José L.A. Gurulé. He had an early and keen interest in the subject of religion. Since he was the individual directly responsible for bringing the first Presbyterian missionary to preach in Las Placitas, stories concerning his early religious experiences were especially meaningful to him. Yet the first influence of Presbyterianism on the Gurulé family begins not with Don José but with his uncle, Lucas Gurulé.

Lucas Gurulé is one of the ordinary people in this history who lived an extraordinary life. He was born in the old village of San José de las Huertas in the year 1798. Although we have no information concerning his early years, he probably moved to Algodones after 1823, along with other families from the San Antonio de Las Huertas land grant. After 1860 we know that he lived in Las Placitas and that he was an important community leader. But to understand why Lucas is important to our story, we have to turn to another man also destined to lead an extraordinary life. He was José Ynés Perea, son of *Don* Juan Perea and *Doña* Josefa Chavez de Perea of Bernalillo. Born April 23, 1837, into one of the wealthiest families in New Mexico, he would in time become the nation's first ordained Hispanic Presbyterian minister.

José Ynés, like other young New Mexican *ricos*, got his elementary education at a boarding school in Mexico. By the time he was twelve; New Mexico had been occupied and annexed by the United States. Realizing that times were changing and that his sons had to be able to adjust to the new American culture, the elder Perea decided to send José Ynés and his brother Francisco to a Jesuit school in New York. There José Ynés joined a group of students who secretly, and in defiance of school rules, read the Bible. His father, when he found out about the illicit activities, arranged for the boys to be appointed to the United States Military Academy at West Point. José Ynés soon fell out with his military teachers and returned to Bernalillo. There he proceeded to embarrass his parents by avowing his Protestant faith. His parents tried in vain to correct him, and when their efforts had clearly failed, his father sent him off to St. Louis to learn the retail trade by working in a dry goods store.

José Ynés worked for two years in St. Louis. During this time he joined the Presbyterian Church. Then on July 4, 1855, he boarded a steamer and sailed to New Orleans to work for a marine shipping company. At some point in this sojourn José acquired the company of two men from Las Placitas. They were considerably older than he, and probably served him as menservants. These men, brothers, named Antonio and Lucas Gurulé, spent all or part of the next five years traveling the world with Perea and having their horizons considerably broadened by the experience.[5]

There is no way of quantifying the influence José Ynés Perea had on his two traveling companions. There is no reason to believe that either of them ever became Protestants. But José Ynés was, if anything, enthusiastic and persuasive. The Gurulé brothers cannot but have been impressed with the sincerity of the young man's beliefs or with his fierce independence. What is certain *is* that their lives were forever changed by their association with him. It seems that through the Gurulé brothers, and Lucas in particular, the future of the little community of Las Placitas was changed as well.

José Ynés Perea and the Gurulé brothers parted company in 1860. Perea returned briefly to Bernalillo and made peace with his father. He then journeyed to California. Lucas moved to Las Placitas to join other members of his family and, from all accounts, became a highly respected leader.

The stories that include Lucas tell us something about the man, and even more about the nature and ideals of leadership in mid-nineteenth century Las Placitas. To be a leader in a traditional Hispanic village a man had to be his own master able to take charge during a crisis and willing to challenge authority if need be. Lucas demonstrated all of these traits in a story Batchen entitled "The Panic of 1862" in which Lucas faced down the powerful *patron* of the area, another member of the Perea family named José Leandro Perea. The incident began in February of 1862 when the people of Bernalillo heard that Confederate forces were approaching. An army of Texans had routed the Union forces at the battle of Valverde, and was headed northward up the Rio Grande. Sure that the hated Texans would rob him and take all his men as prisoners of war, José Leandro Perea packed his family into several carriages and headed north to Colorado. Before he left he secretly buried two leather bags filled with gold in his chicken yard, and left two young men to guard his house and property.

When the Perea family returned in the spring, José Leandro discovered that one of the bags of gold was missing. Without revealing the reason for his fury, he summoned the young men whom he had left behind to guard the house and accused them of stealing. They declared their innocence and, threatened with a terrible flogging, named other men who had worked around the place as the possible culprits. These men were summoned, accused and, when they did not confess, flogged.

By now everyone in Perea's employ knew of the local inquisition. The men of Las Placitas feared the time when they might be accused. They had good reason to fear José Leandro. Many of them rented sheep on shares from him and were deeply indebted at his store. He was in a position to make life very difficult for them if he chose. Lucas Gurulé tried to calm them. He pointed out that most had been far away caring for José Leandro's sheep in the Jemez Mountains. The others in Perea's service had either been busy in the hills above Las Placitas with their own flocks, or had been with the wool wagons on their annual trip up the Santa Fe Trail.

José Leandro Perea would not rest until he found his thief. One person after another was dragged before him, accused of the crime, flogged and pilloried until, in desperation, he accused someone else. The day finally came when seven Perea aids marched into Las Placitas to seize the two Chavez brothers, Manuel and José. The villagers were outraged. Manuel and José Chavez were two of the most honorable men in Las Placitas. At this point Lucas Gurulé stepped forward. He called for his brother Nicolás and announced that the two of them would accompany the Chavez brothers to Bernalillo and act as their advocates. Lucas, after all, had been around the world. He knew something about legal matters, and he knew that *Don* José Leandro, no matter how powerful, had no right to hold and torture innocent men. Lucas had the independence to do this, because he had never had his name on the Perea account books.

When the company of men reached Bernalillo, Lucas demanded that José Leandro give the Chavez brothers a lawful hearing before the mayor. Perea was speechless. He had never before been addressed this way by someone of a lower class. But he didn't want to open the matter to public scrutiny. Without apology or explanation he dismissed the four men and ended the inquisition.

So Lucas was remembered not only as the kind of man who was his own master, but as one who was not afraid to challenge authority. Such a man could be trusted to lead the community in a crisis. And according to the tales recorded by Lou Batchen, he was called upon to do just that the following year during a harrowing Indian attack. In 1863, while the American military forces were busy defending the territory against the Confederates, the Navajos stepped up their raiding. In a daring daylight attack, a small party of Indians swooped down upon a group of young Las Placitas shepherds, killed two of them outright, kidnapped two others, and ran off with their sheep. They then rounded up the only three horses in the village and rode off.

Lucas knew that the Indians would head for the larger flock of sheep being guarded by his brother, Nicolás, and his son, José Aron. He called together all of the able-bodied men of the village and, armed with bows and arrows, they rushed off in pursuit. By the time they caught up with the Indians it was already dark, and a pitched battle was in progress between the Indians and the older shepherds. The villagers routed the Indians, but not before they had run off with the rest of the sheep. Lucas sent Nicolás and José Aron back to the village to help in the search for the missing flock and the two little shepherd boys. Then he and his men tracked the Navajos through the mountains in hopes of catching up with them. It was to no avail. The Indians had horses and they far outpaced the men on foot.

The villagers eventually recovered most of the sheep, though dozens had been needlessly slain by the Indians. They also found the mutilated body of one little shepherd, slain like the sheep. The other was carried off by his captors. According to local legend, the Navajos took the boy to their winter camp at Canyon de Chelly. He escaped in the turmoil that followed Kit Carson's raid on this

Navajo stronghold in 1864 and eventually made his way back to the village.[6]

It would be hard to imagine that young José Gurulé did not admire and wish to imitate his uncle. Lucas embodied the traits of a man *con mucha verguenza* (modesty, strength, fairness and independence), and very early in his life José began demonstrating many of the same traits, along with some Protestant ideas that might have come from his uncle, as well.[7] By the tender age of fourteen he was so well known as an independent, free thinker that someone gave him a new middle name—Librado—meaning liberated. From that time on he was known as José Librado Aron Gurulé. In later years people mistook the initials L and A in his signature for an H, and with his youthful rebelliousness only a distant memory, he became known to the Las Placitas community as José H.[8] In his earlier years, however, his independent free-thinking got him into a number of youthful scrapes.

The first of these escapades concerned his aunt and her saints.[9] She was, we are told, a pious lady devoted to her sizeable collection of old carved wooden *santos*. She had inherited them from her mother and her grandfather, old Miguel Trujillo, a *Santero* (maker of religious images), who had carved the village's first statue of San Antonio de Las Huertas. About the year 1865, Petra left the village on an extended absence. She left her precious saints with her sister, José's mother. José tells us that he knew that they were idols, and he could not sleep with them in the house. One night when everyone was asleep he took them out of the chest where they had been placed for safekeeping and buried them in different places throughout the village.

No one suspected that they were missing until his aunt returned. There was an outcry when his mother and aunt found that the saints were missing, and José admitted what he had done. He tried to retrieve them, but he had forgotten where he had buried them. The few that he found were so badly decomposed that they were ruined.

Another episode concerned his experiences as a young student at the Mission Church in the San Felipe Pueblo. José first learned to read and write from an old man named Pedro Sarna who lived at Ojo de la Casa. Sarna used to accompany the young boys of the village when they went to the hills to tend sheep. There, using charcoal and a dried and stretched sheep's skin, he taught them their letters. José enjoyed this first taste of learning so much that, when he was about twelve, he went to San Felipe to live with his mother's brother, Juan Bustos, and study under a priest he called Father Baron. The good father permitted him access to all the books in the San Felipe Mission Church and the rectory. That, José recalled, was the one great privilege he craved—to learn to read the holy books, not only for his own knowledge, but to be able to teach others.

He did, in fact, teach the young Indian children at the San Felipe Pueblo; and with the chile, corn, and beans that he was paid for his services, he was able to pay Juan Bustos for his board and room. It disappointed him that he had to restrict his teaching to religious songs and verses, prayers, veneration of the saints, and implicit obedience to one's elders.

José was particularly intrigued with the church record books and longed to find the entry of his own baptism. Such research was forbidden, and whenever José attempted to examine the books he found himself being scrutinized by Indians who seemed to watch his every move as if they divined his intentions. One day during an Indian ceremonial, when everyone was engaged elsewhere, José stole into the Mission Church, retrieved the record book and hid himself while he searched for the entry of his baptism. He found it, but his eye caught another entry that he desperately wanted to read, as well. It was too long and complicated for him to read quickly, so clutching the forbidden book under his clothing, he ran to the home of Juan Bustos. He didn't feel safe even there. So he continued to his parents' home, fully intending to return the book to the Mission Church before anyone discovered its absence.

The account that José read and copied recorded a case of presumed witchcraft at the San Felipe Pueblo. He had no sooner finished copying it, however, than he heard the ear splitting yell of a mob of furious Indians invading Las Placitas. They marched to the house of José's parents, Nicolás and Catalina Gurulé, and demanded to see young José. No one in the village understood, of course, why the friendly Indians of San Felipe Pueblo had suddenly turned against them. Lucas Gurulé fought his way through the angry mob to his brother's house, determined to do whatever he had to do to defend his nephew. Standing before the closed door, he faced the Indians defiantly and courageously. Then the door opened and José's mother emerged holding the book. She strode resolutely toward the leader of the Indians and placed the book in his hands. With the precious book once more in his possession, the Indian leader had no trouble persuading his companions to leave the village peacefully. The Indians restored the book to its honored place in the Mission Church, but some years later the Church was badly damaged by a sudden rain that washed away the portion of the wall and roof where the book was stored. The Indians who found it, soaked and muddy, took it to the pueblo for safety. So far as the people of Las Placitas knew, it was never seen again.[10]

Besides any individual concerns that José Gurulé may have had with the Catholic church, there were other more general problems that were shared by all Hispanic New Mexicans. New Mexico was always desperately poor in its ability to deliver religious services to its people. In 1760, shortly before the founding of San José de las Huertas, New Mexico had thirty Franciscan missionaries. After Mexican independence this number declined to only nine.[11]

For the first one hundred years of its existence, the Las Huertas community, first at old San José de Las Huertas and later at Las Placitas, had no church or chapel, no cemetery, and no regular religious services. It was only in 1795 that Las Huertas was assigned to the Mission Church at San Felipe Pueblo. From that time on the Franciscan priest from the Mission led the yearly celebration in Las Placitas of the fiesta of San Antonio, but the rest of the time the villagers had to travel to San Felipe for services such as baptisms, marriages, and funerals.

New Mexico's Hispanic villagers filled much of the religious void in their lives with a self-sufficient folk religion. In addition to a rich literary tradition of semi-religious legends and folk tales, they used wood, gypsum and paint to make simple paintings and sculptures of Christ and the saints to decorate their home altars. The simple, stark, and often bloody images reflected the harsh realities of their frontier existence and the ever present specter of death in their lives.

One of the harsh realities that the Las Huertans had to face on a regular basis was the sixteen-mile round trip to the San Felipe Mission Church that had to be made for every marriage, baptism, and funeral. Like all frontier folk, they were resourceful in meeting the problem. Godparents took babies for baptism, to relieve the newly delivered mother from having to make the long trip. When the baby got hungry, the godparents found a Pueblo woman with a nursing baby and asked her to share her milk with the Hispanic newborn. This was never a problem, and in celebration of the event the Pueblo family always invited the Hispanic couple to share the noon meal. With a bit of haste on the return trip, the godparents were usually able to return the baby to its mother before it had to nurse again. Babes that were stillborn or that died before they could be baptized were buried under the water spout of the house—to be baptized by the water from heaven.[12]

Marriages were festive affairs. No one seems to have objected too strongly to the long trip to and from the San Felipe Mission Church if, in the first place, they could afford to pay the priest for the ceremony. Funerals were another matter entirely. The deceased, wrapped in a shroud, and laid upon a funeral "ladder," had to be carried all the long way on the shoulders of the pallbearers. Men were in charge of preparing the body for burial, and only men made the trip to the cemetery. They had to stop and rest at frequent intervals, and when they did, they erected a small shrine of rocks to mark the spot of the *descanso*, or resting place. Batchen tells us that some of these little shrines were still in evidence in the 1930s.[13]

Nothing so angered the people of Las Placitas as the need to carry their loved ones so far for burial. Even after Our Lady of Sorrows Church was built in Bernalillo in 1856, most families continued to carry their dead to the San Felipe Mission Church. Burial there was free, but in Bernalillo the priest charged what, for those times, was an exorbitant fee of $4.00. The villagers asked for their own plot of sacred ground, but to no avail. Over the years patience gave way to impatience and finally to anger. The final insult came with the burial of Concepción (Chonita) Tafoya. Bad weather had prohibited making the trip promptly. When the funeral procession finally got under way, one of the pallbearers became nauseous from the smell of decay. He tripped, and the badly decomposed body fell off the ladder and broke open. That night the outraged villagers called a meeting. They appointed a committee to meet with the priest in Bernalillo and demand that he bless ground in Las Placitas for a cemetery. This time their pleas reached the diocese in Santa Fe. Placitas got its cemetery in the early 1870s, but not before many of its residents were disillusioned with the local clergy's lack of responsiveness to their needs. (One of the first things the new Presbyterian members of the San Antonio de Las Huertas land grant did after the 1894 founding of their new Presbyterian Church in Las Placitas was to consecrate their own cemetery on the outskirts of the village.)[14]

The years of less than benign neglect of Las Placitas ended suddenly in 1867 with the arrival in Bernalillo of a group of five Italian Jesuits, three priests and two brothers, assigned to the area by Bishop Lamy. Several of them spoke Spanish, having served earlier in Spain, and were familiar with traditional Hispanic culture. The Jesuits had been invited to New Mexico to teach and help train the clergy, and many local Hispanics, knowing about the colleges the Jesuits had opened elsewhere in the United States, hoped that they would open a school in Bernalillo. The priests especially were eager to train some young men who could later be ordained to the priesthood. Father Gasparri, the head of the mission, was deeply disappointed when his hopes to establish such a seminary collapsed. It would have been an appropriate undertaking for the society, he wrote, but "apart from wishing and talking about it, nothing more was done."[15]

In the meantime, the Jesuits had the care of twenty-three different villages, many of which, like Las Placitas, had rarely seen a priest. To respond to their needs, the priests traveled to one village, then another, in a wide circuit, much like the first Protestant missionaries would do a decade later. The priests also began giving parish missions at which they preached fiery sermons designed to stir up the souls of sinners and get everybody thinking about religion. One of the largest of these revival meetings was in Algodones in the spring of 1868.

For the Las Placitas villagers, whose spiritual lives had been so long neglected, the revival services must have been an electrifying experience. In late February 1868, two men, possibly newly inspired by the Jesuit's revival meeting in Algodones, stopped off in Ojo de la Casa on their way to the mountains to fast and pray. They talked to the villagers about their mission, and a woman named Juanita Zamora was so moved by their example of self-sacrifice and penitence that she determined to do as the two men had done. Shortly before Easter she quietly left the village. Her husband and friends from the village searched for her throughout the days and nights of Holy Week. Knowing that she had carried no warm clothing or food with her, they feared that she would die from exposure. It was something of a miracle, then, when the search party finally found her just at dawn on Easter morning, famished and exhausted and nearly frozen, but alive and ever so grateful to see her family.

Holy Week of 1868 was also memorable because Father Gasparri came from Bernalillo to choose several boys to play the part of angels in the Easter pageant. This was the first time that boys from the village had ever been given such an opportunity, and the excitement of the moment was recalled years later in stories told to Lou Batchen. José Gurulé was one of the fortunate boys who went to Bernalillo with the *padres*. Preparation for the Easter pageant took eight days, during which he and the other boys rehearsed their roles, were fitted for their elaborate costumes, and shared the priests' monastic lifestyle.[16]

The Jesuit influence upon the Bernalillo area was all too short. A complication about acquiring ownership of the Bernalillo Church led to the order moving its headquarters to the San Felipe de Neri Church in Albuquerque. The Jesuits left Bernalillo shortly after Easter in 1868. It must have been a devastating loss to the people whose lives and spirits they had touched. One cannot help but wonder about the effect of the excitement and spiritual awakening offered by this brief exposure to Jesuit teaching and preaching. It may have created, in at least one young man, a great yearning for something more deeply soul-stirring in the way of religion. Without intending to do so, the Jesuits may have helped to prepare José Gurulé and others for the introduction of Presbyterianism a short while later.[17]

What is sure is that by the early 1880s, when José Ynés Perea, recently ordained to the ministry in September 1880, introduced Presbyterianism to Las Placitas, the villagers were hungry for spiritual guidance. They were also deeply concerned about education, and none more so than José Gurulé. The main reason was the desperate and uneven struggle that the Las Huertans were making to get and keep title to their land.

CHAPTER III
The Struggle for the Land

Land was everything in New Mexico. It was the means of survival, and so it was identity, security, home. The most respected occupation was that of farmer-rancher. It was simply a matter of scale whether one was a *rico* or *a pobre*. Without land a person was nothing. With land that same person, rich or poor, could hold up his head with pride, secure in his or her own worth. Land was definitely worth fighting for.

The settlers of Las Huertas held title to their land with just such intense pride. The extent and boundaries of the land grant were among the most important bits of information passed down from generation to generation. But from 1840 until 1907 the San Antonio de Las Huertas grantees were locked into a bitter struggle with land speculators for title to their land. They soon discovered that the old survival skills that had seen them through over 150 years of hardship on the remote New Mexican frontier were not good enough. The speculators had the advantage of money, education, and access to the American legal system and a knowledge of English. The fight appeared to be hopeless, but the San Antonio de Las Huertas grantees were not without resources. They could appeal to God, as they had always done in times of need, for strength, wisdom, and guidance, and they could try to help themselves by getting the education and knowledge of Anglo-American ways necessary to compete on an equal level. Apparently they did both. It was surely not coincidental that in July 1882, as the struggle for the land intensified, José Gurulé invited the Presbyterian minister José Ynés Perea to preach in Placitas, and that shortly after that members of the community petitioned for a Presbyterian school teacher.

Land speculation in the area began some years before the American conquest—in 1828 after gold was discovered in the Ortiz Mountains. After both gold and copper deposits were discovered in the San Pedro Mountains in 1839, desire to possess these riches mounted to fever pitch. By the time American annexation put the titles to all of the land grants made under the previous Spanish and Mexican governments into question, Mexican speculators had already wrested some of the most valuable lands from their less sophisticated countrymen. After 1848 land grabbing by fair means or foul became a way of life, and no area seemed to offer greater promise because of its perceived mineral wealth than that stretch of the Sandia and Ortiz mountains that was included in or bordered by the original San Antonio de Las Huertas land grant (SADLHLG). In the knock-down drag-out fight for this mineral wealth no one paid much heed to the rights of the San Antonio de Las Huertas grantees except the grantees themselves.

It wasn't meant to be that way. The Treaty of Guadalupe-Hidalgo, signed between the United States and Mexico at the end of the Mexican War, contained specific safeguards for the former Mexicans living in the annexed territories. The United States not only guaranteed them automatic American citizenship but guaranteed that their lives, property, and religion would be protected as well or better under the new government as under the old. The problem did not lie so much with official intentions as it did with the lawlessness of the New Mexico frontier.[1]

It also lay with a problem of multiple land titles. In 1839 and 1840, some of the descendants of the Las Huertas settlers requested and received grants of land at San Pedro and Tejón, which were within the original San Antonio de Las Huertas land grant. Multiple, overlapping titles may have seemed a source of extra security, but as it turned out, they became a terrible liability in the years that followed.[2]

The struggle for control and ownership of SADLHLG begins with one José Serafin Ramirez, an influential politician residing in San Antonito on the eastern side of the Sandias. In 1844, when he was the acting treasurer of New Mexico, Ramirez began acquiring title to potential mining claims in the Sandia, San Pedro, and Ortiz Mountains.

SADLHLG was made up mostly of agricultural and grazing lands, but the lands on the eastern boundary had gold, lead, and copper deposits. Around the Town of Tejón there were extensive deposits of coal. Ramirez could only get control of these mining properties by getting title to at least some portions of SADLHLG common lands. In order to simplify this procedure he set out to divide and conquer by first getting title to the San Pedro and Tejón properties. He began by buying out the Las Huertas settlers at San Pedro. When some of them refused to sell him their rights he forced them out at gunpoint. They sued, but the wily politician apparently used his extensive contacts to have the court cases settled in his favor.[3]

In 1854, the United States Congress established the Office of Surveyor-General to investigate and recommend the approval or rejection of land grants made under the Spanish and Mexican governments. Ramirez lost no time in submitting the San Pedro land grant petition to the first Surveyor-General William Pelham. Pelham was by all accounts an idealist quite unprepared for the realities of the New Mexico frontier. He was also understaffed for the enormous job of reviewing the many complexities of the land grant situation. He approved Ramirez's petition without specific boundaries and virtually without evidence.[4]

With this success, and with amazing audacity, Ramirez then claimed both the Town of Tejón land grant and the *entire* SADLHLG as his separate private property. Pelham approved the Town of Tejón land grant, and Congress confirmed both it and the San Pedro land grant in June 1860. By the time Ramirez submitted SADLHLG in January 1862, however, Pelham was no longer Surveyor-General. There was a new administration in Washington, and the United States was involved in the Civil War.

No land claims were settled between 1861 and 1868. Ramirez died in 1869 and his claim to the entire SADLHLG apparently died with him. Judging from Ramirez's ability to separate poor landowners from their lands, it was just as well.[5]

In the meantime things were far from dull in Las Placitas. The San Antonio de Las Huertas grantees were well aware of the existence of minerals on their grant lands. They had all heard tales of lost or abandoned gold, silver, and lead mines. Prospectors swarmed over their lands looking for mineral deposits. Some of the settlers were actively engaged in mining, either on their own claims or as employees of prospectors and mining companies. Others had helped to construct a huge sluice to bring water across the mountain for placer mining.[6]

The amount of mining in the area brought economic good times to Las Placitas throughout the 1870s, but nothing topped the "discovery" of a vein of gold in the main street of Las Placitas in 1878. That find brought hundreds of gold seekers to the community, including Governor Lew Wallace who bought into the project and temporarily moved both himself and the capital of New Mexico to Placitas while he joined the search. A Bernalillo doctor and Colonel Francisco Perea, brother of José Ynés, were also caught up in the tide of excitement that swept the area. Newspaper correspondents descended on the village and kept the telegraph wires humming. There were stories that the adobe mud in Las Placitas was so rich in gold that the people had torn down their houses and shipped the bricks to the smelter. Before the excitement was over some of the miners had made plans to bring a spur of the railroad from the main line at Bernalillo and to ship in coal for the furnaces from Hagan or Madrid. Hopes faded as the outline of a fraud began to surface. Later ore samples sent off to Denver to be assayed showed no trace of gold. The Governor and his partner lost interest and returned to Santa Fe. Others left and the village returned more or less to normal. But the San Antonio de Las Huertas grantees had seen too many prospectors and land speculators not to be very nervous about losing control of their lands.[7]

In May 1881, a B.C. Wade of the law firm of Wade and Chaves resubmitted the 1861 petition for title to SADLHLG. Judging from a sketch map submitted with the petition, mining was again very much a motive in wanting to get the grant approved. Specifically, the boundaries claimed a mine called the Real de Dolores at the base of the "Old Placer" (Ortiz) Mountain.[8]

Lucas Gurulé, now an old man of 83, was one of three witnesses called to testify in preparation for the hearing before the Surveyor-General. Questioned extensively about the genuineness of SADLHLG documents, Lucas said that he had seen them before on three occasions. The first was in 1821 when they were examined at the Palace of the Governors in Santa Fe by an inspector from old Mexico who had come north to report on the status of the Spanish land grants. One of the matters the inspector had to settle was a dispute between the San Antonio de Las Huertas settlers and their ancient enemies the Apaches over lands to the east of the Sandias. To settle the dispute the inspector read aloud the grant documents including the 1768 Act of Possession, the only document to identify the eastern boundary. He then accompanied Lucas and other San Antonio de Las Huertas grantees on a tour of the grant and pointed out to them the exact boundaries.

Lucas saw the grant papers again in 1861 in the office of José Serafin Ramirez, and in 1872 in the home of José Leandro Perea. He swore that the papers presented with the 1881 petition were the same as those he had seen in 1821 in Santa Fe. This was important, because the original grant papers were no longer in the governmental archives. The papers submitted with the petition were signed copies of the originals. However the Act of Possession, the only document to lay out the exact boundaries of the 1768 San Antonio de Las Huertas land grant, was torn at each and every reference to the eastern boundary. Because of this the eastern boundary had to be established by oral testimony.

When asked to identify the grant papers Lucas replied that, because of his age, he could not read them. When he was asked if he could read when he was younger, Lucas replied that he could read and write a little. He and the other two witnesses, both of them men from the Town of Tejón, claimed that Tejón was part of the original San Antonio de Las Huertas land grant. They apparently hoped that if SADLHLG were approved they would be able to reclaim title to the lands. Such was not to be the case. The petition never went to trial. Three years passed and a new

Surveyor-General, George Julian, contacted Attorney Wade to ask him if he wished to submit any more information. Wade replied that he had withdrawn from the case.

Julian reviewed the case and dismissed it. He gave as his reasons for denying the grant that the grant papers submitted were copies, that the Act of Possession was mutilated and the eastern boundary was illegible, that there were discrepancies in the testimony of the three witnesses, and that the testimony of Lucas Gurulé was unreliable, in part because "by his own admission, he could read but little." Julian's decision was delivered to Placitas on Christmas Eve 1885.[9]

The news must have been devastating to the SADLHLG heirs. With a stroke of a pen they had been denied their heritage. Worst of all, their respected leader Lucas had been humiliated by having his testimony disregarded because he *could not read*. Never people to take defeat lightly the San Antonio de Las Huertas grantees determined to fight the decision and to do it, as far as they could, on their own terms. In a hastily called village meeting they elected a new and younger leader, one who *could* both read and write. It was Lucas's nephew, José Gurulé.[10]

No matter how much Lucas and others may have been involved in giving testimony for the 1881 petition, they obviously had not been in control of the proceedings. Someone else representing one of several powerful mining companies interested in getting control of mines in the Ortiz Mountains must have hired the Wade and Chaves law firm to present the petition to the Surveyor-General. Then, for reasons of his own, this unknown person lost interest and withdrew his support for the petition. Had the San Antonio de Las Huertas grantees sponsored the petition they would surely not have withdrawn it before it ever came up for a hearing!

The problem, like everything else that confronted the San Antonio de Las Huertas grantees in the last years of the nineteenth century, was their lack of money. It cost a great deal to hire an attorney to represent them and to pay for a survey of their lands. José Gurulé told Lou Batchen in later years that he traveled many times to Santa Fe to talk with lawyers and ask their advice. He had no money to offer them, but he was an influential community leader respected by local politicians. He surely figured that he could cut some kind of deal.[11]

By this time the San Antonio de Las Huertas grantees must have been quite frantic with worry. In 1881 an attorney for the law firm of Thomas Benton Catron had filed a partition suit for the Town of Tejón land grant common lands. This meant that the District Court of Bernalillo County had to order a sale of the Tejón common lands in order to divide them equitably among all owners. The settlers at Tejón had no desire to sell their lands at any price, but they had no money to defend themselves against the court order. José Gurulé told Batchen that he traveled frequently to Tejón to advise kinsmen to "fight, fight for your homes and your lands!" Dispiritedly they answered him, "No podemos remediarlo" (There is nothing we can do to change it). In 1886, the patent to the Town of Tejón land grant passed to the estate of José Leandro Perea and then to his son-in-law and business partner Mariano S. Otero.[12]

Getting a lawyer who would defend the San Antonio de Las Huertas grantees was no easy business. Seven years passed during which time the Office of Surveyor-General was replaced by the Court of Private Land Claims. Finally in February 1893, just one month before the cut-off date for submitting land claims, Don José Gurulé found his lawyer. He was none other than Tom Catron, who agreed to represent the grant heirs for a fee of not less than one-third of the grant.[13]

It was a strange bargain that Catron must have made with the SADLHLG representatives José Gurulé and Francisco Trujillo. Stranger still, Mariano S. Otero joined Gurulé, Trujillo, and the SADLHLG heirs as a plaintiff in the suit. The odd partnership, like so many things in New Mexico, was surely a matter of politics. Catron and Otero, who clearly had their own reasons for supporting the petition, could have called in some political debts with the SADLHLG heirs. The heirs probably had little choice in the matter. With the deadline for submitting their claim just one month away, they may have felt that any deal was better than to lose their land by default. The petition, numbered 90, claimed a territory of approximately 40,000 acres and included the Town of Tejón land grant.

Almost immediately Antonio José Gallegos and 62 other San Antonio de Las Huertas grantees represented by the law firm of G. Hill Howard and Earle Jeffries filed a rival claim. This petition, numbered 269, claimed a total of 130,000 acres and included not only the San Pedro and Town of Tejón land grants but parts of four other grants—all with valuable mining properties. The suit listed various mining and railroad interests controlled by Catron and his associates as defendants in the grant.

There is still much to be learned about the motives of the individuals behind the second petition. If initiated by Gallegos and other San Antonio de Las Huertas grantees on their own, it was an act of amazing bravado for them to file suit against the wealthiest and most powerful companies and individuals in New Mexico. Instead, the petition looks suspiciously as if it may have been sponsored by a rival mining company interested in snatching control of SADLHLG from Catron and Otero. Whatever the case, the court quickly consolidated the two cases under the Gurulé/Catron petition, essentially eliminating the Gallegos/G. Hill Howard petition.

Litigation dragged on for several years. José Gurulé, Francisco Trujillo, and Antonio José Gallegos spent many hours testifying before the court concerning the exact boundaries of SADLHLG. All clearly hoped to regain the Town of Tejón lands, if not the San Pedro land grant as well. In October 1897, when the Court of Private Land Claims actually confirmed SADLHLG to include the Town of Tejón land grant, the government refused to enter a decree. It argued that the previous confirmation of the Town of Tejón land grant back in 1860 deprived the Court of Private Land Claims of any jurisdiction over that portion of SADLHLG. Catron had probably known from the beginning that that would be the case, but he apparently did not relay this information to Gurulé and Trujillo or the other SADLHLG heirs.

Gallegos appealed the decision to the United States Supreme Court, but failed to have it filed and docketed. The Supreme Court dismissed the proceedings in March 1900. The government, whose position was to keep as much land in the public domain as possible, held out for two separate surveys before it finally approved the boundaries of SADLHLG. The original 1768 San Antonio de Las Huertas land grant may have covered hundreds of thousands of acres. However, as finally patented in 1907, SADLHLG contained a paltry 4763.85 acres, of which Catron, by then the largest individual land holder in the history of the United States, took the eastern one third.[14]

CHAPTER IV

A New Teacher, A New Church

Lavinia Thompson had been having an absolutely dreadful time. For the last year and a half she had tried her best to establish an elementary and a Sabbath (Sunday) school for the children of Peña Blanca, and she felt that she hadn't made very much progress at all. In her first report to HOME MISSION MONTHLY, the journal of the Board of Home Missions of the Presbyterian Church USA (PCUSA), written early in 1892, she had noted that the women and children were somewhat receptive. "But to revolutionize this place, the men must be reached. I have felt very unhappy about my Sabbath School. I have received only thirteen due to the opposition of the priest."

The local Catholic priest had mounted a full scale campaign of opposition to her school. It grieved her that he had collected and destroyed all of the Testaments that she had distributed. He had even offered rewards to the parents of her pupils if they would take them from her school. As in other communities, he had so threatened the village people that many of them were afraid even to be seen talking to her.

Other things were not going well either. Even after teaching for a year at the mission school at Laguna she was still shocked by the presence of dirt floors in the houses. She had insisted that the owner of the building she used as her schoolhouse in Peña Blanca put down a proper wooden floor. The constant dust in the air hurt her lungs. Still, months had gone by and the job wasn't done. The owner's excuse was that his mother had died and the priest had charged him so much money for her funeral that he couldn't afford to keep his promise.

Some months later Lavinia reported that the number of pupils had risen to 28 in the regular school and 21 in the Sabbath School. Besides an elementary Christian education, she taught them to recite, in English and Spanish, the catechism, the Ten Commandments, and the Lord's Prayer. Her sister and brother-in-law had sent her a $75.00 organ from back home. With it she taught her children to sing hymns. She also greatly appreciated the fact that the Presbyterian Church had arranged to have a wooden floor put down in her classroom. They had charged it against the rent paid to the owner for using the room. Still, the efforts of the priest to block her every move were deeply disturbing.

Lavinia's distress did not go unnoticed by the Board of Home Missions, nor did the fact that she was a good teacher. When it seemed as if the effort was hopeless, they recommended that she be transferred to another community where there were more children of school age and where the opposition from the "Romanists" would be less intense. That community was Las Placitas, and it had been waiting for a teacher for several years.[1]

Sometime shortly after José Ynés Perea's first visit to Placitas in 1882, the villagers had petitioned for a Presbyterian mission school. Many people in the village wanted an education for themselves and for their children, particularly an American style education with instruction in English, and in school-poor New Mexico this was the most direct route to the desired end. The villagers were so eager to get a Presbyterian school and teacher that they were willing to put up with the opposition of the local Catholic clergy. In their petition to the Board of Home Missions of PCUSA they noted, "In this part of the country we are not afraid of the priest or his threats."[2]

For poor New Mexican village folk an education was one of the rarest of commodities. Las Placitas had had a school teacher since 1876 in accordance with a territorial law that required each village to pay a teacher 50 cents per pupil per month in goods and services. In 1880 that teacher was, in fact, José Librado Aron Gurulé. Don José, the most qualified person for the job in the village, was a good teacher, but no one knew better than he that he knew no English and was as much bewildered by the new customs and the alien legal system introduced by the Americans as his neighbors. If the Placitas villagers were to survive and prosper in the new American society, *Don* José knew that they needed a teacher who could teach them English and American ways.

Presbyterian school teachers were both very much in demand and hard to come by in northern New Mexico. True to their practical Scottish origins, the Presbyterians understood the importance of education to the Hispanic people and used it as an opening wedge to break into the Catholic religious monopoly. But supplying schools and teachers for all of northern New Mexico was more of a financial commitment than the Board of Home Missions PCUSA was willing to take on. Its leaders argued that its resources should be used to preach the Gospel to the many English-speaking people that were flooding into the Territory. The Board of Home Missions of PCUSA finally resolved the problem in 1877 by passing the responsibility for financing the schools to the ingenuity and imagination of its newly created Woman's Executive Committee of Home Missions. "Let our women then assume the work, to them so strikingly appropriate, and support the mission schools . . . so far as the women supply the means." [3]

The Woman's Executive Committee (with a name change in 1897 to the Woman's Board of Home Missions—while still subsidiary to the Board of Home Missions) did its best to meet the demand for village "plaza" schools, but its resources to pay teachers, secure rooms for them to live in, and rent comfortable schoolhouses were very limited. The number of women willing to undertake such a hard role must also have been limited. Teachers had to be willing to live alone in a Spanish-speaking community. Besides teaching, they had to serve as physician, nurse, minister, sister, and friend—knowing all the while that they might be exposed to such infectious diseases as diphtheria, tuberculosis, and smallpox.[4]

Word reached José Gurulé that a teacher was available in August 1893, and he lost no time in yoking up his team of oxen and heading down the trail to Bernalillo and the railroad station to get her. We have no way of knowing exactly what happened when they met, but let us imagine that when the train arrived in Bernalillo he helped her unload her few personal belongings along with her meager school supplies—a few Testaments, some slates and pencils, her school benches, and her beloved organ.

They would have greeted each other with smiles and gestures but few words. Pleasantries would have strained Lavinia's newly acquired Spanish, and José Gurulé, reserved before this strange woman, would have been equally tongue-tied. We can be sure that he smiled broadly to reassure her as he loaded her things into the wagon. He would then have helped her into the cart and they would have headed out of town, back in the direction of Las Placitas.

She would have wondered about her new assignment. What would it be like? It would have to be better than what she had experienced at Peña Blanca, if *Don* José's eagerness to come get her was any indication of the reception she would receive from the rest of the Placitas villagers. Glancing sideways at the man beside her she would have noticed the first thing that anybody noticed about him—his missing left forearm. Averting her eyes to keep from embarrassing him, she would have wondered what dramatic event had brought about that loss. Just looking at him—the smiling eyes but the firm cut of the jaw—would have convinced her that he would protect her from the kind of problems she had experienced in Peña Blanca. Concluding that he would be her champion, she would have breathed a sigh of deep relief.

Later she would have heard the story of how a gun had accidentally discharged while he was unloading a wagon. It happened during a trip to the salt lakes in the Estancia Valley. The blast tore through his arm, leaving the lower part hanging loosely from a single tendon. Shocked and in terrible pain, José knew that he had to act immediately or bleed to death. While the others in the party rushed to the scene of his accident, he took the knife he always carried with him and cut through the tendon, completely severing the lower part of his arm. Others in the party helped him tie a blanket around the bleeding stump so tightly that it served as a tourniquet. Later, after the wound was dressed, he buried the severed arm on the spot where he had lost it.[5] Lavinia had correctly measured the strength and courage of the man beside her.

José Gurulé would have been just as curious about the woman sitting next to him. She might have seemed a bit frail, but he had good reason to know that even frail women could be surprisingly strong and resourceful. The Placitas women planted the gardens, plastered their houses, prepared the meals, spun wool and made clothing, bore numerous children, fought alongside their men during Indian attacks, and still had energy to kick up their heels at the fiesta dances. Frail looks weren't necessarily a sign of frail character. He would have had to admire her courage. To have come so far away from her home and family, to face life all alone in a strange community where she could just barely speak the language, would require some special kind of dedication. Yes, he must have concluded, she will be able to do the job that needs doing.

Hearing the sigh and noticing the way the stress lines in the teacher's young face were beginning to melt away, Gurulé must have concluded something else. She needed the Placitas community as much as it needed her! They had to have a teacher, it was true; but she had to have a school. Without pupils, how could she fulfill her mission? He had heard about the treatment she had received from the Peña Blanca priest. Well, just let the priest in Bernalillo try anything like that! He and the rest of the villagers would see to it that she felt comfortable and welcome. Prodding the oxen to move a bit faster, he would have been eager to get her back to the village and set up in the little adobe building they had just bought from Don Pedro Pino to use for a school. Maybe, he would have thought, she can begin teaching tomorrow.

Lavinia did start to work immediately. With several years of experience already behind her, she knew just how to go about her task. Following the instructions given to her when she first arrived in New Mexico, she opened school promptly each day with prayers and singing. She followed this with classes in reading, writing and arithmetic—the "Three R's." Teaching demanded every ounce of creativity she could muster. At first, in Laguna, she had had to communicate entirely through sign language. Now she could speak enough Spanish to introduce herself to her pupils and tell them what she expected of them. From that point on, she was on her own. The Board of Home Missions of PCUSA had given her absolutely no guidelines for conducting her classes, and nothing resembling a recommended course of study. With no blackboard, globes, maps, or standard reading books, she based all of her lessons on parables and passages from the Bible, acting out the more obscure parts until her students learned the English meanings. At the same time she taught by example, stressing what she believed to be proper cleanliness, dress, and behavior. There was one thing that she was very strict about. The students had to try their best to speak in English. If they failed to do so, they received demerits.[6]

School and Lavinia's duties did not end with the school day. In the evening she taught more classes in reading, sewing, and singing to the adults of the community. On Sunday she taught Sunday school—though it was not much different from regular school with its religious emphasis. To what must have been a great surprise to the villagers, especially the village women, she even conducted the Sunday Church service whenever a minister could not make it to the village. In between these activities she visited the homes of her pupils and of prospective pupils to get to know them and the community and to further the cause of Presbyterianism. [7]

Despite the long hours, Lavinia was happy. Freed from the hostile presence of the priest and surrounded by bright eyes and shining, eager faces, she must have rejoiced in the good fortune that had brought her to Las Placitas. With a heart full of love and gratitude, she embraced each tiny pupil, secure in the knowledge that she was doing what God had commanded her to do. Her students responded with like joy in her presence. The little building soon overflowed with students of all ages.

Even more desirous of an education than their children, the parents must have set a good example by their interest and willingness to accept new ideas. Like most Anglo-American newcomers, Lavinia would have been prepared to find the native New Mexicans lazy, frivolous, and backward. Actual experience quickly changed these negative stereotypes. Like other mission teachers she concluded that it was only a lack of opportunity that prevented them from being as well educated as anyone in the country. Even when she did not experience immediate results she was patient. John Menaul, who regularly visited the village, would have urged her, as he did other Presbyterian missionaries, to respect the strength of Hispanic culture and "make haste slowly." Lavinia surely agreed wholeheartedly with Elizabeth Craig, a fellow Presbyterian school teacher, who wrote that same year to HOME MISSION MONTHLY that "Truth forbids my seeing great results, but in faith I can look forward to the time when there will be wonderful changes in New Mexico."[8]

Lavinia also learned much from the people she had come to serve. Alone and far from her home and family, she admired their simple, gracious, and generous hospitality. No matter how poor the home, there was always food for a visitor and room for an orphan or an "old one." She would have strongly disapproved of the drinking and fighting that so often accompanied the village *bailes* (dances), but she must have loved it when groups gathered in the evening to sing. In her regular visits to the homes of her students, she often joined in simple pastimes around the corner fireplace—finger plays or stringing chile. The Placitas villagers became her family. She was at home.[9]

Lavinia's residence and daily presence in the village must have been a major factor in the Placitas community's decision to organize a Presbyterian Church. Though not very many villagers were ready to commit themselves to a new religion, most were happy with the education they and their children were getting at her capable hands. The problem now was the lack of a Church building. In her report to HOME MISSION MONTHLY in 1894, Mrs. Frederick Pierson, corresponding secretary for New Mexico, noted that "The Mexicans of Las Placitas greatly desire to secure a church. The missionary teacher accordingly requested a list of those who would assist in building the adobe part of the structure. Fifteen names were given her, and there are still others who will add their names. These people are very poor, and will need help to roof and seat their building." Instead of constructing a new building, however, the villagers remodeled the building they had purchased and used for the Las Placitas Mission School. They removed the center partition to enlarge the interior space, and then, upon hearing that the San Felipe Pueblo Church had an extra church bell, a number of people made contributions to buy it. [10]

Writing to HOME MISSION MONTHLY in 1896, Lavinia Thompson reported that the Mission at Las Placitas had prospered since the Church was organized two years earlier. The village consisted of about three hundred inhabitants and the congregation numbered more than forty members. More than half the pupils were members of the Church. Some of the older pupils, especially among the girls, were beginning to feel an ambition to acquire an education. One of the pupils, a married man of 25 (Juan Baros though she did not name him) was resolved to become an evangelist. He had been studying to prepare himself for the work. Finally, she reported that a Junior Christian Endeavor Society had recently been organized through the help of a Christian Endeavor Society at Jemez Springs.[11]

Lavinia Thompson spent only three years in Las Placitas. In 1896, she left the community never to return. The records of the Board of Home Missions of PCUSA, noted at the time that she was "one of the most capable and charming personalities that ever came to the field." We have no way of knowing why Lavinia left when she did. It may have been due to an illness, since she was apparently not transferred directly to another school. Her name appears again in 1898 as a school teacher in San Pablo, Colorado. José Gurulé later recalled that "when she left Las Placitas all the people followed her until they saw her enter the train at Albuquerque, nearly thirty miles away. I took her to the depot and when she saw how the people followed, crying, she turned to me and said, 'Brother, I have just seen my funeral.' Her memory has remained with us through all the years." [12]

Lavinia Thompson was replaced in Placitas by Carrie Fenton, the wife of the minister at Jemez Springs. She taught the school until it closed in 1900. The final report submitted to HOME MISSION MONTHLY on the Las Placitas Mission School reported a remarkable change in the community since its establishment. In most of the houses the people sat on chairs instead of the floor, and women sat down at table with their men instead of waiting upon them. Many people were now sleeping in bedsteads instead of on the floor on sheepskins, and the rooms in the homes were kept very tidy with snow-white bedcovers. Referring to Juan Baros, Placitas's resident evangelist, and his wife, Rumaldita, the report noted that women might go out with their evangelist husbands to sing and read with the people. In conclusion, the report noted that the teachers had been much loved and respected, and their influence was everywhere to be seen.[13]

Founders and the Early Church

José L. A. Gurulé and some family members, ca. 1903. L–R, daughters Carolina, Onofre, and Florinda, wife Rosita (Gonzales), and José L. A. Gurulé.
Courtesy Ephraim DeLara and Josephine Ringling.

José L. A. Gurulé was the driving force behind bringing Presbyterianism to Las Placitas by inviting five other villagers to a meeting with Presbyterian minister José Ynés Perea in 1882. Besides José L. A. Gurulé's father Nicolás and uncle Lucas, the other three villagers were Juan Antonio Perez, Preciliano Baros, and Francisco Trujillo. The latter two individuals continued to be actively involved with José L. A. Gurulé in inviting Presbyterian ministers to Placitas in the years after the 1882 meeting, culminating in the organizational meeting that established The Presbyterian Church at Las Placitas on February 24–25, 1894. The Gurulé, Baros, and Trujillo descendants, as well as many other Placitas families, have been active throughout the decades in sustaining and growing the Church.

Ministerial training class at College of the Southwest, Del Norte, Colorado, 1898. L–R, front row: Juan Baros (second from left), Victoriano Valdez. Back row: Santiago Van Wagner, Gabino Rendón, Tomás Atencio. Serving as early pastors at The Presbyterian Church at Las Placitas were Juan Baros from 1906–1914 and Victoriano Valdez from 1917–1922.
Courtesy Christine Baros Gonzales.

The Baros Family ca.1911. Pictured are the children of Preciliano Baros and Placida Lucero de Baros. L–R, front row: Rumaldita Candelaria de Baros (wife of Juan), Elizardo Trujillo, Juan Baros, Christina Baros, Virginia Baros de Salas, Felipita Baros de Trujillo. Back row: Gabrielita Baros, Agustin Baros, Barbarita Baros, Cipriano Salas, Santiago Baros, and Juanita Baros. Preciliano Baros was one of the six villagers who met with Rev. Perea in 1882. His son Juan became one of the two first elders of the newly-established Presbyterian Church and later on its pastor.
Courtesy Christine Baros Gonzales and Vivian G. DeLara.

The José Trujillo Family, ca. 1921. L-R, Julia, José, Francisco (Frank), Albiria (Gurulé), Isabel (Betty), Miquela (Mickie).
Courtesy Josephine Ringling.

José, elected as Church elder in 1914, was the youngest child of Francisco Trujillo, one of the six villagers who met with Rev. Perea in 1882. Francisco and his five living children (Melecia, Daniel, Floran, Virginia, and José) were listed as attendees at the Church's 1894 organizational meeting, where Francisco was elected as one of the two first elders of the Church. Also listed as attending that meeting were Francisco's brother David Tafoya Trujillo and his eldest child Avelina, who would later marry Nicolás Gurulé.

Nicolás Gurulé, aged about 30, ca. 1912.
Courtesy Carrie Sandoval Taraddei.

Nicolás was the oldest child of founder José L. A. Gurulé and was a mainstay of The Presbyterian Church at Las Placitas in its early years by caring for both its spiritual and physical welfare. He served continuously as a ruling elder for 46 years while also serving an incredible 41 years as Clerk of Session. He voluntarily acted as caretaker of the Church building. When a minister could not get to the village, he prepared and led the Church services.

Life in the village changed slowly. Making adobes, ca.1900.
From Juan Quintana family album. Courtesy Carlos Candelaria.

House built in 1860s by Preciliano Baros for his bride Placida Lucero, ca. 1929. It was inherited by son Juan Baros in 1911 and then by Juan's widow Rumaldita in 1914. José L. A. Gurulé moved into the house when he married Rumaldita in 1915. Those pictured include Onofre Gurulé, José Gurulé, and José Trujillo.
Courtesy Christine Baros Gonzales and Sandoval County Historical Society photo archives.

The latest in music technology, ca. 1910.
L-R, José Teodosio Gurulé, David B. Trujillo, and Florencio Sandoval.

Courtesy Tony Lucero and Sandoval County Historical Society photo archives

World War I, with U.S. involved in 1917-1918. Six young men from from Placitas served in the Great War: Private Pablo Baca, Private Emeliano Baldonado, Pvt. Bertura Escarida, Pvt. Juan N. Gurulé, Pvt. Isidiro Lucero, and Private David B. Trijillo.

Pvt. Juan N. Gurulé.
Courtesy Vivian G. DeLara.

Pvt. David B. Trujillo.
Courtesy Tony Lucero and Sandoval County HIstorical Society photo archives.

Two of José L. A. Gurulé's children, a future son-in-law, and a friend, ca. 1915. L–R, front row: Rosenda Gurulé Fraide/Friday, José Teodosio Gurulé. Back row: Gregorio Gutierrez, Hipolito Escarcida (future husband of Onofre Gurulé).

Courtesy Doris "Weda" Baldonado and Robert Gurulé.

Reverend John Mordy served The Presbyterian Church at Las Placitas from 1913-1917. Horses were a vital way for pastors to make their rounds among parishoners they served.

Courtesy Carlos Candelaria.

Three of José L A. Gurulé's daughters and their families, ca. 1921. L-R, Back row: Antonio DeLara, Onofre Gurulé Escarcida and husband Hipolito Escarcida. Front row: Florinda Gurulé DeLara with son Max DeLara on lap, Bentura Escarcida and wife Carolina Gurulé Escarcida, with Onofre's son Eloy Escarcida on lap.

Courtesy Frances and Willie Escarcida.

Congregation of the Placitas Presbyterian Church, ca. 1930. L-R, second row: Roque Salazar and Nicolás Gurulé, with José L. A. Gurulé next to last at end of row. Roque and brother Ramón Salazar helped lead Church services whenever a minister could not get to the village.

Baptism of José Lucero, 1930. L-R, top row: Nancy (Nessie) Simmonds (wife of Reverend George Simmonds), Avelina Trujillo Gurulé (wife of Nicolás Gurulé).

Second row: Eugenia Trujillo Montoya with Josie Lucero (baby), Josepha Trujillo Lucero, Amadeo Gurulé, Adelina (baby), Rosa Gurulé and Lydia Gurulé.

Third row: Carmen Lucero, Elsie Lucero, Amarante Lucero.

Front Row: Bernabé Lucero (with cap), Nina Lucero, John Lucero.
Courtesy Tony Lucero, Helen Sanchez, Jim Madueña.

Right: Breaking ground for the 1930's Church. Lucas Salazar (left) and Nicolás Gurulé.
Courtesy Helen Sanchez.

Left: Nicolás Gurulé and Rev. George Simmonds during construction of the 1932 Church.

Nicolás stands in the entrance above where the steps would be.

Right: Entrance to the new 1932 Church. Note the decorative vigas, an influence of early "Santa Fe Style" more properly known as Pueblo Revival architecture.

World War II, with U.S. involvement from 1941–1945.

Several young men from Placitas served in WWII, with four pictured below. Sadly, three Placitas soldiers did not survive the War: Pvt. Emilio Chavez, Pvt. Leonidas J. Santillanez, and Pvt. David G. Trujillo.

Pfc. Sam Salazar
Courtesy Sam Salazar.

TEC 5 Max Gonzales
Courtesy Vivan G. DeLara.

Sgt. Bill F. Gurulé survived the Bataan Death March and a Tokyo POW camp.
Photo credit: Bill Gurulé, FLEETING SHADOWS AND FAINT ECHOS OF LAS HUERTAS. (New York Carlton Press, 1987).

Sunday after Church, ca. 1941. L-R: Virginia Chavez, Max DeLara, and Christine Baros.
Courtesy Frances and Willie Escarcida.

Just prior to WWII, Max and Christine collected folk stories and oral histories about Placitas to help Lou Sage Batchen record them.

During WWII Christine worked as a riveter in San Antonio, Texas while Max served as Cpl. in the U.S. Army.

The end of an era approaches. José L. A. Gurulé and his second wife Rumaldita Candelaria de Baros de Gurulé, the widow of Rev. Juan Baros. Rumaldita would pass away in June 1942 at age 70 to be followed by José ten months later in April 1943 at age 92.
Courtesy Vivian G. DeLara.

Christine Baros Gonzales. Of twelve children of Rev. Juan and Rumaldita Baros, she was the only surviving child—living to 83 in 1990.
Courtesy Vivian G. DeLara.

Barbarita Baros Lucero, ca. 1977. Last survinging child of Preciliano & Placida Baros and last surving attendee at the Church's 1894 founding. She lived to 95 in 1981.
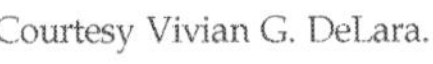
Courtesy Vivian G. DeLara.

CHAPTER V
Other Founding Families

So far it would appear that everything that happened to and for The Presbyterian Church at Las Placitas came about through a single family—the Gurulés. While they appear to have been central to the organization of the Church, their efforts would have come to nothing had they not been joined by a number of other families equally desirous of change. Lou Batchen has left us an interesting record of their earlier history and of the character of some of the Placitans who chose to become Presbyterians.

Two men were ordained as elders at the Church's organizational meeting of February 24-25, 1894. They were Francisco Trujillo and Juan Baros, and both were community leaders in their own way. Francisco Trujillo was born in 1840 on the northeast corner of the San Antonio de Las Huertas land grant in the small settlement of Uña de Gato (named "Cat's Claw" after the thorny wild locust tree). He traced his descent from the original settlers through Nicolás Montoya and José Chavez. The former, he said, was the grandfather of his grandmother, the latter was his great grandfather.[1]

Francisco was only six years old when he began to assume responsibility for his mother and younger siblings. His father, a man from old Mexico, left the family in 1846 to fight on the side of Mexico in the war with the United States. As the eldest child,

Francisco helped his mother maintain the house, care for the sheep and goats, and rear his four sisters. His father returned two years later, and two brothers were born—Joaquin and David. Then in 1854 his father died. Unable to care for so many children without a husband, Francisco's mother portioned out her daughters to relatives. Fourteen year old Francisco bought an old house in Las Placitas and took his younger brother, Joaquin, to live with him. His mother moved to Algodones with her youngest child, David.[2]

In 1861, New Mexico's Governor Connelly called for volunteers to defend the territory against an invading army of Texas Confederates. Francisco Trujillo was one of three men from Placitas who responded to the call. New Mexicans had had little reason to develop any great loyalty to the Union. The Confederacy had fully expected New Mexicans to fight on its side. However, it failed to take into consideration the long standing New Mexican distrust and hatred of Texans. Some twenty years earlier Texas had invaded New Mexico in an attempt to annex it. The mere suggestion that Texans were once again on the move was enough to rouse the fighting spirit of men like Francisco Trujillo. He and his friend Francisco Gonzales marched off to war. Both fought in the Battle of Valverde, and both returned to live out their lives in Placitas.

Upon returning from the war, Francisco went to work for a newcomer to Las Placitas named Juan Armijo. According to Trujillo family legend, Armijo was a Navajo who had been captured as a child and brought up in an Armijo family of Alameda. In time he became a master weaver and a wealthy trader. When he moved to Las Placitas around 1860 he brought with him his wife and family, many personal belongings, herds of cattle and sheep, and several other families, among them the Luceros and the Escarcidas. Armijo presumably left Alameda because he had become a target for thieves (including Navajo raiding parties). He thought that he could protect his property and livestock better if he had them in the mountains around Las Placitas.

Trujillo began by helping Armijo build a large and, for its time, elegant house in Las Placitas. In a short time he became his employer's valued associate, helping him engineer his marketing trips over the Santa Fe Trail to Missouri, calculating the value of the loaded wool wagons, and deciding what kinds of goods to bring back for sale in New Mexico—items such as copper kettles, coffee, sugar, bolts of cloth, and manufactured clothing. After one particularly successful trading trip Francisco brought back a marvelous brocaded silk wedding dress, the first of its kind ever seen in Las Placitas, and presented it to Juan Armijo's daughter, Miquela. The two were married shortly afterwards in the San Felipe Mission Church and settled down to live in the old house that Francisco had bought in the village. Both of Francisco's younger brothers also worked for Armijo. Joaquin, like Francisco, took numerous trips over the Santa Fe trail. Armijo took Francisco's younger brother, David, into his household after his mother's death. David tended goats for Armijo and eventually acquired a flock of his own. Then, based on the fact that only the Trujillo family had continued to live on and farm the old San José de Las Huertas village site, David claimed the entire area for himself and his bride, Juliana Baca of Bernalillo. [3]

Juan Armijo appears to have been the first Placitan eager to bring a teacher to Placitas who could teach the children English. This teacher, a fluent Spanish-speaking Anglo-American prospector named Wes Courtney, arrived in Placitas in the mid-1870s. Courtney married Armijo's daughter Pablita. He disappeared suddenly from the village and the people who knew him believed he met with foul play.

In addition to being respected for his business ability, Francisco Trujillo was remembered in Batchen's day as the wisest *alcalde* (mayor) in the history of the village. In the days before calendars and clocks, every village had its wise man who was able to read important information in the movements of the sun, moon, and stars. As alcalde he kept records, advised the people about the proper time to sow and reap crops, and proclaimed feast days. Above all, he was a good weather forecaster.

Each morning, regardless of the weather, Francisco Trujillo mounted his roof and faced the east at the moment of sunrise. From there he observed the heavens and made deductions from the condition of the sky, the wind, and the previous night's moon. When he descended he summoned the men of the village and uttered the weather forecast, upon which the day's activities were planned. His observations were particularly important during the pre-planting months. When all the signs were favorable for a rainy spring, he told the farmers to plant their fields plentifully, whether they were under irrigation or not. When all signs pointed to dry weather he told them to plant only the land under ditch. The new moon was most important in foretelling the weather. If the crescent rode flat in the sky, that indicated dry weather, as no water could spill from it. But if the crescent dipped it was a sure sign of rain, for water could easily spill out, as from a tilted dipping gourd.

Francisco Trujillo kept a daily calendar. He never proclaimed the fiesta days publicly, but he told someone close to him and asked that the word be spread throughout the village. Even if he had not kept a daily calendar, the villagers were sure that he could have called the fiesta days, because he knew how the wise men of long ago had reckoned them. Once, generations before, Batchen records, when there were no priests or wise men in the village to keep a daily record, they lost track of the date. One old man recalled a method for retrieving it. They must wait for the harvest moon, he said, then count fifteen days forward. That day would be the Feast of Las Cabanas or the Jewish Feast of the Tabernacles, and would be around the fifteenth of October. No one knew how Trujillo had come to possess this special information.

In the days before he became a Presbyterian, Francisco Trujillo made himself personally responsible for seeing that every man, woman, and child was up at dawn for the Fiesta of San Juan on June 24. He led the procession from the village to the nearest arroyo of deep running water. There they all walked into the water and, falling to their knees, completely immersed themselves in commemoration of the baptism of Jesus by John the Baptist. Then they all returned to the village to begin the day's festivities.[4]

In the early 1880s, the village divided over a number of issues. Villagers such as Francisco Trujillo, Nicolás Gurulé, and his son José Librado Aron Gurulé followed the inspired teachings of the Presbyterian missionary, José Ynés Perea; but the schism was more than a quarrel between differing religious factions. It marked a split between village conservatives and progressives, with the progressive men bobbing their hair in the American manner and the conservatives continuing to wear their hair long in the traditional manner. The progressives were more than anything else the individuals in the village willing to adopt new ideas and profit from changing times and new opportunities. According to Batchen, the villagers credited Nicolás Gurulé, father of José Librado, with introducing the use of American-style furniture to Placitas. He made a table and benches for his kitchen by splitting pine logs, joining them together with wooden pins, and decorating them with hand carving. That inspired Juan Armijo and Francisco Trujillo to begin importing American goods to Placitas. The venture was so successful that Juan Armijo was able to enlarge his business and establish an important trading post servicing the communities of La Madera and Tejón, as well as the many prospectors working mines in the Ortiz and San Pedro Mountains.[5]

Armijo's house was famed for its fine hospitality. Priests and politicians were frequent guests, and Armijo himself was something of a minor Republican power. Batchen records that Mariano S. Otero and his political ally Thomas B. Catron visited there on occasion. Armijo died in the late 1870s, before Rev. José Ynés Perea made his first visit to Placitas. Judging from his close association with the "progressive" wing of the village, it is likely that had he been alive, he would have been among the small group who welcomed Perea to the village in 1882.[6]

Juan Baros was a leader of a different sort. He was descended from settlers who made their home at La Madera on the San Pedro section of the San Antonio de Las Huertas land grant. The village of La Madera was built in a clearing on the thickly wooded east-facing mountain slope close to the source of Apache Canyon. The distance between La Madera and Las Placitas was about five miles, and people traveled frequently between the two communities for special events.

Juan's grandfather Manuel Baros had once been head of the La Madera community. A man remembered for his fairness and wise counsel and for the worldly goods that he shared with those less fortunate than himself, he was also remembered as a stern taskmaster. Manuel Baros loved to till the soil. He owned several span of oxen and a good wooden plow. Every spring he offered out his hoard of seed and the use of his oxen and plow to anyone desiring them. When his offer was not accepted he became angry. But many men turned him down because farming was never easy in La Madera. Rainfall, rather than irrigation, determined the harvests. In rainy seasons the bean crop was heavy and corn grew abundantly, but there were many years when there was very little reward for the hours spent in plowing As a result, many La Madera settlers did no more than cut and haul lumber. Manuel Baros regarded this failure to till the land as nothing short of sacrilege. He scolded his neighbors for shirking their farming chores and admonished them to be thrifty and honest and hardworking. [7]

Presumably Manuel passed these traits that meshed so well with Presbyterian ethics and concepts of morality, along to his son, Preciliano. Whether Preciliano also inherited his father's lands in La Madera is less certain. Shortly before he married Placida Lucero in the late 1860s, he built a house with a patio on the west side of Las Placitas. He was a farmer and, Batchen tells us, was remembered as one who had worked hard to accumulate more lands. He was also a trader and, like Francisco Trujillo, associated with Juan Armijo. On his numerous trips to Kansas City and Chihuahua, Mexico, she tells us, he acquired bolts of cloth that Placida made into clothing for herself and their children. He also brought back various pieces of furniture for resale in the early 1870s, and enough copper kettles that Placida had one for every pottery jar in her kitchen.

As a "modern" woman Placida wore a calico dress cut in the latest fashion with a very full skirt worn over many petticoats. She gave up wearing *teguas* (moccasins) in favor of store-bought shoes. Her mother-in-law, a much respected woman named Gabrielita Gallarda, disdained the new fashions and clung to the traditional sack-like skirt and shirt. She refused to put aside her moccasins. Neither would she sleep or eat on anything but her clean, smooth (and she insisted) more comfortable and warm mud floor.

Placida is remembered as one of the first women in Placitas to have a table and benches in her kitchen, and a wooden bed with a homemade wool mattress in her bedroom. To be sure, the furniture was homemade of rough boards split from pine trees, but its use marked the Baros household as both prosperous and modern. Much of this prosperity, we are told, came from the influx of gold seekers who hired Placitans to help them work their mining claims. Other Placitas men got jobs mining coal in the Tejón coal fields once the railroad reached New Mexico. Cash, which had barely existed before, was now essential for all kinds of comforts and conveniences. The only way for many people in Tejón and Las Placitas to get it was to sell small plots of their land.

Placida and Preciliano lost several of their children in the terrible diphtheria epidemic of the late 1880s. Of those surviving, one son, Juan, was installed as one of the first ruling elders at The Presbyterian Church at Las Placitas. Already inflamed with a desire to preach the Gospel, he enrolled that same year in the training school for young ministerial candidates at Del Norte, Colorado. His sister Barbarita became a staunch pillar of the Church and the longest surviving member of the original founders.[8]

Roque Salazar was one of the founders baptized and taken into membership on the night of February 25, 1894. The Salazar family, which has remained one of the most loyal and supportive in the Church's history, had once lived in the neighboring rancho of Tecolote, located where the road to Tejón crossed the Las Huertas arroyo. According to oral testimony recorded by Batchen, Roque's grandfather Juan Salazar moved there with his wife, Petra Gurulé, before either Las Placitas or Ojo de la Casa were settled. He was Alcalde of Placitas in 1863, at the same time that Lucas Gurulé was Captain of the Home Guards.[9]

Juan Salazar was remembered as an industrious farmer with herds of sheep and goats. He was also an imaginative businessman and something of an engineer. When Las Placitas became a sizable village in the 1850s, he built an ox-powered flour mill. It was a simple adobe structure housing two huge grinding stones, centered with a pole, and resting on a frame. Juan charged a fee of 20 percent of the wheat he ground into flour.

The work of driving the mill took a heavy toll on his oxen, which sometimes dropped dead in their tracks. As soon as he could afford to do so, Juan replaced the oxen with burros. They held up better under the exhausting effort, but they were very valuable animals—too valuable to be used up powering a mill. So, in the late 1860s, Salazar decided to power the mill with a water wheel. In those days water flowed throughout the year in the Las Huertas Arroyo. Juan engineered a ditch that would bring water from higher up in the arroyo to the mill and another that would return the water to the creek somewhere below the mill. The wheel, with its wide paddles, was about nine feet in circumference. Smoother and quicker than the old ox and burro-powered mills, the new wheel handled considerably more wheat in a given time. It became a popular meeting place, and Juan was rated a first-class business man.

Juan Salazar also built and operated a sorghum press. His two businesses prospered until the late 1870s. Then nature and trade played a cruel trick on him. A severe drought dried up the water supply and forced him to close the mill. He operated the press sporadically for a few more years, but the availability of commercial sugar put him out of this business as well. By the time his grandson Roque joined The Presbyterian Church at Las Placitas, the Salazar family was once again involved in farming and herding sheep and goats. [10]

CHAPTER VI
The Mission Church

The year 1900 brought a new century and a new era to the little community at the base of the Sandia Mountains. The closing of the school in that year and the departure of the Las Placitas Mission School teacher marked the end of a continuing external Presbyterian presence in the village. John Menaul continued to make regular visits to hold services in the little Church and to moderate the infrequent meetings of the Session until 1902. He was followed by Dr. Henry Thomson, the Reverend Juan Quintana, and the Reverend John Mordy, but except for the Quintanas who resided briefly in the village; their visits to the community were brief and infrequent. The loss of consistent external guidance and encouragement could have meant the end of local interest and support for the Church. Instead the small Presbyterian congregation generated its own dedicated internal leadership.

Credit for much of this strength and continuity must go to Juan Baros, Las Placitas's own homegrown Presbyterian minister. Baros was ordained an elder along with Francisco Trujillo on February 25, 1894 at the close of the meeting establishing the Church. Born in 1870 in Las Placitas, he must have been strongly influenced by the evangelist missionaries Perea, Arreola, and Menaul and by the missionary schoolteacher Lavinia Thompson;

because in the same year the Church was founded he entered ministerial training at the College of the Southwest at Del Norte, Colorado, under the Reverend Francis M. Gilchrist. In 1898 Gilchrist died and the theology school closed. Baros followed the class to Albuquerque, where it reopened in 1902 at Menaul School under Dr. Henry C. Thomson. He graduated in 1906.

Baros had already begun preaching in Placitas by the time 1900 rolled around, and in 1908 he was given full charge of both the Las Placitas Presbyterian Church and the Spanish Presbyterian Church in what was then known as Martineztown in Albuquerque. Baros remained Las Placitas's Presbyterian spiritual leader until his untimely death in December 1914, except for two brief absences. The first was in 1909 when he was assigned to the Nacimiento Church in Cuba, New Mexico. He, his wife Rumaldita, and their baby daughter Christina made the trip north in a covered wagon in the dead of winter. Caught in a blinding blizzard, they were forced to bed down on the open plains. Baros spent the night searching for bits of wood and brush to keep a fire going and his family warm, but he paid dearly for that night of extreme exposure. He contracted pneumonia, and that disease so weakened him that he developed tuberculosis. His second absence from Las Placitas was when the Church sent him to the Presbyterian Sanitorium in Albuquerque. Baros never recovered his health, but his personal tragedy may have been a disguised blessing for the little Presbyterian congregation in Las Placitas. Had he remained in good health, the Synod of New Mexico would have sent this talented, dedicated man to serve many other communities throughout New Mexico. As it was, he lived out the remainder of his life in Las Placitas, serving his congregation as a source of strength and continuity with the larger parent Church.[1]

In the last years of his life Baros must have received considerable support and solace from his friend and former classmate at Del Norte, the Reverend Juan Quintana. Quintana came to serve Las Placitas in 1904, and his wife Juana taught the public school in the village. The couple moved to Cerrillos in 1905 but returned in 1906 to live and teach until 1909, at which time Quintana was assigned to the Spanish Presbyterian Church in Albuquerque and congregations in Pajarito (a community some miles south of Albuquerque) and La Madera on the east side of the Sandias, all of them in addition to the Las Placitas Church. He is remembered as a very strict person, but then Juan Baros had had his stern moments as well. One day while Baros was preaching two young men sitting at the rear of the Church casually lit cigarettes. Baros interrupted his sermon, stepped down from the pulpit and ordered them to leave.[2]

Juan Baros lived to see the former Las Placitas Mission School building remodeled into a small but proper church, complete with a little bell tower for the bell that had been acquired some time earlier from the San Felipe Mission. Bells were not as hard to come by as one might think. They were locally cast of copper from the area copper mines. According to the minutes of the Session of October 1913:

> The Church was renovated during the summer of 1913. An American roof was put on the walls which were raised 3 more feet and new and large windows were placed in the walls instead of the former old ones which were very small.
>
> In order that it may be known to future generations, as a stimulus and encouragement, we place here the names of those who have helped with this work. This brings up the contribution until the 1st day of September, 1913

Days Labor:	
Melicendro Armijo	12
Nicolás Gurulé	13
Cipriano Salas	7
David Trujillo	1
Agustin Baros	3
J.T. Gurulé	8
José Gurulé	6 ½
Ramón Salazar	2
Roque Salazar	½
Juan Baros	2 ½
Florencio Gurulé	1 hour
Andres Armijo	2 hours
J.H. Gurulé	Paid $2.65 for nails
Besides the Congregation paid in cash	$25.67

Bills Bernalillo Mercantile Co.	
I Paid	$25.60
Least Bill	$12.72
Sash and Door Bill (Co.)	$26.46
Baldridge	$8.80
Collected by D. Trujillo	$12.00

Besides the above J. Mordy worked two days with a team hauling lumber.

J.T. Mordy, Moderator and Clerk

Despite the fact that Juan Baros put in two and a half days of labor on the Church, he had but a year to live. The Minutes of the Session of February 7, 1915 read as follows:

> The Session desires in this place to make note of the death of our beloved friend and brother, Juan Baros, which occurred on December 29, 1914, and he was buried the following day. For many years brother Baros was a faithful elder in this congregation. He had completed his studies for the ministry, but was prevented from receiving ordination by sickness. During the long period in which he lingered in consumption he bore his heavy trials with manly courage and Christian resignation. His Christian life was a noble testimony to the truth which he preached. He was an excellent business man and left his family in comfortable circumstances, in spite of the fact that for years he was unable to work. Born in very humble circumstances, he succeeded in gaining an education far in advance of his neighbors, but above all, brother Baros was a faithful Christian and his fair voice became silent while singing his favorite hymn—"Safe in the Arms of Jesus." John Mordy, Moderator.[3]

John Mordy was one of several Sunday School missionaries who visited Las Placitas on an irregular basis during these early years. In May 1913, he noted that he had also been given oversight of the church in Pajarito and "an undefined region east of the Sandia Mountains." This, he added, "rendered it impossible for him to visit the Church (in Placitas) more than once each month." Mordy may have organized the first Sunday School in Las Placitas. The Session records tell us that it was he who first suggested to the Session that members be asked to give a monthly contribution for the minister's salary.

There were 25 Sunday School missionaries in the early days in New Mexico. They often served in the capacity of "Stated Supply" in the small mission churches, preaching at as many as four different places each Sunday, visiting the sick, conducting funerals or marriages, helping out in family crises, and organizing as many as ten daily Vacation Bible Schools during the summer.].W. Winder, "Uncle John" Henry, Ralph Hall, and M.B.S. Legare are among those whose names are remembered in Las Placitas. Legare, who worked full time among the Spanish people, was particularly fond of Las Placitas. He boarded with the Gurulé family for over a year while serving the little community.

These missionaries, who often traveled circuits of fifteen to twenty-five communities, usually made their rounds in an automobile with an open top, removable side curtains, and a running board on each side. Before each trip they filled the indispensable chuck box on the running board with food and cooking utensils. While the missionaries were always invited to share a meal with one of the families in the villages where they were known, there were times when they had to prepare their meals in the open country or along a stream in the mountains. They never went anywhere without a water bag and blanket roll, and sleeping in the open was a pleasure even if the night's rain left a puddle of water on the top of their tarpaulin. Like all campers, though, they found it not so pleasant getting up on a cold or rainy morning and repacking gear soaked with rain or covered with snow.

Roads away from the main highways were little more than rutty, twisted trails. Flooded arroyos or mud holes were a seasonal problem, and in dry weather the automobiles often got "high centered" on a rock or oversize rut. There is a story of one Sunday School missionary who cracked the oil pan on his car while driving down an arroyo. As resourceful in the ways of the world as he was in the ways of the Lord, he patched the hole with some chewing gum carried for the village children, refilled the crank case with cooking oil and a melted can of Crisco, and reached his destination without further mishap.[4]

The Las Placitas community missed the continuing presence of the Mission School teacher as much as anything. Not that the community was left without a school, because New Mexico State law now assured each village a public school with a teacher paid through state funds. It was a law easier to pass than to fulfill. Schools in rural areas were rarely able to pay teachers for more than four and a half months of the year—so the children spent far less time in class than in the nine-month Presbyterian mission schools. Only one-third of the children of school age attended public schools, and then only through the third grade.

So why was the school closed when it was still so badly needed? The answer lies in the fact that in 1893 the nation was plunged into one of the worst depressions in the history of the United States. The Presbyterian Church USA (PCUSA), forced along with all other publicly supported institutions to do some drastic belt tightening, decided to close many of the plaza schools. The action was not so much an abandonment of the national Church's traditional commitment to education as it was a new approach to the matter. With schools like Menaul turning out bright, well-educated young Hispanic graduates, church leaders hoped in short order to supply the public schools with Presbyterian teachers paid through public funds rather than by the church. The plan succeeded to such a degree that many Hispanic Catholics came to see public education as "Protestant" education.[5]

Las Placitas did continue to have a public school. For at least one year the teacher was also Presbyterian—Juanita Quintana, wife of the Reverend Juan Quintana. Most families agreed that it was adequate for the first few years. But for many families, like the Gurulés, the Trujillos, and the Luceros, being educated meant something more than an elementary education. They wanted to assure their children a higher level of intellectual and moral challenge and the opportunity to learn to speak and write good English. That meant sending them away to boarding schools in Albuquerque or Santa Fe.

José L. A. Gurulé (often referred to now as José H. Gurulé due to his two hand-written middle initials sometimes looking like an

H) was particularly concerned about his younger daughters, Florinda and Onofre. Since they had lost their mother Rosita in 1906, he had found it difficult to give them proper care, even with a hired woman helping out in the home. The girls, understandably, were not as concerned about their upbringing as their father was. They loved to do chores for him, like running barefoot down the hot and dusty road to get the mail. Most of all, they loved to help him harvest the fresh produce he freighted to the mining camps or to Bernalillo for sale. The best times were when they put on their brothers' pants and climbed up into the trees to pick fruit. Their father would load it into his wagons and, by the time he got back from town, they would have picked another wagon load for him.

Don José needed and appreciated their help, but it still worried him that they were being passed from the care of one married sibling to another, and that they were not learning English. Their older sisters had attended the Allison-James School for girls in Santa Fe, as had David T. Trujillo's daughter, Josepha. But that was very far from home. So, when Onofre was twelve and Florinda ten, José sent them to the Harwood Girls' School, a Methodist boarding school in Albuquerque, from which Florinda graduated eight years later. Some years later José Gurulé sent his stepdaughter Christina Baros to Harwood as well.

Thus began a long tradition of Las Placitas Presbyterian families sending their sons and daughters away to religious boarding schools to receive a higher education. For boys and later for girls as well, the preferred school was the Menaul School in Albuquerque. Paying for boarding school was never easy. Even relatively prosperous families like the Trujillos and the Gurulés counted their wealth in land, livestock, and farm produce, and not in the cash that was becoming more and more essential to modern living. The schools were understanding, and accepted produce in exchange for tuition. After all, they had to feed their students, and what better food could they give them than the milk, eggs, vegetables, dried and canned fruit, and meat from their own homes? The students also helped to pay their tuition by doing chores at the school, like waiting tables and helping in the kitchen.

The year 1914 seems to have marked the passing of one era and the opening of another. In January of that year the Session elected three new elders: Nicolás Gurulé, Cipriano Salas, and José Trujillo. Salas did not remain active in the Church, but for Nicolás Gurulé and José Trujillo, their election marked the official beginning of many years of devoted service to the congregation. In 1915, the major social event of the fall was the marriage of Rumaldita Candelaria de Baros, Juan's widow, to widower José H. Gurulé. This marriage united the two most influential families in the Church and made Christina Baros (later to become Gonzales) and Florinda Gurulé (later to become DeLara) stepsisters. In 1917, José H. Gurulé's son, Nicolás, became the Clerk of the Session, a responsibility he fulfilled faithfully for an astonishing forty-one years. He voluntarily assumed the job of caretaker of the Church, keeping it always clean and orderly, starting the fire in the stove before each service, opening and closing the doors, and ringing the bell. Through the years that followed, he, José Trujillo, and a bit later Roque and Ramon Salazar prepared and led the Sunday service whenever a minister could not make it to the village.

In 1917, six of Las Placitas's young men marched off to serve their country in the First World War. They were: Pvt. Pablo Baca, Pvt. Emeliano Baldonado, Pvt. Bentura Escarcida, Pvt. Juan N. Gurulé, Pvt. Isidro Lucero and Pvt. David Baca Trujillo. When they returned, they found the community severely stressed.

The years 1922 through 1924 were particularly hard for the village and the Church. The mining boom that had brought prosperity to the area since the 1870s was over, as were jobs in the mines that had brought in necessary cash. Gone were the days when David T. Trujillo and José H. Gurulé could wet down wagon loads of fresh produce from Placitas gardens and haul them through the mountains to the mining camps, returning with cash in their pockets. Other men, like Roberto Fraide/Robert Friday, who had been a butcher in San Pedro during the heyday of the copper mine, had no recourse but to return to Placitas and look for some other kind of work. Most devastating of all, because there was no changing it, the villagers no longer had access to their old common lands, which were now either in private hands or part of the National Forest. Without pasture land on which to graze their sheep, goats and cattle, many village men had had to sell most of their livestock, thereby depriving their families of a major source of food and cash. To find work, men had to leave their homes for as much as ten months of the year to herd sheep and cattle in Utah, Wyoming and Montana, travel the west as itinerant sheep shearers or migrant farm laborers, mine coal, or cut ties for the railroad. Some men, like Roque Salazar, moved their whole family to Colorado for a couple of years to plant, tend and harvest sugar beets.

Family members who remained at home were hard pressed to keep their lands and homes intact. The corporate nature of the village broke down without the men, who traditionally had helped each other and shared both equipment and labor. Survival had never been easy and had required the villagers to make full use of every available resource. The village women, who had always done their share of the work, took over even more responsibilities. They tended the gardens and the field crops with the help of the old folks who remained in the village and of their children, who tended and herded the animals, cut wood, picked fruit and vegetables, and hauled water. Spring and early summer were the leanest times. By then the stores put up the previous fall were nearly depleted, and the summer crops had not yet begun to come in.

In 1922, morale in the village was so low that the Church had to take special steps to restore hope and breathe life back into the congregation. First, the Session voted to enlarge its membership to include two new elders—José H. Gurulé and Ramón Salazar. It also decided to hold a series of Revival Meetings during Lent. Revival services, known as *Revivamientos* in Spanish, truly renewed the spiritual life and fellowship of a congregation. Ministers from different communities exchanged pulpits so that the members of the congregation could hear someone new and different preach the Word. There was much singing and time for socializing as well as for worship. Before or after the service, the women of the Church prepared a meal and invited the visiting ministers to eat in different homes. In Placitas the revivals were conducted by the well-known and respected Presbyterian evangelists Gabino Rendón and Tomás Atencio. They were well attended and must have accomplished their purpose because activity in the Church definitely revived.

In 1923, the Reverend Acorcinio Lucero replaced Reverend Victoriano Valdez, who had served the Church since 1917. During

Lucero's first year in Placitas the congregation voted to reorganize the Sunday School under what appear to be its first elected church officials: Superintendent, José H. Gurulé, and Assistant Superintendent, Barbarita Baros de Lucero. The Church also elected Agustin Baros as its first Secretary-Treasurer and named several teachers to take charge of the different classes: Carolina de Escarcida, children; Frances Salazar, young ladies; and Santiago Baros, young men. The Sunday School voted to add its contributions to the minister's salary "either in money or in products of the land."

The following year, in March 1924, the Session reported to the Presbytery: 4 Elders, 32 members, 3 children baptized. It also noted that:

> This Church, having been almost abandoned for many years and the community having suffered many mishaps in its work, has not been able to carry through a program large enough to raise funds in conformity with our Presbyterian regulations, but it has agreed to adopt the following budget for the year that begins April 1, 1924.

Despite the sincere intentions, the congregation fell short of meeting its financial goals. In 1925, the Session held another series of Revival Meetings and adopted for the first time an "every member canvass" to raise money. But faced with the reality of a desperately poor and struggling congregation, it lowered its budgetary goal from $88.00 to $65.00 for the minister, leaving $23.00 for congregational expenses.

In times such as these, churches like the one in Placitas, as well as the ministers who spread themselves so thin trying to meet the spiritual needs of the many widely dispersed settlements, needed all the help they could get. Fortunately, an innovative solution to the problem had already been inaugurated at the Menaul School. Begun in 1922, the Menaul Gospel Team was one of the most important and influential programs adopted by the Synod of PCUSA in its efforts to help the small Hispanic congregations of northern New Mexico, and keep them spiritually and physically a part of the broader body of Presbyterians. The program also gave ministerial training to some of the school's most talented students.

The Menaul Gospel Team consisted of a group of students who traveled each weekend to poor and isolated communities that could not be visited by a minister. Accompanied by a teacher who helped them prepare the service, the boys (and later girls, as well) preached sermons, read passages from the Bible, sang at least two hymns in quartet, and led the congregation in singing other hymns. For men like Tomás Gonzalez, who was a member of the Menaul Gospel Team during the mid-1930s, it was an inspiring introduction to the ministry. He remembers finding it difficult to think up and prepare a sermon in those early days, so he read long passages from the Bible. That was fine with the congregation. Many of them could not read well, and they were hungry for the reading of the Word. Besides, church was one of the most enjoyable events of the week. No one was in a hurry for the service to end. As for the members of the Gospel Team, they found their visits to Placitas and other villages to be a wonderful break from the study routine at Menaul School, as a chance to stay overnight with a friendly family who treated them as honored guests and above all fed them wonderful home-prepared food.

Members of the Menaul Gospel Team also helped to plan and staff the summer Vacation Bible Schools and occasionally helped to plan special Christmas services in their home communities. But the most profound impact many of the Menaul boys had on the communities they visited may have been upon the young girls, who found the visits of the slightly older, polite, sincere, and very well turned out young men to be thrilling occasions. Though not allowed to have boyfriends (openly) by their strict fathers, the girls were allowed to walk with the Menaul boys from the Church to the bend in the road. That was as far as they could go and still be observed by their watchful parents.

The job situation in the area was somewhat relieved in 1924 when the White Pine Lumber Company opened in Bernalillo, though it was not enough to offset the loss of all the other jobs from other sources. In the meantime, life in the little village went on much as it had in the previous century with only minor changes. Babies were delivered by Aurelia Gurulé, the local *partera* or midwife, while other women assisted or stood outside and sang and prayed for a safe delivery. Presbyterian babies were baptized in Placitas; others (Catholics) still had to be taken to San

Felipe Pueblo or Bernalillo. Baptisms were always big events. The jubilant family usually roasted a little goat and invited friends and family to dinner. Weddings were also occasions for a great celebration, with dancing and merrymaking. It was all good harmless fun for the most part, but everyone remembered the accident that happened when José Trujillo and Albiria Gurulé were married. Someone lit and threw a stick of dynamite of the kind used to make roads. When the stick failed to go off as expected, José Teodosio Gurulé went to investigate. He picked up the stick just as it exploded, and he lost his hand—the same left hand that his father, José H., had lost so many years earlier in the accident with the rifle. The eerie coincidence was discussed for years.

When a person died, the family washed the body and laid it out in a wooden casket made by Benino Archibeque. Then everyone gathered for the *veloria,* or wake. If the deceased was a Presbyterian, Nicolás Gurulé rang the bell at the Presbyterian Church—one clap for every year of the person's life. If the deceased was a Catholic, someone tolled the bell at the Catholic Church. When an old person died, the bell was struck so that there was a dung, a miss, and a dung. When the bell rang steadily, everyone knew that someone young had died. The original Placitas cemetery was reserved for Catholics, but there was now a Presbyterian cemetery as well. Both were officially owned by the San Antonio de las Huertas Land Grant.

Placitas was still very self-sufficient. The only things that people had to buy at the Bernalillo Mercantile were coffee, refined sugar, and flour. José H. Gurulé had two large adobe warehouses filled with the products his workers had put up for the winter—dried and canned fruit and meat, slabs of dried bacon, and preserved vegetables. Since nobody had any money, Gurulé used to exchange his produce for other commodities, which in turn could be bartered for yet other goods.

Gurulé kept a large bull snake in one of the warehouses to catch mice. He called it "his cat." Though the snake was quite harmless to people, his grandsons were invariably startled out of their wits when they encountered it looped over one of the rafters while hunting for something in the dimly-lit building. One day, while their grandfather was in town on business, they killed it and did away with the body. Old José H. surely suspected what had happened to "his cat," but the boys never confessed, and nothing more was said of the matter.

Each family had its own store of dried and preserved foods and homemade wine in the cellar, and everyone tried to have a few chickens, one or two pigs, and two to three goats. A horse was a *must.* Without a horse the family had no form of transportation—either on horseback or pulling a wagon—or any way to haul wood from the mountains to burn in the stove or to sell in Bernalillo.

The men still used horses to tramp out the wheat on hard mud threshing floors. Women ground corn into meal on a metate, beat pinto beans from their pods with sticks, and winnowed by hand. They made clothing for their families, plastered their houses and the churches whenever they needed refreshing, and tended their kitchen gardens. Those men who were able to get permits to graze their sheep and cattle in the National Forest combined them into collective herds and took them to the high pastures of the Sandias in the summer. Their sons, in family groups of three to four, took the lambs and goats to pasture closer to the village. After school the boys chopped wood for the fire, and on Saturdays they went either with their father or alone to dig stumps for firewood in the forest. The girls assisted with the care of the younger children and helped their mothers with the washing, cooking, sewing, and cleaning. Everyone helped to maintain the community irrigation system, and families got together to harvest the crops, dry and preserve the summer's fruits and vegetables, and assist at the yearly *matanza* or hog slaughtering.

The family worked at chores, such as jelly-making and stringing red chile peppers into colorful *ristras* in the long, golden summer evenings. There was always fun in working together. A favorite trick was to bury a watermelon under the huge pile of chiles as a reward and incentive for the children. When their attention and efforts lagged, an adult would say: "¡Appurense, hijos, hay abajo de las pilas de chile una sandía!" (Hurry up, children, there's a watermelon under the piles of chile!) But the children couldn't eat the watermelon until all of the ristras were made. The favorite pastime was still visiting, usually in the late afternoon after the day's work was done, when it was pleasant to sit on a *banco* on the shady side of the house and laugh and talk. On chilly days people gathered around a cozy fire. A favorite gathering place was in front of the house of José H. Gurulé, who was the patriarch of the village. On summer evenings, after their chores were done, children played hide-and-go-seek, "kick the can," and baseball. Boys spun tops and played marbles; girls played jacks, hopscotch, London-Bridge-is-Falling-Down, and jump rope. Girls reserved their dolls for winter in-door play. Sometimes all the children would get together and build a bonfire and tell stories, but all play ended abruptly when a mother or grandmother whistled. By nine o'clock all villagers, adults and children alike, were headed for home and bed.

Placitans still kept San Juan Day with feasting and horse racing and celebrated San Antonio's Day, by virtue of special permission from the Catholic Church in Bernalillo, on November 13 after the harvest was gathered and the wine was in the barrels.[6] Prohibition had technically ended any sales of the fine Placitas and Bernalillo wine, but most families continued to put up enough for their own consumption. And while the Presbyterian families did not attend Mass, many were happy to join in the dancing and merrymaking that followed. There were two dance halls in the village, and lots of dances. Some of the Presbyterians did not really approve of dancing, but a young girl could generally sweet-talk her father into taking her, particularly if this meant that he could keep a sharp eye out for any suitors that might press her with too much attention. A local band, usually made up of a guitar, a violin and an accordion, provided the music. The dancers paid ten cents a dance—unless it was the celebration put on by the *Mayordomo* after the ditches were cleaned in the spring. In that case it was the *Mayordomo* who footed the bill.

Apart from these moments of frivolity, life was serious and work-filled, and a service at the Church was a real social get together. At special times throughout the year the women baked bizcochitos and brought coffee for a social hour before or after the Church service. Occasionally the members would go up to the Sandia Conference Grounds, hold a service, sometimes perform a baptism, and have a picnic afterwards. The most anticipated event of the year was, without doubt, the annual Christmas Pageant, together with the party that followed. This was the one time of the year when the children of the community took part in the service. For many years Christina Baros (later Gonzales) had charge of the program, planning the Nativity Play and rehearsing the children for their roles. Almost every child had a role, and the better speakers got the lengthier parts. Everyone remembers the magic of the beautiful Christmas tree decorated with real candles, but few recall the time it almost caused a terrible tragedy. It happened shortly after Rumaldita Baros and José H. Gurulé were married. Rumaldita's daughter, Christina, was standing on tip-toe to light some of the higher candles when her new organdy dress caught fire. Everyone gasped in horrified surprise. Her mother fainted, her stepfather started to strip off his jacket to throw it over her. But Florinda, her new stepsister, acted most quickly of all. She grabbed the burning dress and tore it off her screaming sister. Florinda had badly burned hands and Christina was very sick afterwards from shock and fright, but to everyone's relief, Christina survived the near tragedy without permanent harm.

As soon as the religious part of the Christmas program was over, the festivities began. The most exciting moment was when Santa Claus arrived. Children and adults alike waited breathlessly for the knock at the door that announced his arrival. Then Santa would burst into the room dragging a big sack filled with toys and little bags of fruit, nuts and candies. In the early days it was Roque Salazar who played Santa. He acted the part with great gusto, bouncing into the room telling everyone stories of the adventures he had had on his way down from the North Pole.

Giving was always simple in this poor community, and there was only one gift per person; but everyone, man, woman and child, Church member or village visitor, received something from Santa—net bags or little sacks of dried fruit, bizcochitos, and empanaditos, or the oranges, apples, nuts, and candy that became available in later years at the Mercantile in Bernalillo. Little girls received dolls made by their grandmothers. Some years bags of toys came from the Presbyterian women's mission field, and in 1931 toys came from the First Presbyterian Church in Albuquerque. On Christmas morning everyone was up early. The children made the rounds of the houses with their little sacks begging for more sweets, and reciting: "*¡Angelitos somos, del cielo* *venimos, pidiendo limosnas, y si no nos dan, las puertas quebraremos!"* (We are little angels come from Heaven, begging alms; and if you don't give them to us, we will break down your doors!)

Easter Services were more restrained and concentrated on Good Friday, when people really thought about the great sadness of the Passion of Christ. If there was a pastor in the village, he held a three-hour service on the Seven Words of Christ. Each one of the elders took a passage and spoke on its meaning. Since the pastors who served Placitas had their main commitment to the Second Church in Albuquerque, however, there were apparently very few Good Friday services in Placitas. People did remember some beautiful sunrise services in the back of the Canyon on Easter Sunday morning. Everyone assembled just as the sun was coming over the mountain. After the service everyone stayed for a picnic.

Easter time called for the preparation of festive foods prepared with eggs, which the women saved up for the occasion. The favorite egg dish for the Easter celebration was *forejas*—bread sliced and cut into small squares which were dipped in egg batter, fried in fat on both sides, and boiled in syrup made from locally grown grapes. *Sopa* (bread pudding), made in the old days from unleavened bread, was another fiesta day favorite.

Many Catholic children attended programs at the Presbyterian Church, especially the very popular Vacation Bible Schools that were held every summer. Some may even have expressed the wish that they could also be Presbyterian. This reinforced the good feeling that most Presbyterian children had about their religion. They felt good that they (or their parents) had *chosen* to take a different course, rather than simply follow village tradition. Many children came from families where one parent was Catholic and the other Protestant, and they had been allowed to make their own choice when they came of age. Still, with the village divided between the two faiths, there were some understandable antagonisms. To an outsider, it might have seemed at times that the village was split into two warring religious camps. These divisions made for some rather intense competition in the village, some lusty arguments, and, when some men had drunk too much of the homemade wine, some bloody brawls.

People loved to argue. In the rather humdrum life of the isolated little village, it was the preferred, and usually safest, method of "letting off steam." Many families were split between the two churches. Brothers argued with brothers, neighbors argued with neighbors; but after the shouting died down, and all the people involved had slept off their peeve, they were all friends again—at least until the next argument. It *had* to be like that because, in the final analysis, everyone was related to everyone else. Everyone was *familia*, and the survival of the family depended on the cooperation of every one of its members. Even more important, the survival of the village itself depended on this cooperation.

Despite the fights and antagonisms, the only incidents of outright discrimination appear to have been on the part of outsiders, such as when Florinda Gurulé, her sisters, and her friend Barbarita Baros attempted to attend the wedding of a cousin in the Catholic Church. The priest recognized them and demanded that they leave because they were Presbyterians. It was an embarrassing incident long remembered. While not strictly discriminatory, the high school in Bernalillo, run by the Catholic Sisters of Loretto, took Presbyterians only when there were not enough Catholics to fill the roster. This meant that the Placitas Presbyterian children whose parents could not afford to send them away to boarding school often had to forego high school, a situation that did not change until the 1950s, when the Dixon Case (so-named because it was filed by a Presbyterian family in Dixon, New Mexico) ended public support of church-run schools.

Fortunately, Placitas children apparently carried few of their parents' arguments over into the schoolroom. Dulcilina Salce, a young woman from Corrales who came to teach in Placitas in the early 1920s, noticed immediately that the community was different from others she had known. A Catholic herself, she was surprised to find so many "other religions," but thought it was beautiful the way everyone got along so well. "They didn't fight over what they were. And I wouldn't let them," she recalled.

Dulcilina was fairly typical of Placitas's early schoolteachers. Just out of high school, she was only seventeen when she started teaching school. In her first year at Placitas she taught all eight grades, but she concentrated on the younger grades because not many children made it into the higher grades. Children from families that had a little more money went away to private schools. During the years Dulcilina taught in Placitas she boarded with the local Chaves family. She had grown up speaking Italian, Spanish, and English and considered it a blessing to be able to talk to her pupils in their own language—to convince them that they should learn English and "to bring them out." According to Dulcilina, if a teacher did not speak Spanish, "She had a hell of a time, poor thing." None of the children spoke any English before they started school, so they all started out with the same disadvantage and needed help, especially help given in their own language. It was very hard for the children to learn to speak English well because they spoke only Spanish with their friends and families.

The second year Dulcilina shared her responsibilities with another teacher and they divided the students into several groups. Each teacher spent about three quarters of an hour with a grade. While this was going on, the children in the other grades studied and did desk work. Occasionally the teacher had the older students help teach the younger ones, but this was not the rule. Besides reading, writing, and arithmetic, Dulcilina taught geography (with maps) and New Mexico history. Girls were easier to teach than boys, she remembered, and they used to stick up for her when mischievous boys tormented her. Childish pranks being what they were, and relatively harmless, everyone, students and teachers alike, remember school days as being really enjoyable.

Helen Gurulé (later Sánchez) and Lizzie Gurulé (later Archibeque), two of Dulcilina's students, were the first to graduate from eighth grade in Placitas. She remembered them as "very busy girls." Helen went on to attend the Allison-James School in Santa Fe for one year. She then transferred to the Harwood Girls' School in Albuquerque. It was strange, she remembered, being away from home for the first time and having to really speak English. Although she could read and write the language, she had never before had any reason or any opportunity to carry on a conversation.

Christina Baros (later Gonzales), another of Dulcilina's students who later attended Harwood Girls' School, remembered that the Placitas school had one pot-bellied stove. The children used it to heat the lunches they had brought from home. Everyone walked to school, and in the coldest weather, the girls wore heavy pants under their skirts. Since there was only the one room, the boys had to wait outside the school until the girls had removed them and readied themselves for the day.

There were about five or six students in the first grade, and about the same in the second and third. The number of students in the entire school varied between 25 and 40. Although for most Placitas children, school attendance was a "must," they sometimes had to miss school, especially in the fall when there was so much work to be done at home. The school was understanding of the problem and extended the school week to include a half day on Saturday to make up the lost time. Some families could not spare their children the luxury of school at all. For them, duties at home were a matter of family survival.

Bell of The Presbyterian Church at Las Placitas. Contributions by early Church members enabled purchase of this bell from the San Felipe Pueblo mission in 1894. The bell is still in use at the Church.

Original Church Building and Early Congregation of The Presbyterian Church at Las Placitas, ca. 1910. Building in background was purchased from Pedro Pino to serve as the Presbyterian Mission School from 1893-1900. With the Church's 1894 founding, the building was used in this form for Church services until the 1913 remodeling. Photo includes L-R: Virginia Baros de Salas, Barbarita Baros, Rumaldita Candelaria de Baros and daughter Christina, Rosita Gonzales de Gurulé and daughter Florinda. On extreme right are Juan Baros—one of two first elders and later its pastor, and José L. A. Gurulé—the driving force behind bringing Presbyterianism to Placitas. Courtesy Helen Sanchez

The Presbyterian Church at Las Placitas from 1913 to 1930. Original Church building remodeled in 1913 with walls raised 3 ft. and American-style pitched roof added, larger windows installed, and bell tower with new entrance added. Picture taken about 1930 just before building was torn down to make way for the new 1930s Church construction. (Building materials shown on right side of photo.) Courtesy Helen Sanchez

CHAPTER VII
New Beginnings

In September 1929, the Reverend George Simmonds took command of the Placitas Presbyterian Church. Simmonds's energy and sunny disposition were the perfect antidote for the doldrums that continued to plague the congregation. His coming marked the beginning of both a new era and a new church building.

Simmonds had been in Albuquerque only a month when he visited the Sandia Conference Grounds in the company of Dr. Ralph Hall. While there he met Nicolás Gurulé, its attendant, for the first time. The two ministers stopped in Placitas on the way up to the camp to announce that there would be a meeting that night in the "little old Presbyterian school house, which served as the place for our services." Simmonds noted in his "Recuerdos" (Memories) that various persons in the Rio Grande Presbytery were very interested in Placitas and its fine church members. They apparently had decided that the congregation deserved a reward for its devotion and service. Four months later, on February 18, 1930, Simmonds filled out an application for a grant from the Board of National Missions of the Presbyterian Church USA (PCUSA) to build a new building for the Placitas Presbyterian

Church. Shortly thereafter he received notice that the Board had granted them $2,400.

From this point on things moved very rapidly. In April Simmonds took Jim Henry, brother of the Sunday School Missionary "Uncle John" Henry and an expert carpenter, to talk with the Placitas Presbyterian Church Elders. They decided to retain Henry to guide and oversee the construction of the new building. Within a few hours Nicolás Gurulé and Roque Salazar had hitched up their teams and excavated the basement of the Church.

On April 30, 1930, Simmonds recalled, he left Albuquerque very early in the morning for Placitas and the Rim to cut timber for the beams of the new Church. He had previously met with the Supervisor of the forest in the Sandias, who had marked some very fine trees that could be cut and hauled to Placitas. Nicolás Gurulé, Roque and Ramón Salazar, Antonio DeLara, José Trujillo, Hipolito Escarcida, and Mateo Ventura all made the trip with their teams and wagons. It was very cold in the mountains, and the logging party got back very late at night. Simmonds remembered that he spent the night either with Nicolás, where he was a frequent guest, or at his father José's home, where he spent "many a happy evening during the six years I served as Pastor." The next day they were off again for the Rim to cut more timber and haul it down to the village. A few days later Simmonds took Jim Henry to Placitas to oversee the construction, and especially the hanging of the doors and windows. Simmonds made the trip up to help as often as he could, and Placitas received the bulk of his time during those weeks and months of construction. Everyone worked willingly, Simmonds remembered, and the meals prepared by the ladies of the Church were wonderful. He wrote: "I'll never forget how good they tasted!"

On October 16, 1930, Simmonds recorded that he had received $400 to pay for plaster and window frames. He recalled that the benches were made in Albuquerque, and that the pulpit furniture was the gift of a Mr. Sommerndike. One of Simmonds's fondest memories was of a blind man who wanted to help in the building. Simmonds recalled how he had someone guide him into the right position so he could help with whatever needed doing. During the razing of the old schoolhouse, Simmonds recalled seeing him perched astride the wall taking the adobes of the wall apart, handling them ever so carefully so that they might be used in the new building. Simmonds concluded his "Recuerdos" with: "I'll never forget the faithful women of the Church who did the plastering. What a beautiful job they did. The people of the Placitas Church loved their church and kept it always in tip-top condition. I feel honored to have been one of its ministers and part of its history." The Church was completed in 1932.[1]

Reynaldo Salazar remembered that he and his brother, Lucas, used to mix mud for the adobes, load it on a sled and take it over to where the men were making the adobes. Each man had a quota of adobes to produce—he thought the number was 500. Reynaldo's father, Roque, and his uncle, Ramón, took turns with Nicolás Gurulé laying the adobes. George Simmonds worked right along with them. He was so strong, Reynaldo recalled, that one time when they were putting up vigas Simmonds lifted the end of one viga, while it took three men to lift the other end.[2]

Willie Escarcida remembered that when his dad took his team of horses to get the vigas for the Church, he took only the front and rear axles and their wheels. The men loaded one end of the vigas on the front axle and then tied the opposite ends to the rear axle. In this way they maneuvered the enormous logs down the narrow, winding trail to the village. Amarante Lucero recalled how exciting it was for the young boys to watch the older men work. He knew the work was really tiring. The men used two-man push-pull saws to cut down the trees, and then stripped off all the limbs before loading the logs onto the wagon frames.[3]

The new Church building, together with the new pastor and his assistants, had an exhilarating effect on the Placitas congregation. The Session, spurred by a renewed sense of purpose and direction, met four times in 1931 and noted, in its annual report to the Presbytery, that regular Church services and Sunday School classes had been held all year without interruption. During 1932, the number of active memberships jumped from 34 to 48, and the Session raised the minister's salary to $100. But times were still hard, nationally as well as locally, and in 1933, as the Great Depression settled heavily upon rich and poor alike, Simmonds and the Placitas congregation came to some hard decisions. In 1928, under the pastorate of Paul S. Warnshuis the

Placitas congregation had begun to make annual contributions to the Presbytery and to the Board of National Missions of PCUSA, but these contributions had lapsed during construction of the new Church.

Now, with the new building completed, the national church expected the congregation to renew its commitment to the Presbytery. Unfortunately, it simply did not have the money to do so. Simmonds resolved the dilemma by taking a 40 percent cut in salary. The overall Church budget, including insurance on the new building and Sunday School supplies, totaled $124.75.[4]

Christine Baros Gonzales recalled George Simmonds as "the missionary Pastor" because he made such an effort to minister to the small, neighboring congregations of La Madera and El Llano. When visiting the little preaching station at La Madera he often took two or three young people from Placitas to assist him with the service and to help him if his car got stuck going through the canyon. While the young people frequently rode their horses through the canyon to attend social events in La Madera, the way was impassable for a car until George Simmonds took it into his head to get a proper road. Somehow he persuaded the Forest Service to build it, with the people of La Madera supplying the labor. The residents of La Madera were so pleased to have the road that they would have gladly performed the work free of charge, but the Forest Service eventually paid them for their labors.[5]

Simmonds's assignment to minister to Placitas and its nearby villages, as well as the Second Presbyterian Church in Albuquerque and the Spanish Presbyterian Church in Santa Fe would have been impossible even for a man of Simmonds's dedication and robust constitution had he not had a lot of help. Fortunately he had the assistance of several student pastors and the Menaul Gospel Team. The Gospel Team, assisted by girls from the Life Service Band, took the entire responsibility for services once a month at La Madera. One of the student pastors who assisted Simmonds in Placitas was Alfonso Esquibel. Another was Porfirio Romero, remembered by the young girls of the time as "the romantic pastor." Romero married Elizabeth Valdez, the pretty daughter of the Reverend Victoriano Valdez, during the time he was serving in Placitas. Victor Manuel Sandoval was another of Simmonds's assistants. Sandoval took full charge of the Placitas Church for one year after Simmonds left, then followed his friend and mentor to San Francisco.[6]

It was during the early years of Simmonds's pastorate that Max DeLara began to collect folk tales and oral histories for Lou Sage Batchen. One of Max's favorite story tellers was his grandfather, José H. Gurulé. He says he can remember, as if it were yesterday, sitting with him under the shade of an old apricot tree and hearing him tell the story of how he had once been mauled by a bear. Sometime before Max was born his grandfather went to check on one of his workers who was herding sheep for him on the other side of the Sandias. When nightfall came, they both rolled up in their blankets and went to sleep by the side of their fire. The sheepherder had a little dog, and in the middle of the night the dog started to bark furiously. José H. raised his head and there, by the light of the coals, he saw a bear. The bear also saw him and charged just as José was shaking clear of his blankets. He caught the bear's tongue, and stabbed at him with his little knife, but it was a very uneven contest. The shepherd heard the commotion, and seeing the bear, started to run away. Then he came to his senses, grabbed his rifle, and shot the bear. It was none too soon, because by this time the bear had inflicted deep scratches down José's back and bitten deeply into his shoulder. In later years Max and his brothers frequently asked to see his grandfather's scars. It thrilled them to think how strong and brave he had been in his youth.[7]

In October 1933, the CCC (Civilian Conservation Corps), a Depression program of the Roosevelt "New Deal," established a camp just above the village in the Sandia Mountains Forest reserve. Thirteen heads of families enrolled from Placitas. The many Placitas men and boys who served in the "CCs" really enjoyed the years they worked for that very worthwhile organization. Only one man per family could serve at a time, and the term of service was limited to two and a half years. For doing all kinds of conservation work in the forest and for building roads, bridges, and picnic grounds, each man received $30 a month. He was given $5.00 for his personal spending, and the government sent the remaining $25.00 home to his family. That sum, small as it was, went a long way toward sustaining a family that produced most of its own food. The DeLara boys, the Salazar cousins, and most other eligible Placitas men took their turns in the CC's, then got jobs in the W.P.A. (Works Progress Administration), another Depression era jobs program, building the new road from Bernalillo to Placitas, and a new school house in the village plaza. Other W.P.A. projects in the area included cleaning ditches, work on the levee, and building the visitor center and stabilizing the archaeological ruins at the Coronado Monument.[8]

Besides being paid by Lou Batchen for helping her collect stories and oral histories, Christina Baros and other village women were paid for making mattresses, a W.P.A. program for village women. The money everyone received for these jobs or others with government organizations like the Soil Conservation Service and the Farm Security Administration brought a minor economic boom to the area. Suddenly Placitas could support three stores and, for the first time in years, the villagers began to fix up their homes and even buy a few luxuries—things like a gas-powered washing machine, an ice box, or a phonograph.[9]

George Simmonds left Placitas and Albuquerque in 1935. Paul Warnshuis, who preached briefly in Placitas before being made Assistant Director of the Board of National Missions of PCUSA in charge of mission work among Spanish-speaking people, remembered Simmonds as someone who brought a missionary fervor and zeal to his work. He also helped Spanish Americans sing their way into the Kingdom. When Simmonds began his ministry, there was scarcely a Spanish anthem in print and almost no choral music in Spanish to be found, anywhere. George produced more than fifty collections of anthems, several sacred song books, and a new hymnal with more than four hundred hymns translated into Spanish. He is remembered fondly in the village as "the singing pastor."[10]

One year later, Placitas came under the care of its equally beloved José I. Candelaria. Candelaria, like his predecessors, had charge of Second Presbyterian Church in Albuquerque, the Placitas Presbyterian Church, the little Presbyterian congregation in La Madera, and the Spanish Presbyterian Church in Santa Fe. During the first years of his pastorate, he held Sunday church service in Albuquerque at 11:00 in the morning, in Santa Fe at 2:30 in the afternoon, and finally in Placitas at 7:00 in the evening. Carlos Candelaria, José's son, remembered that on the first Sunday that his father preached in Placitas, he brought the entire family to introduce them to the congregation. Carlos recalled how peaceful and beautiful the little village was with its little irrigation ditches and the narrow, rose-hedged lane that led up past the Presbyterian Church. Peaceful, that is, until the Church bell began to clang out the happy news that the pastor had arrived. Then the doors of the houses burst open and people flocked to the little Church to meet the newcomers. For both the Candelaria family and the congregation, it was love at first sight.[11]

Candelaria continued and expanded Simmonds's efforts to interest the young people of Placitas in the work and mission of the Presbyterian Church and involve them in church activities. One of the ways he did this was to bring groups of young adults from Second Church to Placitas to attend Christian Endeavor meetings and to help with the summer Vacation Bible Schools. The plan worked, and Placitas youngsters looked forward as eagerly to meeting their contemporaries from Albuquerque and learning from them something of life in the larger city, as they looked forward to visits from the Menaul Gospel Team. The Placitas young people, in turn, visited La Madera to encourage young people from that even smaller, more isolated mission to endure in their faith.

Christian Endeavor classes met in Placitas between 1934 and 1940, usually on Tuesday evenings. They were a favorite activity of the young people and the most eagerly anticipated activity of the week. When there was no adult leader, which was often, the young people planned their own activities and assigned themselves passages from the Bible to be memorized and recited. At other times, each member read a passage from the Bible and commented on its meaning. Then they all sang and prayed.[12]

Slowly but surely, Placitas was becoming less isolated and more a part of the larger world. First, the lack of jobs drove many men and even entire families to travel beyond the valley in search of work. Then in the 1930s and 1940s many government programs came to Placitas to deliver various health services and to teach the women to can fruits and vegetables and practice better hygiene. Closer relations with Menaul and Second Church continued the process of widening horizons. Those who could buy battery-powered radios developed a new awareness and interest in things happening miles and even worlds away. By 1935, there were three telephones in nearby Bernalillo. That meant that when a crisis occurred in the village, the minister could be summoned to help. By 1938, thanks to the W.P.A., he even had a fairly decent, though still unpaved, road by which to reach the village.

Visiting, which previously was the exclusive responsibility of the deacons and a few other church officials, now became a much appreciated activity of the pastor. José Candelaria considered it to be a major responsibility. He traveled to Placitas almost every Tuesday, usually accompanied by Matilda Martinez (later Matilda Tapia), his most faithful assistant. They spent the entire day visiting members of the congregation, and in the evening they led the Christian Endeavor Society and Bible Study classes. They paid particular attention to the sick and elderly, and, when summoned to a deathbed, they prepared the body for burial and later officiated at the funeral. Matilda played the piano for the evening meetings and for Sunday Church services. In 1939, she began training the Church's first choir.[13]

By 1940, Church members numbered 54. The budget had grown ever so slightly to $150, and a fine group of young people, brought up in the Presbyterian faith, given moral and spiritual guidance through thoughtful attendance at Sunday School and Christian Endeavor meetings, many of them well educated at Menaul, were ready to take over the reins of leadership from the aging founders. Instead, they found their world turned suddenly topsy turvy.14

Construction for a new Presbyterian Church began in 1930 on the same location as the original one-room building used for Church services from 1894-1930. Above is the newly-completed Church in 1932. Below is the same western view of the Church as of the early 1960s. Note that the decorative vigas have been removed due to their deterioration.

CHAPTER VIII
The End of Innocence

The bombs that shattered the tranquility of a Sunday morning in Pearl Harbor, Hawaii on December 7, 1941, reverberated around the world. In New Mexico they brought the outside world crashingly home, ending for all time the isolation and community cohesion that had been the source of the villages' strength and salvation throughout the first 175 years of their existence. The breakdown in cohesion did not happen all at once. It had begun eroding in the early 1920s when the need for money and jobs drove the villagers to leave the comfort and security of their beautiful valley to seek employment in the outside world. But these jobs were always temporary, and often only one or two family members left the community. It was hard maintaining the family land holdings with the reduced work force, but family roots were left intact. With the beginnings of World War II, entire families pulled up their roots and left the valley, few of them to return.

The War did solve the unemployment problem. A great exodus of young people to the army, navy, and defense work occurred almost immediately. But, while the village was virtually depopulated, those who remained behind benefitted from the increased flow of money from sons and relatives living, fighting, and working abroad. At least one Placitas man was already in the service when the War began. He was Nicolás Gurulé's son, Bedelio, who, seeing the approach of World War II, had joined the New Mexico National Guard at the end of his second year at the University of New Mexico. His unit, the 200th Coast Artillery Regiment, was stationed at Clark Field in the Philippines when the Japanese attacked. With American defenses all but wiped out in the Pacific, the Philippines surrendered in May 1942, and Sgt. Bedelio Gurulé, along with many other New Mexicans, found himself a prisoner of the Japanese. He survived the terrible Bataan "Death March" and, after four years of captivity, was liberated and sent home. His mother, who had never before left the environs of Placitas, met him at the dock in San Francisco. Bill, as he came to be called later, took advantage of the government subsidized education program known as the "G.I. Bill of Rights," and enrolled at the University of California-Berkeley. He graduated from that institution in 1949 with a degree in International Relations. Bill was one of many Placitans who returned briefly to the village but did not stay.[1]

Of the men from the Placitas area who served in World War II, three died while in service to their country. Their names were: Pvt. Emilio Chavez, Pvt. David G. Trujillo and Pvt. Leonidas J. Santillanez. Pvt. Isaac Sandoval died a few years later in 1951 in Korea. Many other Placitans, men and women, left the village to work in defense industries. At least one woman, Christina Baros Gonzales, worked as a riveter in San Antonio, Texas. For the people who waited anxiously at home for news of their loved ones, so far away in a world they could hardly comprehend, it was a sad and lonely time. And it was the hardest time that the Church had encountered so far.

Reverend Candelaria reported that the village population had dwindled to such an extent that he had had to cut back on many programs. In addition, the difficulty of securing enough gasoline, which was strictly rationed throughout the war years, made it impossible for him to continue making his weekly trips to the village to hold the meetings of the Christian Endeavor Society, now called Westminster Fellowship. Candelaria could go only once or twice a month to call on families and hold a prayer service. Fortunately, the Women's Missionary Society organized by Mrs. Candelaria continued to hold regular meetings and helped to raise the benevolence budget of the Church.[2]

By 1943, the Church was badly in need of repairs, and Candelaria arranged for the Menaul School to extend credit for this purpose until such time as the Church could pay the bill. As usual, the members of the congregation did the work, including the women who did the plastering. The Church budget was now at $233 and included an honorarium of $96 for the pastor. Candelaria returned $24 of his salary to the congregation in the form of a gift.[3]

On April 2, 1943, the Church bell tolled 93 times announcing the death of Elder José L. A. Gurulé, (now known as José H. Gurulé). Nothing symbolized the passing of the old times so much as the death of the feisty old man who had led the village for so many years.

Early in the 1940s Reverend Candelaria added Alameda to his busy preaching schedule. He had begun his ministry to that community with prayer meetings in the homes of local residents. In October 1944, they asked Candelaria to start a Sunday School, and the Alameda Church acquired a good sized house in which to hold regular church services. Amadeo Maes, a retired minister, came to help in Placitas in 1945 so that Candelaria could give more time to organizing the Alameda church. Like Simmonds before him, Candelaria continued to travel to La Madera every two weeks for services and Sunday School classes, but despite his efforts and those of the Menaul Gospel Team, the ministry failed when La Madera was all but abandoned during the War.[4]

The year 1945 brought victory for the United States—in Europe on May 8 and in Asia on September 2. With the painful, costly war finally ended, the Placitas men and women who had served their country rushed joyfully home to renew family ties only to find that both they and their village had changed. Without realizing just when and how it had happened, most had become accustomed to a faster pace of living, with conveniences and excitement completely unknown to the little village. Observing with fresh eyes the poor and simple lives of their parents, they could not imagine themselves living the same way. Most had also acquired new skills and knowledge, and they wanted jobs that offered a challenge and opportunity for advancement. They also wanted cars, money in their pockets, and the possibility of someday acquiring a house with all the modern appliances that were still unheard of in Placitas.

As for Placitas, it had changed for the worse. A twelve-year drought had killed most of the apple trees. Between the drought and the lack of men in the village, the irrigation system had broken down and the neglected farms and gardens were dry and choked with weeds. There was no going back to the old days when villagers could graze their sheep, goats and cattle freely on the Forest Service lands that had once been part of the San Antonio de Las Huertas land grant. Now the Forest Service permitted only a limited number of head of livestock to graze, not enough for the two families, the Maldonados and the Luceros, that had once supported themselves entirely by raising cattle. Since there was no place else to graze their livestock, they had to abandon this business.

So Lucero men, like many others in Placitas, went off to seek their fortunes in Albuquerque and beyond. Some families simply moved down the road to Bernalillo to take jobs with the city, county, or state. Others went to work in the mines in Madrid and Cerrillos, and when those mines closed, they worked in the mines in Grants. Finally, many families moved to California or to Denver to work in factories. Knowing that they would not likely ever return, they sold their homes and land to outsiders.

Those who remained in Placitas had to scratch for jobs in the tight New Mexico economy. Sam Salazar, who had learned to operate heavy equipment while working for the W.P.A. and the Soil Conservation Service, found no market for these skills, so for a number of years he drove a school bus for Santo Domingo Pueblo and worked as a janitor and maintenance man. In time many Placitas men, like Salazar and Max Gonzales, found positions with the Veterans Administration, Kirtland Air Force Base or Sandia Laboratories, or with other governmental entities. Making the long daily commute to town was difficult, but the reward of maintaining roots in the little village, of keeping a few head of livestock, raising a little garden, and staying close to family and church, made it worthwhile. Meanwhile, with the passage of time, and exposure to alien beliefs and cultures in the outside world, the old animosities that had existed in the village between the Catholics and the Protestants faded. Mixed marriages were common among those who stayed in the village—there was not that large an eligible pool to choose from—and tolerance within the family extended to civic and community ventures. Still, everyone rather missed the excitement of the old contests between the different faiths.

The continuing drain of persons and talent from the Church rolls is reflected in the Minutes of the Session. In December 1946, both the Church treasurer and Sunday School teacher left for California. The Session chose a new treasurer, but could find no one to take over the teacher's job. The situation was, if anything, worse a year later. In April 1947, Reverend Candelaria noted that the exodus from the community continued and included the newly elected leader of the Sunday School and his family. Now there was no one left to teach the Vacation Bible School except the pastor. Barbarita Baros Lucero, who usually played the organ for the Church, and Matilda Martinez, who assisted Reverend Candelaria, must have been away, also, as there was no one to help with the music. Candelaria hoped that none of the women, who had long been the backbone of the congregation, would have to leave the village to earn their livelihood. Meanwhile, the drought continued, making life very difficult for everyone.[5] That year some Anglo newcomers attended the Good Friday and Easter Sunday services as guests and showed a great deal of interest in the Church. A year later there was a new Anglo member. Betty Lou Kelly, from the Evangelical and Reformed Church of Plymouth, Pennsylvania, moved to Placitas following her marriage to Herminio Baros—just one of many Anglo spouses to follow.

Pressure from the outside world took different forms. First there was a pressure from within to bring in modern conveniences to the Church and to the village. The Church got its first plumbing in 1945 when the men of the Church brought in a water line to the Church basement. A year later the Placitas community, at the suggestion of the pastor, circulated a petition to the Rural Electrification Authority (REA) to extend electric power from Bernalillo. There was no immediate action on the electricity, and the church continued to be illuminated with gasoline lamps, but the pressure to modernize grew. In 1949, the pastor acquired an oil heater to replace the old wood stove, and the men of the Church put in pipes for a drain for the basement sink, though the building still had no sewer or septic tank. That year the men also cleaned and repaired the Church privy.

Another kind of pressure came from the Presbytery. Church funding on the national level had been drastically cut since the early days of the Depression, and support for the mission program had never recovered from this loss. In 1947, Paul Warnshuis called a special meeting of the Session to discuss the adoption of a benevolence budget fully twice that of the one raised in 1946. He acknowledged that there would be some who would affirm that it was more than the Church could raise, but, he insisted, that attitude could not be permitted to prevail. Without a much larger benevolence budget the missionary program would be cut and the Placitas Church could lose its subsidy from the Board of National Missions of the Presbyterian Church USA (PCUSA). "If there are any churches which should gladly accept the full quota assigned to them and definitely plan to pay every penny of it or even more," he told the Session, "it is our mission churches—and of course, our Spanish churches. Freely we have received—Yea, so freely ... Freely we must give."[6]

But meeting a quota was not easy for the tiny congregation, and the Presbytery accepted the fact. Although the Committee on United Promotion had asked the Session in a letter to accept the sum of $50 as its computed share of the world wide benevolence budget, that sum was crossed out and amended in pencil to $30. Despite a budget that now amounted to $333, the largest in the Church history, the congregation responded generously to a request from Bedelio Gurulé—he of the Bataan Death March ordeal—to send food to the needy of Europe. This project, instigated by a former member of the congregation, had a more immediate appeal than the more institutionalized benevolence budget. The congregation could indeed understand and identify with sending food to the needy.

In June 1950, the Placitas Presbyterian congregation received a new lease on hope and faith through the ministry of Antonio Jiménez, a layman from the Methodist Church in Las Cruces. Reverend Candelaria had come to know Jiménez personally, since his wife and Mrs. Candelaria were first cousins, and the two women had taught together at the Howchen Methodist Settlement School in El Paso. Through that connection Candelaria had learned of Jiménez's tireless and dedicated work as a circuit-riding evangelist in the southern part of the state; how, as a Watkin's Products salesman, he had preached the Gospel at countless, isolated homesteads, and how he had preached at prisons and not only brought many hardened souls into the light of Christianity, but converted some to become fellow ministers of the Lord. Now Jiménez was seventy years old, an age considered by many in the church as too old for active service. Candelaria knew otherwise. He knew that Jiménez loved preaching the Gospel as much as he loved and appreciated people and that the congregation in Placitas, along with the small congregation that had been meeting for a year in Bernalillo, needed someone with just his kind of love and dedication to lift its spirits and help its people through the trying times. Ministering to the two small congregations that in his words "listened with their hearts" restored Jiménez's faith in himself and made him feel needed, wanted, and productive. He also felt it was a way for him to repay his tremendous debt of gratitude to the Presbyterian Church for having enrolled seven of his ten children, several on partial scholarships, at the Menaul School.

Although Jiménez was originally hired on a part-time basis, both congregations were so pleased with him that they asked the

Board of National Missions of PCUSA to employ him full time. The Placitas Session further offered to pay him any surplus of contributions over debts until such time as the Board could provide him with a full-time salary. Jiménez and his wife moved into a little house in Bernalillo that he rented for $20 a month, and shortly thereafter he found property next door that would do for a little church. The organization of the Bernalillo Presbyterian Church was a mixed blessing. Fully half of the Placitas congregation had moved to Bernalillo or Albuquerque, and attending services in Placitas was a difficult matter. In a tribute of love and concern by those who remained in Placitas, the Session voted to raise a subscription to help their brothers in Bernalillo buy the Pilgrim Holiness property for a church, even though this further reduced their own membership.

Jiménez had accepted the position in Placitas on the condition that he be ordained by the Rio Grande Presbytery. That condition was not fulfilled. In May 1951, Jiménez submitted his resignation, but he agreed to stay on until another minister was found. After the new minister, Kenneth J. Green, arrived in September, Jiménez returned to Las Cruces to preach for the Baptists. He served them as an "officially designated" Bible Teacher until a year before his death at the age of 101.[7]

The year 1951 also brought an official end to the Placitas ministry of José I. Candelaria, although Candelaria continued to take a fond and special interest in the Placitas Presbyterian Church until his retirement in 1962. José Candelaria is remembered affectionately by Placitans as a man of great warmth and charm. Vivian Gonzales DeLara was told that when she was a tiny child she crawled down the aisle one Sunday while Reverend Candelaria was delivering his sermon. He picked her up, held her gently in his arms, and finished his sermon without missing a word. Vivian's mother, Christina, recalled that when he first came to the Church he wanted to organize a choir. One Sunday during service he asked if there was anyone who would like to join, and the entire congregation left their seats and came forward. Paul Warnshuis in his "Memoirs of Mission in New Mexico" attributed Candelaria's fine ministry to two things. First, he obeyed Paul's injunction to Timothy "to be steady, endure suffering, to do the work of an evangelist, and fulfill His ministry." The second was his adherence to the motto he had framed on the wall by his desk: "There is no limit to the good a man can do, if he doesn't care who gets the credit for it."[8]

In Candelaria's final report he reviewed the changes that had occurred in the village during the seventeen years he had pastored the Placitas congregation. Most evident was the depopulation of the village brought on by the war, the drought, and the lack of jobs and opportunity, factors that had robbed the Church of most of its lay leadership. But while there was little hope that the Spanish population would increase, other Anglo families were moving in. In 1940, there were only three families of Anglo extraction in the village. In 1951, there were at least ten Anglo-American families, and more were constantly trying to buy property to build summer homes. One family raised dogs and another planned to open a craft shop, but most of them had their work elsewhere. Two or three of the Anglo children were coming to the Sunday school, and the Anglo adults occasionally came to the Church for special programs, though there had been no special effort to enroll them in Church activities. Candelaria could foresee the need for bilingual work in the near future. The youth work that had been virtually abandoned for a decade had been reestablished through the organization of both Junior and Intermediate Westminster Fellowships. Meetings were held once or twice a week, sometimes in a Roman Catholic home.

Candelaria noted several pressing needs. The program of religious education needed strengthening for both children and adults. The outside walls of the Church building needed to be replastered and a ceiling was needed in the small basement room. The building also needed a sewer or septic tank and a better outdoor toilet. The village needed a monthly well-baby and pre-natal clinic, something he hoped could be housed at the Church in cooperation with the State Health Department. To do this during the winter months, the Church would have to improve the heating system, since the oil stove in use in the basement was not adequate. He recommended the installation of a small oil furnace. Candelaria also recommended that the new pastor be given an adequate travel allowance to cover the three point field that included Placitas, Alameda and Bernalillo. With a resident pastor, he hoped that a 4-H Club could be established for the boys and girls who had no other opportunity for self-improvement during their leisure time. Concluding his report, he wrote:

> We are passing through a transitional period especially in the matter of language. The predominance of English among the second generation of our people is demanding that we do most of our Sunday School and young people's work in English. However, we still find in Martineztown and more so in Placitas and Bernalillo, a good many small children who know very little English, and some who do not use it at all. We have to be cautious how rapidly we make the change, because of this, and also because we still have, even in Martineztown, at least 75 percent of the families who use Spanish in the home almost exclusively... There are many adults in these communities who will not respond too freely to English preaching . . . To continue reaching them with the Gospel, we still must go on using the Spanish in the regular preaching or evangelistic services, and make use of the English language when and where there is a demand for it, or when we are sure it will serve the purpose of the church to do its greatest and most effective work in reaching the unreached, or conserving those already in the church.
>
> Transportation and communication facilities have brought favorable changes. It has brought our fields of labor closer so that the extension work . . . has become much easier. Placitas ... has had more frequent and better service than in the buggy days.
>
> Health conditions have changed a great deal since the founding of the work, but they are still unsatisfactory. Outside toilets are numerous. A large number of homes are without sewers. Infant mortality is still high, and malnutrition is quite prevalent ... Child delinquency has increased rapidly since the last World War ...
>
> Religious conditions have changed, first in the attitude of our Roman Catholic friends toward our Protestant people. The Spanish Roman Catholic constituency are a great deal more tolerant than they were fifty or sixty years ago. Although we still have a number of our people who

> are illiterate and many who have only an elementary education, the Roman Catholic people have been raising their educational level and are doing more reading; yet we cannot say that they are even beginning to be intensive readers, unless it is the small percentage of those who have pursued higher education. The newspapers or anything in politics constitute the chief attraction for reading . . . The economic conditions for our people have gradually changed for the better, and although they are below the average, the standard of living has greatly improved ... A large number in the city of Albuquerque have succeeded in business, and after a fashion, in politics. Common labor is underpaid, and only recently have labor unions begun to organize this labor group. Discrimination in employment is quite often brought to our attention.

Placitas's next minister, English-born missionary Kenneth Green, had worked for fifteen years with the Worldwide Evangelization Crusade in Bogota, Colombia, and so spoke fluent Spanish. Quiet and reserved, he loved to take long walks in the countryside. He found the local geology fascinating and often returned with his pockets full of different kinds of rocks. Green took a very business-like approach to the ministry and projected it into the life of the church. As soon as he had moved his family, consisting of a wife and five children, into the little manse in Bernalillo where Jiménez had lived, he persuaded both the Bernalillo and Placitas congregations to set goals for themselves. In Placitas the goals were: 1) To increase the number of Sunday School teachers and so improve the efficiency of the Sunday School, 2) To better the Church attendance by means of special programs from time to time, 3) To have a special Personal Evangelism Course with instruction given weekly, so as to prepare members and young people for evangelizing the district, and 4) To improve the Church building by bettering the drainage system of the kitchen in the basement of the Church.

Green also began quietly to break down the insularity of the village. Realizing that most of the women had never left the environs of the village, he occasionally gathered a few of them up and took them off to attend meetings in Santa Fe or Albuquerque, or to help him preach in Bernalillo or Cuba. These excursions were rare and much appreciated treats and long remembered by those invited to come along.[9]

Green's efforts to instill confidence in the congregation's ability to meet its financial commitments appear to have been successful. In December 1951, he encouraged the members to accept a proposed budget of $333.96 for 1952, explaining that if 20 members each gave fifteen cents a week throughout the year it would be covered. The members not only met that goal, they exceeded it. The following March treasurer Florinda DeLara reported that 22 members had promised to give one dollar a month to the Church for a year. In May the congregation resolved unanimously to participate in a national quota of 25 percent of Church receipts for the edification of churches and seminaries, with the goal that the Church would be included in the Honor Roll presented to the General Assembly of the Presbyterian Church when it met in New York later that year.

Ken Green's next move was to encourage the congregation to become better organized at accomplishing these goals. The members held their first designated work day to paint the interior, the windows, and the doors in September 1953. Then in November the Session agreed to celebrate Thanksgiving Day with a special dinner to promote Christian communion and to raise funds for the Church. In December, when Dr. Paul Warnshuis, Secretary of the Board of National Missions of PCUSA, wrote explaining the serious financial condition of the Board and asking the congregation to raise its pastor's salary to $250 annually, the Session approved the proposal unanimously.[10]

In January 1953, the Session set three more goals: 1) To gain more members for the Church and for Our Lord Jesus Christ, 2) To put a ceiling in the basement of the Church, and 3) To start a library of books in Spanish for the congregation. August saw the installation of an electric motor in the Church to power new electric lights and plans for a clothing sale in October to raise money. Thanksgiving was again celebrated with a fund raising dinner. In December, when once again the Board of National Missions of PCUSA asked the congregation to increase its contribution toward the pastor's salary, this time from $250 to $350 a year, the members agreed to do so, "trusting in the Lord and the good will of all the members." Clearly, the congregation was coming of age.

A very special service, held on the first Sunday of February 1954, marked the sixtieth anniversary of the founding of The Presbyterian Church at Las Placitas. The occasion was a sentimental homecoming for several of the Church's pastors. The service began with Reverend Victoriano Valdez leading the congregation in prayer. He was followed by Reverend George Simmonds reading from Scripture. Then Reverend Candelaria told the story of José Gurulé's meeting with J.Y. Perea and read the Minutes of the organization and first Session of The Presbyterian Church at Las Placitas. After Reverend Green read letters from various executives of the Presbyterian Church, and Reverend Candelaria introduced the many honored guests present in the congregation, the choir from Second Presbyterian Church sang an anthem. Reverend J.C. Ottipoby, Moderator of the Synod of New Mexico, gave the sermon.

Ottipoby, a Comanche Indian trained as a chaplain for the armed forces at Harvard, chose as his text the words of Moses to the children of Israel as they stood at the frontier of the Promised Land: "Ask now of the days that are past" (Deuteronomy 4:32). A fairly typical Placitas incident occurred as Ottipoby was explaining how he had first discovered Las Placitas Presbyterian Church—while returning a dog to the village. At that precise moment a black dog walked in the door and to the front of the sanctuary. George Simmonds, quick-witted as ever, quipped, "Is this the dog?" An amused Ottipoby replied, amidst the hearty laughter, "Maybe."[11]

Green served the Placitas Presbyterian Church faithfully for three years, setting it on an upward path toward financial responsibility and independence, but the years in New Mexico were not easy for him. His wife was seriously ill, and the poor little house in which they lived in Bernalillo had a leaky roof and was in a constant state of disrepair. Though he never complained, he realized that he must move his wife to a place where she could receive better care. He resigned his position with the Board of National Missions of PCUSA in July 1954, the same month that electric lights were installed in the Church. Before he left he turned his keys over to Florinda DeLara, who taught Sunday

School every Sunday until November.[12] In that month Reverend Rodolfo Torres, a Mexican minister recently retired from the Presbyterian Church in Monterrey, took over the pulpit.

Torres's ministry was another example of Reverend Candelaria's wise and concerned stewardship. What the congregation did not know was that, with Green's departure, the Board of Missions of PCUSA had decided to give up trying to support the three struggling churches. Candelaria persuaded the Board to give them one more chance, and recommended Rodolfo Torres to be the new pastor.

Candelaria had met Torres in 1953 when he was pastor of the large Presbyterian Church of El Buen Pastor in Monterrey, Mexico. At that time Torres told him that he was in ill health and weary of the responsibilities of his large congregation. Realizing that the Placitas, Alameda, and Bernalillo churches needed a strong, dedicated Spanish-speaking minister like Torres to hold them together, Candelaria invited him to accept a call to serve them. For Torres, the idea of ministering to these three small, rural congregations in neighboring New Mexico sounded like the perfect retirement job. He accepted the call and with his wife and four children traveled to Bernalillo in August 1954 to take over the three-point field.

The reality of New Mexico turned out to be vastly different from the dream for the Torres family. Sam Torres, Rodolfo's son, recalls the shock of their arrival. The Bernalillo Presbyterian Church had only one family with four children as members. The church was a small garage-sized building located behind the equally tiny manse. Except for a few pews, it had little resemblance to a proper church. The manse was even worse, as the Greens had found. The small adobe building had deteriorated almost beyond hope of repair. Things were not much better in Alameda. The congregation was larger, but it had no church. Services were held in what had once been a bar or dance hall. Placitas did, at least, have a small church, but the building was in a state of serious disrepair. The small congregation, struggling so desperately to support itself financially and spiritually, was old and weary. Torres could hardly have found a greater contrast from his large and prosperous congregation in Monterrey.

The challenge was daunting, and the entire Torres family went to work with a fierce determination to restore life to all three churches. Eloisa Torres, an accomplished musician, worked side by side with her husband, and the music she produced, at the piano and leading the congregations in song, worked a miracle in restoring joy and faith. Their son, Sam, set about trying to rebuild a young people's fellowship in Placitas. The schedule they set for themselves was exhausting. Sundays would begin with a service in the morning in Alameda. Torres would hold a second service in Placitas at 2:00 in the afternoon. In the evening, he would hold a third in Bernalillo, if anyone turned up at the little church. His wife was often so exhausted that she wore sunglasses during the service so that no one would notice her napping.

During the week the Torreses spent each day in one or another of the villages, visiting families during the morning or afternoon and holding a prayer or Bible study meeting in the evening. Eloisa encouraged women's groups in Placitas and Alameda to meet together on a regular basis. Torres also broadcast his sermons in Spanish over a local radio station in order to reach the many scattered Hispanic Presbyterians in Albuquerque who no longer could, or would, attend church regularly.

Torres discovered early on that the congregations were small because the young people were no longer interested in coming to church. With the outside world offering many distractions, church was no longer as appealing. There was another problem as well. The overwhelming influence of English in the schools had made it very tedious for them to sit and listen to a service conducted entirely in Spanish. They found the old literary Spanish of the Bible, in particular, to be very hard to understand. Torres predicted that if the three little churches were going to survive, they would have to become bilingual.

The Torres family served all three churches until December 1957, when Torres resigned to accept the call of two small churches in Arizona, one in Miami and the other in Globe. His health problems had worsened, and he hoped that he would feel better in the warm, dry winters of Arizona. His years in Placitas had been years of stabilization and consolidation. By the time Torres left, the Church had 28 communicant members and a budget of $650. The biggest item was the minister's salary of $350, but there had also been substantial increases in the costs of heating and lighting the Church, expenses brought about by the change from wood and kerosene to oil and electricity.[13]

Electricity brought more than extra costs to the village. It made possible the conveniences that before had been only the stuff of dreams—better home lighting, electric washing machines, refrigerators, stoves, and irons. It also brought the outside world directly into everyone's parlor. Families spent less time gathered about the kitchen table talking to each other and more time listening to the radio or watching television. While the images of the world beyond the village were often wonderful and amusing, they were as often troubling and unsettling. In the growing generational split, the young people welcomed the changing times as much as their parents and grandparents regarded them with fear and suspicion. With automobiles providing heretofore unheard of mobility and television providing packaged entertainment, young people were less interested in forming Christian youth fellowship groups. Too many activities competed for their attention. No longer confined to an isolated village and required by necessity to live by the values of their parents, they embraced an increasingly secular outside world.

The arrival in August 1958 of Placitas's new pastor, the Reverend Harry S. Willson, was every bit as electrifying as the new wires that traversed the town. Willson burst upon the village with an abundance of religious zeal, a fluent command of Spanish, a sense of mission, and the intense social activism that would characterize the coming decade of the 1960s.

Willson and his wife, Christine, had received the Working Fellowship for Study offered by what was then called the Board of Foreign Missions of PCUSA while both were students at Princeton Theological Seminary. Under this fellowship they spent a year in Spain, where they learned to speak Spanish and acquired a deep distaste for fascism and the Spanish dictator, Franco. Upon their return, and graduation from Princeton, Harry accepted an appointment with the Board of National Missions of PCUSA to take charge of the Placitas Church, the Bernalillo Church, and the mission in Alameda. The Willsons knew virtually nothing about New Mexico before they accepted the assignment, so they were as unprepared for what they found as the Torreses had been before them.

In Bernalillo, which they had expected to be their headquarters, they found a struggling congregation of three members and a manse that was, as Christine described it later, small, falling down, and inadequate in every way. "It was *desolating*, but we did have a wonderful view of the mountains from our back windows. I suppose that saved the day." Ten miles down the valley, the mission in Alameda was more promising. The once sleepy little town was booming with the northern growth of Albuquerque, and new housing developments were going up on all sides. Money had been appropriated by the Board of National Missions of PCUSA and during the Torres years the Alameda congregation had raised about $2,000 for construction of a new church and manse. The third part of the Willson's charge was, of course, Placitas.

After a few months the Willsons moved to Alameda, and shortly thereafter the Presbytery gave up the Bernalillo ministry. Four years later Alameda had a new manse next to a new brick church building. The seating arrangements for 100 worshippers were filled to capacity almost every Sunday. Placitas had not been neglected. The congregation, assisted by summer youth groups from Amarillo, Texas, the Synod of Michigan, and some of the larger Albuquerque churches, had renovated the interior of the Church and replastered the exterior. On January 1, 1963, the churches at Alameda and Placitas became self-sustaining. Yoked in a shared financial relationship, they were no longer dependent on financial aid from the Board of National Missions of PCUSA. It was an impressive achievement for a young pastor.

According to an article in PRESBYTERIAN LIFE, the success of the churches owed virtually nothing to the fact that Harry Willson spoke fluent Spanish. Members of his congregation credited it to his vigorous theological teachings that focused on immediate issues. Willson was proud of the mix of cultures at Alameda. They had, he believed, significantly shattered social sameness. People from many walks of life with widely differing incomes and lifestyles worshipped and worked together confidently and easily.

The situation at Placitas was quite different, the article continued. That church was located in a small, almost solidly

Spanish-American community peopled mostly by the heirs of the old Spanish land grant. Anglos had begun moving into the area, but, as Willson soon discovered, the older members of the Church had decided against welcoming them because they "have a church of their own in the valley and many churches in Albuquerque." Willson refused to accept this un-Christian like attitude. He and some members of the congregation whom he referred to as his "theologically oriented shock troops" determined to turn the situation around. They questioned the reluctance of the older members to accept change and open their hearts to newcomers so seriously and effectively, the article continued, that Placitas adopted an open racial policy and welcomed Anglos into its membership. One member of an old Spanish family was quoted as saying, "At that moment, the Church turned the corner and rounded into the 20th century."[14]

There was another side to the story, of course. Willson's genuine concern and sincerity, his comfort with the Spanish language, and his willingness to make frequent visits to members of his congregation endeared him to many. His keen mind and very serious, intellectual approach to Christian devotion and service excited others. But in Placitas he was dealing with a deeply conservative congregation, the history and nature of which he little comprehended when he first arrived. It was a congregation that had survived the lean years of the Depression, the trauma of the war years, and the depopulation of the village in the post-war years, only to be met with an even greater challenge—the beginning of extensive Anglo migration into the Placitas area. For the first time this congregation had reason to worry about its *cultural survival*. Any kind of change was frightening, and Harry Willson, if he represented anything, reflected the disturbing, turbulent changes of the 1960s.

With an enthusiasm and lack of caution characteristic of the young and inexperienced, Willson began changing things. The first thing was the Session. When he arrived in 1958 it had only two very *old* elders, Roque Salazar and Nicolás Gurulé. During his first meeting with the elders in August 1958 Willson suggested that they elect at least one more. They agreed, and in November Elizardo Trujillo was ordained. Willson also suggested that, in deference to the growing number of Anglos in the congregation, the first service of each month should be in English. This move apparently met no resistance, so the following June Willson proposed a plan already adopted in the Alameda Church that called for carefully planned bilingual worship services each week. After much discussion the Session rejected the so-called "Placitas Plan," but at another meeting later the same month, it approved a motion to try it out for six months. The following November Willson asked for the election of a fourth elder, and for the introduction of the rotary system used throughout PCUSA whereby elders serve no more than two terms and then go off the Session for at least a year before becoming eligible for reelection to the ruling body.

That suggestion sent shock waves through the congregation. In an action that was almost unthinkable, their young pastor had told the two most senior and respected members of the Placitas Presbyterian Church, Nicolás Gurulé and Roque Salazar, to relinquish their positions of authority.

Nicolás Gurulé was deeply offended, as was the whole Gurulé family. In the forty-six years that Nicolás had served continuously as a ruling elder he had been the mainstay of the Church, caring for both its physical and spiritual welfare. His family had been responsible for founding the Church. The land on which the Church stood had belonged to his family. His children had served the Church faithfully. More than any other member of the small congregation, Nicolás Gurulé *personified* the Placitas Presbyterian Church. It was hardly surprising that he and most members of the congregation regarded it as *his* church. And if the Church did not specifically belong to Nicolás Gurulé, the congregation believed most sincerely that it *did* belong to the Spanish-speaking congregation. In the eyes of many, Willson's insistence on a rotating board of elders was not only an insult to two venerable old men but a direct challenge to the community's identity and autonomy.

Willson, interviewed in 1993 about this first crisis in his ministry, commented: "They didn't understand (the rule of rotating elders) and thought that I had made it up. I was just trying to go by the way the system works. That is part of being a young pastor and not paying any attention to the fact that something that has been done for fifty years, rightly or wrongly, matters to people. I don't know what I would do today, but what I did then was totally inevitable, which was to offend him."

It is ironic that, with Willson's fluent command of Spanish, the next crisis lay with the continued use of that language in the church services. According to Willson, he preached in Spanish for the first two years but, like Torres before him, gradually came to believe that by so doing he was limiting both his message and its relevance to a rapidly changing community and a rapidly changing world. In his words: "I had always believed, before it became something of a fad in the 1960s, that the church had to be socially relevant . . . and if people can't talk to one another, that matters . . . You are stalled out before you start, because you can't communicate. I knew everybody in the village. I knew how everybody was related to everybody. I spent a lot of time in Placitas. It just didn't make sense for the church not to be dealing with how we were going to mix these two people who were living there together. That became the great issue."

Willson continued: "There was a period where I prepared a sermon, and I didn't know what language I was going to preach it in until I stood up during that second hymn, and instead of singing I looked (to see) how many don't know any English, and how many don't know any Spanish. If it was three to one, either way, I would do it in that language. Whatever language I preached it in, I still talked for four or five minutes to summarize it in the other language . . . . I liked preaching. I loved the language—I love both languages."[15]

Apparently the matter of language was less a concern to some members of the Church than it was to others. Amarante Lucero remembers that his mother, Barbarita, one of the Church's founders, loved to go to church whether the sermon was preached in Spanish or English. She felt that her spiritual needs were met even though she could not understand everything that was preached. Some of the new Anglo members of the congregation felt the same way. They had chosen to move to an Hispanic community and to join a Spanish-speaking congregation, so it did not disturb them that they could not follow the sermon. Madeline Randle remembers, with some amusement, sitting through a sermon in which the only words she understood were, "as I was saying,"—words that Willson had let slip into his otherwise flawless Spanish. George Randle does not remember any communication problems, either. "Typically we alternated between (services in) Spanish and English, but . . . if there was any problem in any language we would use both languages. That was true in church and it was true in village meetings. We always used to conduct them in both languages as was necessary. At church and community meetings I went to, the intent and the sincere desire was to communicate. We used all the systems we had to do that."[16]

Of course, as we all know, even if we don't think about it, language is far more than a method of communication. The term "mother tongue" reflects the fact that it is the sound of our earliest and sweetest memories of home and family. As such, it is the language of our most profound feelings. For this reason, the language we hear and speak in our spiritual home, the church, takes on a significance far beyond mere words. For Placitas old-timers, the displacement of Spanish in the service meant the loss of a sense of connectedness with the institution that, more than any other, represented love and security. By the same token, the introduction of English for the Anglo members of the congregation meant that they could find in the Placitas Presbyterian Church their own spiritual home and family. The generation of young people that had grown up speaking Spanish in the home and English in the schools and in their jobs were caught somewhere in between.

The painful and hesitant transfer from Spanish to English took several years to accomplish. In the meantime Willson's agenda of current social issues continued to excite some while it alienated others with its challenge to tradition and continuity. One change everyone liked was his decision to move the Sunday service from the afternoon to 8:30 in the morning. Attendance tripled instantly. Then Willson, calling himself a teaching elder, tackled some challenging subjects in the adult Bible Study class that met weekly on Tuesday or Wednesday nights. One subject that he recalled was "the Church and its changing ministry." Later the group began a dialogue between the local Protestants and Catholics. The Catholic priest in Bernalillo declined to take part, though the dialogue had been sanctioned by the Archbishop's ecumenical commission. Despite the implied disapproval, at least one

Catholic family in Placitas opened its home regularly to the weekly dialogue.

It was at the very end of Willson's ministry that a near tragedy occurred. The Church building came very close to collapsing during the funeral service for Jeanie Escarcida. Some weeks earlier, the Church members had begun enlarging the Church by deepening the shallow little basement. In the process, they left the central sustaining post supported on a narrow column of earth. The service for the popular young girl drew almost the entire village to the Church. As recalled by Reverend Willson, "I had never seen such a crowd of people in that building. Then I felt it go—hoooh—and I knew instantly what had happened. I said, 'We must all get out!' It was a marvel that nobody panicked." Willie Escarcida, father of the dead girl, recalled how he suddenly realized that the Church building was about to collapse. Putting aside his own terrible grief, he stood up and, in a voice of authority, directed the people to keep calm and file out slowly. They finished the service outside. According to Willie, somebody went down to the basement after the funeral and saw the post just swinging loose. The dirt column supporting it had vanished. [17]

Not surprisingly, Willson's concern with social justice led him to strongly support the Black Civil Rights movement, and in a precipitous move, without informing either the Placitas or Alameda Sessions, he left town to join the civil rights march on Selma, Alabama. No objections were raised when he returned, but many members of both congregations were upset by his social activism and involvement in politics. Willson's later stand against United States involvement in the Vietnam War further offended members who had served in the armed forces and whose sons and neighbors were serving in Vietnam.

The matter came to a head after Willson and several members of the Alameda congregation got into a heated argument on the front steps of their church following a Sunday service. The Alameda church promptly "fired" Willson by withdrawing its monetary support. Although Willson still had a loyal following in Placitas, he could not survive on the salary from only one church. For a while he made up the deficit by teaching at the Albuquerque Academy, but ultimately he and the Placitas Session agreed that he should resign. He announced his decision from the pulpit on June 12, 1966.[18]

Reverend Paul Stevens and Reverend John Orr, both from the Synod of New Mexico, were present at the special congregational meeting called to consider Willson's resignation. Stevens explained that the Placitas Church had become self-supporting only as a "yoked-field" with the Alameda Church. If Alameda dissolved the partnership there was no way to provide for the ongoing life of either church. It was a question of both money and manpower. Willson resigned on July 31, but served as a temporary "Supply" until December 12, 1966. At the time he left, the revised roll of the Placitas Presbyterian Church showed 42 members, fully half of whom were now Anglo Americans.[19]

Recent Times

New Mexico's Hispanic Presbyterian Pastors, ca. 1955.
Bottom row: Trinidad Salazar, Julian Durán, José Inéz Candelaria, Maicelio Cruz, Amador Martinez, Tomás Gonzales
Second and third rows: Higinio Ruybalid, unknown, Melandrino Lopez, unknown, Joe L. Medina, Acorcinio Lucero, Alfonso Esquibel, Porfirio Romero, Epifanio Romero, Eluid Valdez

Reverend George Simmonds (served 1929–1935).

Reverend Kenneth J. Green (served 1951–1955).
Courtesy Kenneth Green.

Reverends José I. Candelaria (1937-1952) and Harry Willson (1958-1966) at dedication of Alameda Presbyterian Church.
Courtesy Carlos Candelaria.

Reverend George Jacob Adams (1972-1980), Heritage Sunday, April 17, 1994.

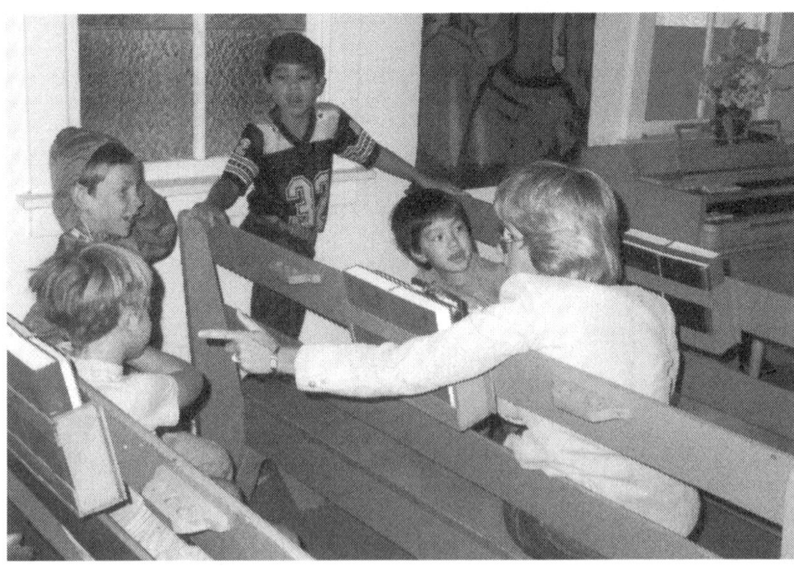

Sally Curro teaching Vacation Bible School in the Upper Room of the 1932 Church, 1983.

Kendall Schlenker and Miguel Molinar, Sr. seat the vigas in the new addition, 1983. 1932 bell tower in background.

Like the 1932 church before (now our Upper Room and Basement), the 1984 Church addition was truly built by the congregation. Young and old, Hispanic and Anglo, worked together as *familia.* Romaine McGough and Ed DeLavy in conversation, while Elsie DeLara and co-workers get ready to stain the vigas.

We paid off our mortgage with enchilada suppers—

and parking lot sales, 1986. Right: Norma Martinez.

Old flows into new in graceful harmony, as the congregation celebrates its first Christmas in the new sanctuary, 1984.

Christmas angels Anna Schoen and Chloe Hoses.

We celebrate our holidays. Christmas pageant, 1988.

The children have just completed the annual decoration of the Christmas tree. Center: Rev. Jim Anderson. Front row, center: Mae Anderson.

Easter Dinner, 1990. Left: Kendall Schlenker, Suzanne Forrest (behind table).

Easter Egg Hunt, 1990.

And we reach out to the community—

Church float in the Fourth of July Parade, 1993.

A parade fixture: Mothers' Day Out sells snow cones and pop at the parade to support their cooperative day nursery.

The Placitas Artists Seriers presents a marimba concert by Steve Chavez. Hosted by the Church since 1986, the series enriches the cultural life of the entire community.

In the mid-1980s, youth activities rate high.

Left: Clowning.

Below: Sledding in the Sandia Mountains.

Bottom: Birdwatching trip to the Bosque del Apache. Rev. Jim Anderson on the left.

Vacation Bible School, 1993.

Swimming party hosted by the Brock family. Jack Brock, Karen Bowen, and Julie Curro.

Camping at Sandia Conference Grounds. Sonja Brock and Kevin Fowler lead the youth in a camping retreat.

Hispano Religious Singers, 1994. L–R, top row: Bert DeLara, Vivian G. DeLara, Donna Perea, Kevin Fowler, Vivian D. DeLara, Viola Duran, Willie Arriola. Bottom row: Norma Martinez, Geri Salazar, Eric Perez, Anna Howarth. Janice Fowler missing from photo.

Pastor Jim Anderson, 1995.

Above: Members of the Founding families came from far and wide on Centennial Sunday, 1994. L–R: Vivian G. DeLara, Joe and Barbara Trujillo, Frank and Catalina Trujillo, Josephine Ringling, Charles DeLara, and Miquela Trujillo Rodriguez.

Left: One of eight new banners by Bunny Bowen, which were dedicated on Centennial Sunday, 1994.

"One Hundred Years of Placitas Fashions" Centennial Fashion Show, May 14, 1994. Julie Curro models her grandmother's wedding dress.
Courtesy Sally Curro.

Below: Centennial Quilt, designed by Wilda MacLauchlan and stitched by the ladies of the Church. The diamond blocks record the names and dates of all the pastors from 1894 through 1994.

Outside Church sign erected after completion of the 1984 Church Addition. It proclaimed the title of Las Placitas Presbyterian Church, by which the Church became known thereafter, along with its acronym LPPC.

CHAPTER IX
The Tenuous Years

So it had happened. Both the Church and the Placitas community had rounded a corner and entered, not just the 20th Century, but the mainstream of American life. That fact did nothing of itself to assure the continuing survival of either. After centuries of relative isolation during which both village and Church were insulated from all but the strongest currents of change, both were now beset with new and perplexing problems. The future of both depended upon the willingness of the native Hispanos to accommodate to the changing times and the willingness of the incoming Anglos to respect the prior rights and customs of their Hispanic neighbors.

For the village, the most difficult fact was that of having been "discovered" by the outside world as a haven of beauty and peace—far enough from Albuquerque to avoid the congestion and confinement of city living but close enough to permit commuting to work. A rhapsodic article published in NEW MEXICO MAGAZINE in March 1969 entitled "Upstairs Albuquerque" called it "a retreat away from the sound, the fury, the air of industry and heated competition . . . an upstairs of the metropolis—[a romantic place with] remnants of old barns, log-hewn, roofed with shingles or rusty tin . . . reminders of days past, of customs obsolete." The Hispanic residents of the village, as described, appear as remnants from a colorful past, peculiarly irrelevant to the "gentlemen of leisure and enterprise, ladies involved in garden clubs . . . the man in the business suit, in the Volkswagen or Renault, the office-commuter, knight errant of the bumper-to-bumper trail." [1]

The new Anglo residents of the mid-1960s were neither as homogeneous nor as superficial as the article implied. Some did take the highway to Albuquerque daily, but many had retired from the urban workforce, and others came to Placitas to farm or practice arts and crafts in home studios. Some brought with them considerable wealth while others sought out the area because, in addition to peace and beauty, it offered the means of surviving on a very limited income. The first Anglo families bought or rented homes right in the old village. Later arrivals found land east of the village at the entrance to the canyon, and the area quickly became known as "Gringo Gulch." Other areas settled at about the same time were called Placitas Heights, Ranchos de Placitas, and Rainbow Valley. Ranchos de Placitas differed greatly from the others. With its minimum lot sizes, community water well, and restrictive covenants it was a harbinger of developments to come.

Most perplexing to Placitas old-timers were the newly arrived "flower children" of the mid-1960s. In the grapevine of the counter-culture, New Mexico was known as the place where "it" was happening, "it" being the back-to-the-earth communal farm movement. This was not the first time a generation of societal drop-outs had found New Mexico. Beginning in the 1910s people like Mabel Dodge Luhan and D.H. Lawrence settled in Taos and tried, quite superficially, to live the simple lifestyle of their Native American and Hispanic neighbors. But while this first generation of social rebels applied their wealth to updating their housing, the hippies of the 1960s genuinely tried to live off the land. The simple farming technology used in earlier times was still very much in evidence, inexpensive homes could be made by adopting the native building tradition of earth, timbers and stone, and land in depopulated villages like Placitas was cheap or available for squatting. Above all, the state's great natural beauty and relatively mild climate offered the promise of a very agreeable alternative life style to the young college-age dropouts of the era. Whether escaping from a life they perceived to be materialistic, aggressive, and wasteful; escaping from the draft; or escaping from the consequences of political protest activity, they gravitated to the state in droves. Communes sprang up all over New Mexico, and a substantial number of hippies found their haven in Placitas.

The first group of newcomers bought land southeast of the village and, because they built houses in the shape of geodesic domes, some of them made out of car bodies and the like, the area became known as "Dome Valley." Other young men and women joined them and they formed a loose sort of community.

Another group of hippies calling themselves "free men" settled in the area that had once been Ojo de la Casa. According to an article in the ALBUQUERQUE JOURNAL written in 1969, they called themselves a "Christian village" and tried to put Christianity into practice by living on and from the sod in a communal group like the early Christians. They were mostly vegetarians by choice or by necessity, and grew their own corn, squash, beans, other vegetables, and fruits using ancient handmade tools resurrected from the fields. The author of the article wrote that he had found nothing "camp" or wild about their clothing, and no indications of heavy drug use. He described the group's leader as "a man of considerable grace and charm, a former university professor of international relations."

The idealistic picture was far from the truth. The colony was no more a Christian settlement than its leader was a university professor. This individual, who called himself Ulysses S. Grant, dressed in an outfit reminiscent of a Civil War uniform and rode around the area on a white horse. A charismatic but despotic leader, he demanded, and for the most part was accorded, total control. The colony became known as the "lower farm."[2]

A third communal effort developed around the old village site of San José de Las Huertas. A young couple occupied the old Montoya family house on the property, and Romaldo Montoya, grandson and grandnephew of two of the Placitas Presbyterian Church founders David T. and Francisco Trujillo, helped them plant a garden. Montoya no longer owned the land. His mother had sold it some years earlier. According to an Albuquerque attorney who was part owner of the land in 1981, an earlier owner of the property gave permission for them to remain as long as they used the surface water for farming. That way, he said, the water rights were maintained on the property.[3] The young couple was soon joined by other young men and women and for one year they tried to maintain a true commune. After the commune broke up due to conflicting goals and personalities, successive waves of occupants shared the area. They lived a simple lifestyle without power or running water, constructed make-shift homes of "found" materials, and dressed in an adaptation of western pioneer garb. Marijuana was the drug of choice. They called their area Towapa, a word of Pueblo origin meaning "down at the village."

The new Anglo residents of Placitas were, then, a varied lot. But despite the hippie image and a few bizarre examples, such as the man calling himself Ulysses S. Grant, they had quite a lot in common. Though ranging all the way from the very wealthy to the deliberately dispossessed, they shared a common desire to live and enjoy a rural life style, a love for the natural beauty of the land, a distaste for the conformity and restrictedness of life in the city and suburbs, and a desire to share, if only by proximity, the simple life of an Hispanic village. While they did not understand the sheer weight of their intrusion or the cultural differences that separated them from their Hispanic neighbors, there was an abundance of good will.

The Hispanic villagers, beset on all sides by strangers, took it all in stride. While some were offended by the forms of dress and undress and the odd behavior of the hippies, they respected their efforts to farm, even if they sometimes found them amusing in their expectations and lack of experience. All who tilled the soil cooperated in many ways. The Hispanic Presbyterians who remained in the Church after the turbulent Willson ministry resigned themselves to sharing it with the Anglos who began coming in ever greater numbers to their services. So long as they proved themselves to be good church-going people they were valued as an asset to the community.[4]

Generally speaking, the hippies were opposed to all forms of organized mainline religion, but at least one hippie couple must have attended the Presbyterian Church from time to time. In November 1970, the wife wrote a letter of thanks to the Church from Portland, Oregon, where they had moved after leaving Placitas. They had joined the Maranatha Church, she explained, and been "born again," but the Placitas Presbyterian Church had been "the first beacon lights we saw while far out to sea." She wished that the Church would carry the Gospel to the communal farm in Placitas, and wondered if anything was being done there. As if in answer to her concerns, the Session minutes record that Ulysses S. Grant had that same month requested four hymnals from the Church. His request was approved. The following month Grant reportedly shot and killed two members of his group and disappeared.[5]

To a surprising extent each group accepted the others' differences without undue friction. Much of the credit for the tolerant behavior must go to the Hispanos. Their long established tradition of accommodation and acceptance, making it possible for them to live peacefully in a multi-cultural environment without sacrificing their own cultural identity, probably had its origins in the post-Pueblo Revolt period. At that time the Pueblo Indians and Hispanos had had to learn to live in fairly close proximity, to share and cooperate in matters of mutual benefit, without trying, or even threatening, to change the culture of the other. It was a tradition worth emulating.

But, while no one particularly wanted or welcomed change, either in the village or the Church, change was inevitable. The next major change in the Church came when the pastoral search committee was unable to come up with a bilingual minister. From the beginning, the Presbyterian Church in New Mexico had lacked enough Spanish-speaking ministers to serve its numerous Hispanic congregations. That was the reason men like Juan Baros were sent out to serve as ministers even before being ordained. The situation had grown worse with time. To meet the needs of the Placitas, Bernalillo, and Alameda Presbyterian churches from the late 1930s to the early 1950s, Reverend Candelaria had had to draw on the services of ministers from Mexico or of Mexican descent from other faiths, as in the case of Rodolfo Torres and Antonio Jiménez. Even these men were available only because they were already semi-retired. So when the pastoral search committee was unable to come up with a single Spanish-speaking candidate, the question of whether Church services in the Placitas Presbyterian Church would be in English or Spanish became irrelevant. In the meantime, Reverend Floyd Sovereign, a former missionary who did speak Spanish, served the congregation as Temporary Supply. Sovereign, whose regular position was

Chaplain at the Presbyterian Hospital, stepped in often over the next decade to minister to the people of Placitas when they were between pastors. Much loved by the congregation, he provided a vital source of continuity. In consideration of the Church's very limited budget, he accepted only the cost of his gasoline for his services. Reverend Candelaria, who also helped out as needed, accepted the nominal fee of $10 as guest preacher.

In May 1967, the pastoral search committee recommended David Hammack, a friend and former teaching associate of Harry Willson at Menaul School, as its choice for preacher. Hammack had come to New Mexico in the mid-1950s from the Board of National Missions of the Presbyterian Church USA (PCUSA) to teach science at the Allison-James School in Santa Fe. When that school closed in 1959 he moved to Albuquerque to teach chemistry, mathematics and physics at Menaul. In 1964, he decided to enter the ministry and enrolled at San Francisco Theological Seminary. Hammack had just completed his studies in 1967 when he heard that Willson had left the Placitas-Alameda field. Since he wanted very much to return to New Mexico, he applied for the position. Both the Placitas and Alameda churches voted to call him to their service and Hammack was installed as pastor in Placitas on July 16, 1967. He and his family took up residence in the Alameda manse.

The change from bilingual to all-English services was a great disappointment to the older Hispanic members. Some, who had access to transportation, transferred their membership to the Alameda Presbyterian Church or the Second Presbyterian Church in downtown Albuquerque, but for most it was too far away from home to be an option. Many simply ceased coming to church. Officially the membership had grown to 59, but among that number were many who no longer supported the Church, monetarily or by their presence. The Session tried to fill the gap by scheduling a quarterly Spanish communion service, usually provided by Tomás Gonzalez from Second Presbyterian Church, but just paying his gasoline bill put an almost impossible extra burden on the already overstretched budget. Morale sagged, and once again the future of the Church looked bleak.

The congregation met some of the extra expenses by holding a fund-raising enchilada supper in May 1968. Then, in hopes of restoring a sense of life and purpose to the congregation, the Session announced an entire year's activities. These consisted of an October "Fun Night" and potluck supper, followed by a Christmas Eve reception at the Church. Another fund-raising enchilada supper was held in April, and Easter was celebrated with a breakfast at the home of one of the parishioners. Various unscheduled "happenings" consisting of singing and dessert were planned, along with a scheduled work day. Other activities, to be scheduled later, were a Sunday afternoon picnic and a series of study sessions.

In recognition of the concern that the Spanish heritage of the village might slip away if not carefully preserved, several members of the Placitas Presbyterian Church revived the old tradition of Las Posadas on Christmas Eve 1968. Directed by Flavio and Grace Trujillo and Willie and Frances Escarcida, the procession reenacted the entrance of Joseph and Mary into Bethlehem and their search for a place to spend the night. It began at the Placitas Presbyterian Church at the conclusion of the Christmas Eve service. Mary led the procession, seated on a donkey, with Joseph following behind. Bonfires and *farolitos*, little lanterns, sparkling in the cold night air, marked the route. At the first "Inn," everyone sang in Spanish the traditional words to Las Posadas: "We have arrived after a long journey, and beg for a place to rest." From inside the house came the response: "Who comes to our doors so rudely on this stormy night? Is it to annoy us?" From outside: "Who will give us poor tired wanderers a place to rest?" Again, from inside: "I am getting angry of these bothersome people. Go away and don't wake us." Several similar stanzas followed, then the procession moved on to the second stop, and repeated the songs. At the final stop, the Placitas Elementary School, a manger with shepherds, some live sheep, and the three wisemen awaited them. Triumphantly the group sang "Happiness and Joy. Today the Queen of Heaven reigns in your house, because of the wanderers Joseph and Mary. For as it was said, here you see us giving thanks to Mary and Joseph." Everyone sang more carols to the Christ Child, then filed inside the school for refreshments and a party. It was a joyous reenactment of an old tradition, and everyone in the village, Protestants and Catholics alike, rejoiced in its rebirth.[6]

In 1969, the celebration included another old Hispanic tradition, *Los Comanches*, or Comanche dancers, and a Santa Claus. According to this tradition, the "Comanches" were the poor children of Bethlehem who danced for the Christ Child, because they had no gifts for him. Mary Arriola's father, Eduardo Valdez, remembered the dance steps, the music and the words. Rosy-cheeked and chubby Romaldo Montoya played Santa. Romaldo's cousin, Tony Lucero, remembers that even if there wasn't any snow, the older boys and men would hose him down so that he would come in dripping, as if he had just arrived from the North Pole. In order not to conflict with the Las Posadas procession and the party at the elementary school, the Presbyterian Church scheduled its formal Christmas service for December 22nd that year, the last Sunday evening before Christmas.[7]

David Hammack remembers his years at Placitas as a very good time. Because he was the first non-Spanish-speaking pastor in the history of the Church, and many of the old members spoke almost no English, he sometimes found communication difficult. That didn't stop him from forming close relationships with his parishioners, however. He devoted several days each week to making calls on different families. There was not much evening activity, but there was a regular morning Bible Study class attended by women. During his ministry Sunday Church services began at 9:30 and were attended by anywhere from ten to thirty of forty people. Everyone sang one hymn in Spanish and from time to time someone read the Scripture lesson in Spanish. Occasionally an outside minister, most frequently Tomás Gonzalez, conducted a Spanish service. Gonzalez was also present to conduct funeral services when members of the old Hispanic congregation died. Hammack remembers that one such occasion took place on a bleak and snowy winter day. He vividly recalls the pallbearers loading the casket on a pick-up truck, and the desolate procession of mourners that filed out through the snowy landscape to the little cemetery to see their dear friend and neighbor laid to rest.

Hammack's attention to two different churches was taxing, but, with better cars and roads, not nearly as much so as it had been for his predecessors. Each Sunday he went directly from the Placitas service to the service at Alameda. Although he was unable to lead the Sunday School for adults and children that followed the Placitas service, members of the congregation planned and conducted it very successfully. Hammack remembered with particular appreciation the high level of music provided by Byrdis Danfelser, who took over the music program following the departure of Harry Willson.

The final years of the 1960s were turbulent, and often violent, years for both the nation and for the State. In northern New Mexico a Texas-born evangelist named Reies Lopez Tijerina organized and led a protest movement against the loss of Hispanic land grants, many of which, he claimed, were now incorporated into the state's national forests. In 1967, when the protest threatened to become violent, state officials and ordinary citizens got a major case of the jitters that did not abate until well into the next decade. Elsewhere the Black civil rights movement heated up, along with protests against the Vietnam War. Placitas remained sheltered from the storm, but Hammack found it increasingly difficult to separate his social conscience from his theological beliefs. When the struggle became too intense, he resigned from the ministry. Hammack's last day in Placitas was September 15, 1970.

Once again Placitas was without a spiritual leader, and once again Floyd Sovereign stepped in to fill the gap. In the meantime the congregation faced another crisis. Its long established relationship with the Alameda Church was about to end. The Northminster Church in north Albuquerque was in the path of the new 1-40 Interstate. Since it had to be torn down, the Rio Grande Presbytery decided to sell the Alameda Presbyterian Church and manse and combine its congregation with the Northminster congregation in the new Shepherd of the Valley Church. This meant that Placitas could no longer be "yoked" financially with another church. The congregation would have to come up with all the costs necessary to keep the Church going or be forced to close its doors. There was no going home again. The Session asked to go back on mission aid, but the Board of National Missions of PCUSA denied the request. The Board did offer to send representatives to talk with the Session about establishing a stronger sense of mission within the congregation. A minor form of help came in the request of a group of local Episcopalians to share the Church building on Sunday mornings. The Session accepted the request, agreeing that the Episcopalians could hold their service at 11:30 A.M. after all of the Presbyterian services were finished. The Episcopalians agreed to contribute $5.00 weekly for their share of the utilities.

After considerable discussion of the problem, the Session concluded that the new pastoral search committee should look for a half-time pastor. It also began consideration of another vexing matter—that of housing for the new pastor. The first thought was that the Rio Grande Presbytery might give the Placitas Presbyterian Church the proceeds from the sale of the Alameda manse as a down payment for a manse in Placitas. In January 1971, the Placitas Presbyterian Church made a formal request to the Rio Grande Presbytery, which was denied. Then Sam Salazar came to the rescue. He had a little adobe house across the street from the Church that he had built for his daughter. She was not using it, so he offered to rent it to the Church until something more permanent could be found or until he needed it again. It needed some fixing up so, Jeanne Army recalls, several people from the Church got together and built shelves and put in a bathroom. Then they painted and varnished until the little house sparkled.

In May 1971, the pastoral search committee found the minister it was looking for in the person of Reverend George Jacob Adams. Adams was a missionary who had served the Board of Foreign Missions of PCUSA first in Korea and later in Japan. Now he was nearing retirement and, after forty-five years in the Orient, wanted to return to the United States. He asked a friend at Menaul to circulate his resume. When it came to the attention of the Placitas Presbyterian Church, the Session opened correspondence with Adams. He prepared a taped sermon and sent it to the Church. It was played first to the Session and then to the entire congregation on Sunday, August 29. After listening to it, the congregation voted unanimously in favor of issuing Adams a call.

Adams could not come immediately. He and his new wife, Michiko, were expecting a baby and, in view of a past miscarriage, he didn't want to subject her to a long trip until after the child's birth. The Church answered by return airmail—"By no means would we think of asking you to come sooner. Please come in

February or even March." Kenneth Kei Adams was born in Sasebo, Japan on January 1, 1972, and the Adams family arrived in Albuquerque April 7. Wilda and Kendall Schlenker met them at the airport and took them to their home, where they stayed until the Church members had finished their work on Sam's house.

New Mexico, so different from Korea and Japan, was a strange new experience for the Adamses. They were delighted with their cozy little four-room home. In his memoirs written for this history, George writes: "The thick adobe walls, combined with the nice furnace, made for very comfortable living year around, as anyone who has been fortunate enough to live in a Spanish-style adobe home will testify. It was warm in winter and cool in summer, even without air conditioning."

It was not, however, without some problems more characteristic of New Mexico than Japan. Michiko recalled her horror at opening the cupboard door under the sink to confront a hissing snake. George writes: "Fortunately George was able to negotiate with Sir Snake to release the can of Dutch Cleanser. The snake had evidently been able to squeeze through the hole in the floor that was needed for the pipes."

Another cultural shock that he and Michiko experienced was encountering the Placitas "flower children." He recalls that they could be seen at almost any time in Placitas village—shopping at Lizzie Archibeque's little Mountain View Grocery Store or hitchhiking to Bernalillo. They were always on foot, usually dirty and unkempt, and quite often had a small child in tow.

Adams was favorably impressed with the ecumenical environment he encountered in Placitas and Bernalillo. Ministers of several different Protestant faiths and a Catholic monsignor, all members of the Bernalillo Ministers' Alliance, attended his installation. The family felt so welcomed by Monsignor Charewitz that Adams invited him to a meal at the manse. A few short weeks later he was stricken with a fatal illness. George and Michiko attended his funeral. Adams also approved of the fact that the Placitas Presbyterians were sharing their church with the Placitas Episcopalians and their Christmas Eve pageant with the Placitas Catholics.

Most of all, George remembers the dedicated women who conducted the Vacation Bible School, the wonderful generosity of members of the Church who personally and anonymously underwrote the repairs on the manse, and the faithful and worshipful piano music provided by Sally Curro. An accomplished musician, Sally inherited the music program and the choir from Byrdis Danfelser in November 1971. From January 1972 until 1979, she played the piano each and every Sunday, with very few exceptions, one of them being the week her daughter, Julie, was born. "Too often," Adams writes, "such devoted faithfulness goes unnoticed and unacknowledged."

Although the Adams pastorate was a time of adjustments and continued growth, more and more Spanish-speaking members left the Church. Spanish services, originally scheduled for once a month, had never been possible from a financial point of view. There were several ministers and laymen who offered their services free of charge, but the Church could not afford to pay even the cost of their gasoline more than four times a year. In 1973, the Session decided to hold a Spanish service once each quarter. The disaffection of the Hispanic community may have been behind the 1974 decision of the San Antonio de Las Huertas Land Grant Association to resume control of the Presbyterian cemetery—an action no doubt motivated by a desire to reserve the limited space for members of land grant families.

In the meantime, Anglo families came and went. In the typically transient world of Anglo culture, families moved to Placitas, only to vanish a few years later from the congregation. In some cases death or divorce divided a couple and the remaining member found it more convenient to live in Albuquerque. Some had job transfers, others moved in order to put their children in city schools. Whatever the reasons, the newcomers stood in stark contrast to the deeply rooted Hispanos.

Despite the somewhat more affluent congregation, finances remained the most critical aspect of Church survival. The effort to pay even a half-time minister strained the budget to such an extent that when asked in 1972 to increase its giving for General Mission, the congregation voted to decline until all expenses were paid. Negotiations to buy a plot of land adjoining the Church for a manse had to be set aside until funds were available. The Church was not averse to accepting help from outside. In 1974 a work camp of young people and leaders from Immanuel Church in

Albuquerque spent a week fixing up the church grounds.

In 1974, George and Michiko resolved the problem of the manse by deciding that they should live in town. Michiko had begun teaching Japanese language classes at the University of New Mexico extension in the evening and worked days at the University Library. Since George was still on a half-time basis at the Church, it seemed more reasonable for him to commute than for her. He fulfilled his obligations to the Church by spending three days a week in Placitas, keeping regular office hours and doing his home visitations. The Church agreed to compensate him $200 a month for travel and rent.

In the meantime, inflation took its toll. By 1979, the Church budget had reached $11,457, over two-thirds of which went to the pastor. Jo Proett, who took over the job of Church treasurer in January 1976, would not have been able to pay the bills if one member had not regularly paid the insurance on the Church building and another had not picked up the propane bills. Many other members contributed their labor. Ed DeLavy had no sooner joined the Church than he built and installed a replacement for the footbridge over the acequia. Still, in March 1980, a special meeting of the Session decided to give members a choice whether the "One Great Hour of Sharing" collection should go back into the Church "in our hour of need" or if it should go elsewhere. The funds that had been raised or donated for the manse were used to pay for a new railing and stairs and to fix the electrical wiring.

During the last years of his ministry in Placitas, George Adams agonized over whether he could marshal the major effort to get the Church on a sound financial basis and give it the leadership it needed in other ways. Finally, and with great reluctance, he announced in May 1980 that he would turn the pulpit over to another pastor. He told the congregation that he would retire effective June 1. This time there was no gap between spiritual leaders. The Reverend Jim Anderson had heard about the Placitas Presbyterian Church through his wife's uncle, the Reverend Tomás Gonzalez. He had also helped George Adams with stewardship efforts and had preached in Placitas once or twice. Tomás Gonzalez recommended him to the Presbytery of Santa Fe, and Jim moved immediately into the pulpit as Interim Pastor, giving his first sermon that same June. Youthful and vigorous, he saw a great future for the faltering Church. He lost no time in putting his ideas in motion.[8]

CHAPTER X
Rebirth

By 1980, it had become a matter of simple arithmetic. The Placitas Presbyterian Church must either grow or die. Jim Anderson knew that, and he brought up the matter with the Session as a condition of accepting the part-time appointment as interim pastor. "Do you want to grow?" he asked them. He was shocked when they really had to think about it. Reverend Adams had faced the same reluctance.[1]

The fear of growth was hardly surprising. In Placitas growth meant mainly bad things. It meant the loss of intimacy and cohesion and connectedness—the sense of being a family. After the traumatic years when so many families had left the Church, the congregation had again stabilized into a new and close-knit bi-cultural fellowship that everyone wanted to preserve. No one wanted to cope with more change—and no one wanted to see the Church become a large, impersonal institution full of strangers.

But choice time was over. With a membership of only 55, and many a Sunday seeing no more than 20 in attendance, the Placitas congregation could not possibly continue to pay the costs of a full-time pastorate. Making matters worse, the last years of the 1970s and the early 1980s were years of rampant inflation. As the price of everything shot up, so did the costs of operating the Church and paying the pastor. He, like everyone else, had to have a living wage to support himself and his family. That the Church survived at all was due to the disproportionate giving and loving stewardship of one particularly generous family. Without the outside support from the Board of National Missions of the Presbyterian Church USA (PCUSA) that it had enjoyed for years, the Church had just two options. It had to find more people to share the costs, or expect those already in the Church to double or even triple their giving. For many the latter was not a possibility, so the answer to Anderson's question was obvious. The Session voted for growth, but with little enthusiasm.[2]

Before the Session adjourned, Bob Allen, representing the Ministerial Committee of the Presbytery of Santa Fe, reassured the members that he was confident that the Church could grow to a membership of 200 and employ a full-time minister. He then announced that special grant money was available for church redevelopment on the national level and asked all elders and deacons to fill out a self-assessment questionnaire.

Anderson lost no time in getting started. He believed firmly that things would get accomplished only if he gave different individuals specific responsibilities. With this in mind he made each elder chair of a different committee. The committees were: Christian Education, Stewardship, Building and Grounds, Parish, and Worship and Music. While it was not the first time that the Session had been organized into committees, past efforts had long since lapsed into oblivion. The Church became a hive of activity. Anderson also went to work improving the Church's visibility in the community. He asked for a large sign for the front of the Church stating the times of services and suggested that one might be installed in Bernalillo as well. He also asked for newspaper coverage. Next, Anderson announced that the General Assembly of PCUSA was taking the initiative in helping churches to buy land and asked if any land adjoining the Church were available. If so, he said, the Church should try to buy it.

In August Anderson called a special congregational meeting to ask for approval to purchase land for future Church expansion. He also asked to change the Sunday meeting time from 9:30 to 9:45 in order for the Sunday School to meet at 9:00 before the regular service. The congregation approved both changes. By

September Willie Escarcida had found out that approximately one-half acre of land east of the Church might be available from Bernabé Sandoval. The Session approved a motion to get a binder on the property until the Church could get a loan from the Presbytery of Santa Fe.

In January 1981, a revitalized congregation approved a budget for the coming year just short of $15,000, changed the Sunday worship time to 10:00, and voted to switch to natural gas in order to economize on fuel costs. By May the Session had negotiated with Nick and Helen Sanchez to purchase property belonging to them across the road from the Church. It agreed to pay them their very modest price and authorized payment for a survey and title. It also applied to the Presbytery of Santa Fe for funds to pay the other half of Anderson's annual salary so as to make him a full-time minister.

Other things were happening in the Church. Jim Anderson had a passionate concern for young people and his efforts to expand the Church's youth ministry were immediately evident. Inspired by his vigor and his vision, Sunday School leaders injected new enthusiasm into their classes. Other members of the congregation, most of them young adults with school age children of their own, sponsored such new after-church activities as swimming and skating parties, clowning and drama workshops and productions, movie nights, and hikes and nature outings. As in the past these activities attracted, and were open to, all children in the community regardless of their religious affiliation. In all of these activities Jim led by personal example, hiking and skating with the kids, and helping to construct new facilities. At one point he broke an ankle while helping build a basketball court across the road from the Church for use by the entire Placitas community, but the accident neither slowed him down nor dampened his enthusiasm.

When Jim discovered the Sandia Conference Grounds had fallen into disuse and might even be sold, he led a rescue effort that restored youth camping for the entire Presbytery of Santa Fe. Over the years Anderson, with members of the congregation and others in the Presbytery of Santa Fe, updated and added to the simple camping facilities, and in the summer of 1994 they completed work on a modern kitchen building adequate to the task of feeding a camp full of hungry youngsters. In order to make the camping experience available to all children regardless of means, the congregation voted to pay a portion or all of the camping fee for any Placitas youngster desirous of attending camp. The Church also sponsored several delegates to the Presbyterian International Youth Triennium at Purdue University in Indiana.

The Music and Worship committee added more music to Christmas and Maundy Thursday programs and introduced occasional evening "hymn sings." Jo Proett and Didi Acosta, two fairly recent members, shared the responsibility of playing the piano for Sunday services with Sally Curro. For several years Matilda Tapia renewed her earlier commitment to the Placitas Presbyterian Church by coming up once a month from Second Presbyterian Church to play as well. Sally directed and accompanied the Choir, assisted by Didi. While Didi established a youth choir, Sally helped organize a youth quartet consisting of trumpet, trombone, flute, and clarinet. The music in the Church became so exuberant, in fact, that it showed up the frailties of the old building. During one memorable Christmas program the local Brownie troop participated with a dance. The girls' lively movements caused the old floor to vibrate so much that the lighted candles on the piano began to topple. Fortunately, someone from the congregation rushed to rescue candles, piano, and pianist, and the program proceeded without further incident.

The reorganized Church school was going so well that the congregation decided to carry it through the summer. Vacation Bible School, a regular event cherished and attended by children from the entire Placitas community—Protestant, Catholic, and non-church-going, was particularly successful. Other good things were happening as well. Dorothy "Bunny" Bowen made and donated a series of batik banners and paraments for the Church. El Buen Samaritano United Methodist Church made a gift of Spanish hymnals, and the old upright piano was rebuilt. Amarante Lucero, a former resident of Placitas now living in Albuquerque, volunteered to conduct a service in Spanish, and Willie Escarcida agreed to do the work of converting the old propane furnace to natural gas. Because the Church school was growing rapidly and the tiny basement room was too small to accommodate the different classes, the Church accepted the gift of a mobile home for an expanded Sunday School and Church office. Soon even that space seemed too limited, and Anderson suggested the formation of a building committee.[3]

Anderson remembers that at first it was just "pie in the sky" speculation. Only eighteen months earlier the Church had faced bankruptcy. But the congregation was increasingly optimistic. In December 1981, the women in the Church gave a very successful fund raising enchilada supper at the elementary school, and planned another for the following February. In January the congregation approved a budget of $22,000 which was $7,000 more than the previous year.

An important break came when the Church succeeded in buying the property owned by Bernabé Sandoval. For a while it had looked like he wouldn't sell, but when the Church discovered that he had cashed the check for $7,000 given him earlier in payment, Sandoval had no choice but to go through with the transaction. From that point on plans for the new building took on their own special momentum. Someone contacted the Department of Architecture at the University of New Mexico, and a well-known architect specializing in adobe building prepared some sketches. One or two other architects did the same, but the problem, as always, was cost. Finally Ed DeLavy, a member of the Church and a talented artist, came up with the solution. An architect friend of his named Lou Castillo agreed to design an addition to the old Church, in accord with the Church's requirements, and accept a portrait by Ed as his fee. The most important requirement was that the new addition not detract from the charm and simplicity of the old structure.[4]

Castillo proved to be both capable and cooperative. In short order he designed an elegant addition within the financial limitations fixed by the Session. When the plans were presented to the congregation for approval, the only comment was that the kitchen should be made larger. The congregation may have been as incredulous as Jim Anderson, who, when he first saw Ed DeLavy's sketch of the new building, found it hard to believe that it could ever afford anything that big.[5]

Now the Church was on a roll. Each successful step in the process seemed to engender more confidence and optimism. To raise money for the new building the congregation decided to hold three enchilada dinners a year. The dinners not only brought in money but served as a social gathering bringing people from the entire community together to work and eat and get to know each other. Other fund-raising events followed, one hot on the heels of the other. Moreover, success breeds success. The rapidly growing congregation provided more justification for an expanded building. One of the happiest developments was the return to the fold of some of the old Hispanic families. Finding more opportunity in the greater Albuquerque area, other Hispanic members moved back from California and resumed their affiliation with the Placitas Presbyterian Church.

Two important matters of business remained. The first was arranging funding for the new building. In a special and momentous meeting of the congregation in July 1982, the congregation voted to build. Two months later the Session voted to apply to PCUSA for a building loan. Anderson also filled out a request for a construction grant from the "Advance in Mission" fund-raising campaign.

The second matter was funding for a full-time pastor. The Session applied to the General Assembly Redevelopment Fund for a grant to help it make the transition. In rather short order it was informed that the request had been approved and that the Church would receive $10,000 a year for three years. In January 1983, the Session appointed a pastoral search committee. No one seriously questioned that Jim Anderson was the proper choice, but there were certain necessary legalities. One of them was that an interim pastor had to resign for a period of six months before he could be considered for a full-time position. The Session asked the Presbytery of Santa Fe to waive this rule, which it did. In March 1983, the congregation voted by secret ballot to call Jim Anderson to the post. The ballot contained no mention of Jim's *alter ego*, his attractive, hard-working and unassuming wife, Mae. She had already become a much loved and appreciated addition to the Church and everyone knew that they were voting for her as well.

Work on the new addition got under way almost immediately. By May the septic tank was in the ground and in July the irrigation ditch was moved to make way for the new addition. The cornerstone was laid on August 21, 1983 in a ceremony followed by a potluck luncheon. By the time of the Halloween party in October, the building was 16 adobes high. The bond beam was poured in November, and by the time of the Christmas party, half of the decking was on the roof of the new sanctuary. The remarkable pace of activity was possible only because of the even more remarkable efforts of the congregation, led by Jack Brock who chaired the building committee.[6]

The Church could not afford a contractor, so Kendall Schlenker, a member of the congregation with some rather extensive experience in adobe building, offered to take time off from his law practice to do the job. He also secured the services of two men from Mexico, Miguel Molinar, a skilled adobe and tile worker, and his son, Lalo, and a skilled carpenter from Farmington, Charlie Little. All three had recently helped the Schlenkers build their own Placitas home. Other members of the congregation who worked on different phases of the operation were Jim and Mae Anderson, Jeanne Army, Leland Bowen, Jack Brock, Sally Curro, Antonio DeLara, Vivian DeLara, Ed DeLavy, Willie Escarcida, Leah Gragert, Bryson Harding, Anna LePre, Ed and Romaine McGough, Bruce MacLauchlan, Steve Nolan, Bob Pramann, Jo Proett, Darrell Sever, Anna Salazar, Reynaldo Salazar, and Sam Salazar. Charles DeLara, Dick Kribs, and Bill Proett, though not members, were among the most loyal of volunteers. Most of the member work was done on the weekends, but Reynaldo, since he was retired, worked right through the week. While others were working on the new building, Ed DeLavy dedicated himself to fixing up the grounds, beginning by cleaning up the little pile of ruins to the east of the Church. He reinstalled the foot bridge over the irrigation ditch and built the rock wall all along the south side of the ditch.[7]

Saturdays saw a substantial part of the congregation at the building site, with many women sanding, sealing, staining and varnishing the vigas and other woodwork and the men helping out in whatever else needed doing. Members who could not engage in the hard physical work of construction helped out in other ways, not the least of which was by preparing hearty noon meals for the laborers. Many village people unconnected with the Church also helped. A few years earlier when the Catholics had restored their parish hall a number of the Presbyterians had helped them out. Now they were repaying the favor, with interest. A few of the Catholic old-timers also confided that they wanted to help out with the adobe work, "Just to be sure that it was being done right." It was a time for healing, for forgetting past hurts, and for making new friendships. Presbyterians and Catholics, Hispanos and Anglos, old-timers and newcomers, young and old, worked shoulder to shoulder building the new house of worship in the best Placitas tradition. Despite the differences, the occasional disputes, everyone was still *familia*. [8]

In January 1984, the congregation approved a budget totaling $34,542, more than double what it had been in 1981. The Church was now ready for its heating system, a roof, and plastering. Money continued to flow in through the enchilada and posole dinners, bake sales, flea market and parking lot sales, and other efforts at fund-raising, and many more individuals contributed services and expertise to the project. Larry Montaño, a skilled plumber and son of members Gilbert and Julia Montaño, volunteered much of the plumbing work. Robert Boyd, a heating contractor and father of Dorothy Bowen, came from Virginia to oversee the installation of the heating system. David Hammack, the former pastor now turned electrical contractor, designed the electrical system. Leland Bowen designed and installed the new sound system.[9]

By September the new building was finished and ready to be dedicated. The Church had just passed its ninetieth anniversary. It was a proper time to be reborn. In celebration of its birthday and in memory of her mother, Ruth Warren, Sally Curro gave the Church a new Yamaha upright piano. The Mora Presbyterian Church loaned it some pews from the old, and now closed, Holman Presbyterian Church, and Ken and Neysa Sauve helped bring them down from Holman.

The Dedication was on September 30, 1984 at 3:00 p.m. It featured, in addition to a moving worship service led by many people from the congregation, a reading by Christina Gonzales of the Church history that she had compiled. George Simmonds, the 94 year old former pastor, sang a hymn he had composed in honor of the occasion entitled, "Bless This Church." He also told the congregation about his early days in Placitas and about helping to construct the 1930 Church. On January 20, 1985, the memorial gifts established during the building program were dedicated in another special worship service. The choir of the Second Presbyterian Church sang, and Reverend Simmonds, back in town to celebrate his seventy years in the ministry, sang two solos. [10]

That same January the congregation approved a budget amounting to a hefty $55,306, including loan re-payments. There were now 92 members. The addition, which had added 5800 square feet of new space to the 2100 square foot 1930 Church, had cost $160,000. Just under $65,000 of that amount had been raised in cash by members and friends. To everyone who entered the serenely beautiful new sanctuary, who listened to the choir and reflected on the perfect acoustics, and who realized that only a few years before the Church had almost ceased to exist, it seemed like nothing short of a miracle. It was, indeed, a miracle—a miracle of faith and love.[11]

A large sign was erected outside the Church that proudly proclaimed the name of **Las Placitas Presbyterian Church**. While the Church had informally been referred to over the decades as Placitas Presbyterian Church, the word "Las" was again officially included in the Church's title as an acknowledgement of the historical names of the village founded in the late 1830s and of The Presbyterian Church at Las Placitas founded in 1894.

In the years since the new sanctuary was dedicated, Las Placitas Presbyterian Church has continued to grow, but not too fast as was once feared. The congregation still breaks up in the middle of the Sunday service for the "passing of the peace"—as it did for years in the old Church—so that friends and neighbors can shake hands and sometimes embrace, and greet each other in a true ritual of friendship. The hubbub startles newcomers, who wonder what has happened, until they are engulfed themselves in the outpouring of fellowship and love. The Church continues to respect its Spanish language origins with a reading of the scripture first in English and then in Spanish. One Spanish hymn is a part of every service, and the Hispano Religious Singers, accompanied by guitar and accordion, frequently augment the music provided by the regular choir. A new Yamaha six-foot grand piano, the gift of the Sally Curro family (replacing Sally's previously-donated Yamaha upright piano), is used in concerts as well as in Church services. A beautiful old organ, the gift of the

Proett family, is available to add its sonorous voice to Sunday worship. From 1988 until 1994, the Choir enjoyed Mark Wallace's enthusiastic and inspired directing.[12]

Las Placitas Presbyterian Church has also become something of a village hub, providing meeting space for a multitude of local groups and organizations ranging from Jardineros de Placitas to Alcoholics Anonymous. In 1985, a group of artists in the Church began organizing art exhibits to hang in the Fellowship Hall. Two of the most significant developments originated by the Church for the entire community are the "Mothers' Day Out," cooperative nursery school and day care center, and the Placitas Artists Series. The latter began in 1986 when the Music committee of the Church sponsored two benefit concerts to help pay medical expenses for a local child severely burned in a fire. One of the concerts featured a visiting operatic tenor from China, the other a newly organized string quartet. The new sanctuary proved to be ideal for chamber music, and an idea was born to combine the art exhibits with a series of musical performances featuring the Helios String Quartet. A group of interested volunteers formed a Board of Directors and in 1987 the Placitas Artists Series, with the Helios String Quartet in residence, became a treasured addition to Placitas's cultural life. The Series has since incorporated as an independent tax-exempt organization, but it continues to hold its concerts in Las Placitas Presbyterian Church. Both the Church and the Artists Series value their mutually supportive relationship.

On February 24, 1994, Las Placitas Presbyterian Church celebrated its one hundredth anniversary with a quiet and reverential prayer service on the actual anniversary of the Church's founding. Centennial Sunday followed on February 27 honoring all descendants of the founding families as well as all who had served the Church through the years as elders and deacons. Many families returned to the Church to join in the celebration, with one family coming all the way from Oregon, and another from Colorado. On Heritage Sunday, April 17, the Church honored its past ministers. George Adams and his wife, Michiko, journeyed from Texas so that George could take part in the service. Several sons of former ministers attended including Carlos Candelaria, Paul Sovereign, Antonio Jiménez, II, and Samuel Torres. Matilda Martinez Tapia represented both herself and her brother, former minister Victor Manuel Sandoval. Vivian Gonzales DeLara, granddaughter of Juan Baros and a loyal member of the congregation since her birth, was also present. A joyous potluck luncheon completed the centennial celebration on May 14th. The program that followed, "100 Years of Placitas Fashions," honored all Placitas women.

In the meantime, Reverend Jim Anderson had asked Suzanne Sims Forrest, a member of the congregation and a professional historian, to research and write a centennial history. Published by the church in 1995, it was entitled *Century of Faith: One Hundred Years in the Life of the Las Placitas Presbyterian Church.* Suzanne presented the book's copyright to the congregation in appreciation of the loving fellowship she and her husband, Jim, had enjoyed during their ten years of membership. It was her wish that its sales would be a source of continuing revenue for the Church.

Now the story of the first one hundred years of Las Placitas Presbyterian Church has been told. It is a wonderful story, full of love and dedication and an abiding faith. Throughout the Church's history we can sense God's loving presence working through its elders, deacons, and ministers. From José Gurulé to Juan Baros, Nicolás Gurulé, George Simmonds, José Candelaria, Jim Anderson, and all the others who have labored in His vineyard, we can see His hand guiding their efforts and providing the right person, at the right time, for the work that needed doing. During these hundred years the Church has grown from poor but protected isolation to the responsibilities and rewards of full participation in the American mainstream, and it has done this without losing track of its unique history and the value of its bicultural heritage. Its young people carry this legacy of bicultural affection, tolerance, and respect with them as they move beyond the village to college and jobs in the broader world. As a legacy, it is inspiring. Future generations of Las Placitas Presbyterian Church goers would do well to keep this legacy warm in their hearts and strive to do and be as much for their Lord, for their community, and for their brothers and sisters in Christ as have those who preceded them.

1932 Church Building   1984 Church addition

Sketch by Dick Kribs of Las Placitas Presbyterian Church (LPPC) after the 1984 addition. South-facing side of the Church was the original entrance, and the historic street address for LPPC remains 7 Paseo de San Antonio.

CHAPTER XI
Los Pastores de Las Placitas Presbyterian Church

JOSÉ YNÉS PEREA
1882 - 1894

Reverend José Ynés Perea, our nation's first ordained Hispanic minister, was Placitas's first Presbyterian pastor. He visited the village intermittently between 1882 and 1894 and officiated at its founding on February 24, 1894.

Perea was born April 23, 1837, the son of *Don* Juan Perea of Bernalillo and his wife, *Doña* Josefa Cháves de Perea. The Pereas were powerful and wealthy landowners who held positions of respect and authority under the flag of old Mexico and later under the American Territorial government. An older brother of José Ynés, Francisco Perea, served four terms, beginning in 1863, as New Mexico's territorial delegate to Congress. Earlier, both Francisco and José Ynés had attended the United States Military Academy at West Point. Francisco was commissioned a Lieutenant Colonel in the United States Army, and during the Civil War he commanded a battalion that defended the New Mexico Territory against invading Confederate forces. José Ynés's and Francisco's cousin the Honorable Pedro Perea, son of José Leandro Perea, was another prominent politician. He was a delegate to Congress in the first decade of the 20th century.

Juan Perea realized, even before American annexation, that the old order was changing and that his children should be prepared to adjust to new conditions. Like other patrician New Mexico families, he sent his sons to boarding school in Mexico for their early education. But in 1849, after the American acquisition of New Mexico, *Don* Juan Perea transferred his sons to the "French School" of Mons. Peugnet in New York City. As it turned out, the school gave his sons more than just an American education.

There, José Ynés was attracted to a group of students who, in defiance of school rules, secretly read from the Bible. Impressed by his scriptural discoveries, José refused to go to confession and soon became known by his teachers as "that Mexican heretic." When *Don* Juan found out about his son's activities in the spring of 1851, he arranged to get both boys appointed to West Point. But a soldier's life was not to young José Ynés's liking. He fell out with his military teachers and returned to Bernalillo, only to embarrass his parents by speaking openly throughout the community of his new beliefs. His mother pleaded with him. His father made every effort to correct him, but to no avail. When the elder Pereas came under intense pressure from the Catholic Church, and other members of the family refused to have any more business dealings with them, *Don* Juan saw no solution but to get his headstrong son out of town. He sent José Ynés to learn the dry goods business in St. Louis, a terminus of the Santa Fe trail over which *Don* Juan sent many loaded wool wagons.

José Ynés worked quietly in Saint Louis for four years, during which time he joined the Presbyterian Church. Then on July 4, 1855, he took a steamboat to New Orleans, joined a marine shipping company, and spent the next five years doing business in all parts of the world. At some point of this sojourn he acquired the companionship of two older men named Lucas and Antonio Gurulé. They may, indeed, have accompanied the young fourteen-year-old when he first set out for St. Louis, as menservants and bodyguards. These men were from Placitas, and they were uncles of José Librado Aron Gurulé.

Perea landed in Boston in 1859 at the height of a religious revival. There he received a letter from his father asking him to come home and reassuring him that his new faith would be tolerated. He returned to New Mexico but went on to live in California until 1864. In 1865, he returned to Bernalillo to be with his father during his final illness. *Don* Juan reconciled himself to his son's new faith and found comfort in the Spanish Bible José had given him. When he died, José Ynés, alone of the eleven children was at his father's side. He was appointed administrator of his father's estate.

After his father's death, José Ynés married Victoria Armijo, the daughter of a prominent Las Vegas physician, but Victoria died within a year of the wedding. Disheartened, José moved briefly to a ranch on the Rio Puerco (at Salazar, where later a Presbyterian school was established), and then to another family ranch eighty miles southeast of Las Vegas on the Pecos River. In 1869, he met John Annin, a Presbyterian missionary, and helped him as translator, intermediary with the local Hispanic population, and friend. In his own words:

> It was in answer to prayer that Mr. Annin came. I had never prayed so earnestly, neither had I ever laid myself down so fully as a sacrifice to the Lord. . . . I had hardly arisen from my knees, making this covenant with the God of heaven, when to my great joy on my return from my sheep-camp to Las Vegas, Mr. Chapman, a merchant, ushered me into the presence of Reverend John A. Annin in Kitchen's Hotel. We then and there commenced earnestly to work.

In 1870, José Ynés Perea and John Annin formally organized a Presbyterian Church in Las Vegas, Territory of New Mexico. Perea heavily subsidized the building and its furnishings and became its one ruling elder. The following year, in order to devote more time to his religious concerns, Perea turned his ranch over to a foreman and became part owner of a general store in Las Vegas. The church soon had 21 members, most of them from distant villages in San Miguel and Mora counties that had been neglected by the priests. These villages later established their own small

Presbyterian congregations. Perea was highly respected for his wealth and because he had seen so much of the world. Still, many Catholics considered him to be the devil and warned their children to stay away from "el Protestante."

During these years Perea actively spread the Gospel. In one of his printed reminiscences he wrote:

> Brother Rafael Gallegos and I rode from plaza to plaza and from one ranch to another, preaching even in the sheep-camps in the counties of San Miguel and Mora for several years. We used to preach even at the wakes of the funerals of victims of small-pox, and would distribute a great number of gospel tracts, Testaments and sometimes Bibles.

During this period he helped to organize the churches of Taos, Rincones, Ocate and El Rito and even pushed his work up through the northern counties of the Territory of New Mexico to southern Colorado. In 1878 Perea left Las Vegas to work as a licentiate and interpreter for Reverend Taylor F. Ealy at Zuñi Pueblo. Ealy's assistant was a Miss Susan Gates. It must have been love at first sight, for on Christmas Day 1878, José Ynés and Susan were married. The pair left in January for a new assignment at Jemez Pueblo. They eventually had eight children and became a preaching and teaching team.

Dr. Shields, the missionary at Jemez, did not particularly want Perea to be with him, and Perea believed that he would be more useful working among his countrymen. He suggested that he work out of one of the less isolated towns along the Rio Grande. Since Albuquerque was "full of Jesuits," he suggested that he work out of Corrales near his family home. The Board of Home Missions of the Presbyterian Church USA agreed, and the Pereas moved to Corrales in April 1879. Perea was ordained to the ministry in September 1880. He thus became the first ordained Hispanic Presbyterian missionary in the United States.

Perea's field extended on both sides of the Rio Grande and encompassed more than twenty-five Spanish-speaking villages, including those on the Rio Puerco and as far as Cubero and Cebolleta. He used a circuit-rider approach. A round-trip whirlwind visit to his dispersed flock took over two weeks. His routine while on these tours was to rise early and ride most of the morning to reach his destination. In the afternoon he visited homes and invited people to the evening services. He often visited with interested people after the service until past midnight. Las Placitas was one of the villages in Perea's field, and he already had contacts in the community through his old companion Lucas Gurulé. In 1882, José Ynés Perea met Lucas's nephew, José Librado Aron Gurulé from Placitas, who invited him to come to Las Placitas to preach. Lucas, by then in his eighties, had moved to Algodones, leaving his old house in Placitas unoccupied. That first meeting, attended by eight people, was held in Lucas's house.

Perea died at his Pajarito home in 1910. His favorite hymn was "*Salvo en los tiernos Brazos-Safe in the Arms of Jesus.*"[1]

JOHN MENAUL
1882 - 1901

Reverend John Menaul was Las Placitas's second pastor. He preached intermittently between 1882 and the founding of The Presbyterian Church at Las Placitas in 1894, then was in charge of the newly established Church until 1901.

In May 1889, the General Assembly of the Presbyterian Church USA (PCUSA) formally established the Synod of New Mexico. By this time John Menaul had already worked nearly two decades among the Navajo, the Apaches, and at Laguna Pueblo. After "retiring" in 1889, he spent fifteen additional years in Albuquerque serving in the Hispanic mission field. James Menaul, John's younger cousin by five years, came to the Southwest in 1881 to serve as minister of Albuquerque's First Presbyterian Church, and in 1889 he was appointed Synodical Missionary for the Synod of New Mexico. Both John and James Menaul were born in Ireland and were brought to the United States at an early age. John graduated from Lafayette College as a physician in 1865, then studied theology at Princeton. He was ordained by the North River Presbytery in 1867. He and his bride, Harriet McMechan, left almost immediately for West Africa to serve as missionaries under the Board of Foreign Missions PCUSA. There they endured such primitive living conditions that Menaul's wife died of disease after three years. Broken hearted, with his own health in ruins, John Menaul returned to the United States in 1870 with his two young daughters.

Menaul's next assignment, which he began the following year, was as a mission school teacher to the Navajos at Fort Defiance, Arizona Territory. Menaul found the language barrier and the Navajos' nomadic ways almost unsurmountable obstacles to his work, but, recognizing the important role that weaving might have as a source of income, he taught his students to use a European style loom and spinning-wheel—skills he had learned as a youth in Ireland. Menaul also met Miss Charity Ann Gaston, another mission teacher to the Navajos, They were married in February 1871. The couple provided a source of amusement to the Navajos, who delighted in the startling contrast between Menaul, who was barely five feet tall, and his bride, who towered above him.

When the mission school closed in 1872, Menaul accepted the position of physician for the Navajo Agency. In this capacity he often found himself administering "modern" health care side by side with Navajo medicine men using traditional healing methods. Menaul did not find that arrangement as difficult as the joint church-government administration of Indian affairs, which he believed severely limited the effectiveness of missionaries. After several years of feuding with the Navajo Indian Agent at Fort Defiance and an equally unsatisfactory experience as physician at the Southern Apache Agency at Ojo Caliente, New Mexico, he and Charity went to serve as missionary and teacher at Laguna Pueblo. The Menauls remained for 14 years in Laguna. According to a contemporary, John Menaul was "a peculiar sort of genius, (who) can preach, teach, and practice medicine, build a house, weave a carpet or blanket, build a mill, and alter a Springfield rifle." At a time when most Anglo Protestants wanted to remold the Indian in the white man's image, Menaul argued that it would "not help the Indian if we pretend he is what he is not." He observed the religious activities of the Pueblos and recognized virtues in their religion that were worthy of imitation by Protestants.

Recognizing that the single most significant obstacle to his work was the language barrier, Menaul first learned Spanish, which was understood by many Lagunas, and in time, the

Keresan Indian dialect. This knowledge enabled him to embark on his most ambitious project—-that of putting Keresan into written form. By 1882, he had translated McGuffey's First ECLECTIC READER so that the Indians could learn to read and write in their own language. He also instructed them in such practical areas as agriculture, carpentry, weaving, and sewing. He was less successful in spreading his Protestant message. When a church was finally organized in 1878, Menaul correctly predicted a meager membership and tribal opposition. The "old ways" were resistant to change, and the hard work took its toll. Menaul retired to Albuquerque in 1889 seriously questioning the value of his efforts at Laguna.

In Albuquerque his cousin, James, persuaded him to enter the Spanish field. Menaul used his fluency in Spanish and his printing press to print Spanish-language religious tracts, hymnals, temperance tracts, and, beginning in 1902, the Synod's bilingual journal, LA AURORA a project he funded largely from his own pocket.

In 1889, he accepted a call to become the first pastor of the newly organized Second Presbyterian Church in Albuquerque. A few years later he also took responsibility for part-time preaching in the village of Las Placitas. In 1904, he returned and took his family to Hinton, Oklahoma to live with a daughter. He died there in 1907, shortly after the death of his wife in 1906.[2]

EPIFANIO ARREOLA
1890 - 1894

Epifanio Arreola, a Mexican-born Presbyterian evangelist, preached regularly in Las Placitas from 1890 to 1894. He officiated at the organization of The Presbyterian Church at Las Placitas in 1894 and, together with the Reverends José Ynés Perea and John Menaul, was largely responsible for its founding.

Very little is known about Arreola's early days in Mexico. He was converted to Protestantism by a visiting missionary while serving time as a prisoner in Mexico City. Sometime after his release, he and his family became members of a Protestant church, though it is not known where. In time he traveled north to the United States with his wife and five grown children and settled in

La Placita de los Martinez, now known as Martineztown, on the outskirts of new Albuquerque. He was considered a "man of the world" because of his travels and his knowledge of the outside world. He was also respected for his Protestant faith. It was not long before he became a leader in the spiritual affairs of the community, where Bible-reading sessions and prayer meetings in different homes were the common practice.

It was Epifanio Arreola, in fact, who established the contact between this community and the Reverend James Menaul. This contact led to the establishment of La Segunda Iglesia Presbiteriana (Second Presbyterian Church) in Martineztown, with Reverend John Menaul as its first pastor. Arreola was elected its first elder. In the years that followed Arreola worked closely with John Menaul in evangelizing other Spanish-speaking communities, among them Las Placitas.[3]

JUAN BAROS
1894 - 1914

Juan Baros was born on October 23, 1870 in Las Placitas. He married Rumaldita Candelaria of La Madera on December 5, 1891. They settled in Las Placitas and had twelve children, all of whom died in infancy save one, Christina Josefa. Juan Baros became a charter member of The Presbyterian Church at Las Placitas at the age of 24 and was ordained one of its first two elders by the Reverend James Menaul. Soon afterward he decided to study for the ministry and enrolled in the theology class of Reverend Gilchrist at the College of the Southwest in Del Norte, Colorado. The theology school at Del Norte closed in 1898, and Juan followed it to Albuquerque, where it reopened in association with Menaul School in 1902. He completed his course of training in 1906 along with his two close friends, Santiago Van Wagner and Victoriano Valdez.

Juan had completed all the requirements for the ministry, but for reasons that are not clear, he was not immediately ordained. Despite this technicality, he began serving the congregations at Las Placitas and Los Lentes, and in 1908 he took charge of the congregation of Second Presbyterian Church in Albuquerque. He remained there for about a year before being assigned to the Nacimiento Church in Cuba, New Mexico.

The family believes the assignment to Cuba, that resulted in a harrowing trip north in the dead of winter, was the beginning of the end for this talented, dedicated man. Baros made the trip with his wife and only child, Christina, in a horse-drawn covered wagon. A severe snow storm forced the little party to bed down for the night, and Juan spent the night searching for wood to keep a fire going. When they finally reached Cuba he was so ill with pneumonia that he couldn't even unload the wagon. The next day being Sunday, he somehow managed to hold services. Baros recovered from the pneumonia, but it had so weakened his resistance and damaged his lungs that he developed tuberculosis. The Church sent him to the Presbyterian Sanitorium in Albuquerque. There his tuberculosis was arrested, but he remained in fragile health. He returned to Las Placitas and continued preaching there.

On Sunday, December 31, 1914, after preaching, Juan came home feeling quite ill. He took off his starched high collar and his necktie, hung them on the mirror of his dresser, and lay down to rest. Just before he passed away, he was heard humming softly the hymn, "*Salvo en los Tiernos Brazos-Safe in the Arms of Jesus*." His collar and necktie remained hanging on that mirror for many years, just as he had left them.[4]

HENRY C. THOMSON
1903 – 1906

Reverend Henry C. Thomson was born in Hanover, Indiana, the son of Harrison Thomson, a math professor at Hanover College. Henry spent his early life in Hanover and graduated from Hanover College in 1861. He taught Latin and Greek there for two years, then served in the Civil War for five months before entering Princeton Seminary. Following his ordination Thomson became one of the first three missionaries from the Presbyterian Church USA (PCUSA) to work in Mexico.

Thomson began his work in Jerez, in the state of Zacatecas. His special interest lay in training native converts for the ministry. To this end, he started a seminary in San Luis Potosí and later taught in a seminary in Mexico City. At this time he also began writing for Presbyterian publications and other religious tracts, becoming one of the first editors of the Presbyterian publication *La Antorcha Evangelística*. In 1875, he became the editor of *El Faro* and later edited *El Farolito*. He also became involved in editorial debates with local Catholic publications. However, it was his teaching that endeared him to those early seminary students who called him *Enrique*. In the 75th Anniversary Book of the Mexican Presbyterian Church it was written of him:

> *Que podemos decir de Enrique Thomson, otro Helenista y Hebreista, con una majestad de patriarca, barba rubia, ojos azules y su mirada penetrante en la interpretación del Antiguo Testamento. Era maestro, sabía enseñar y cuando hablaba, sus discípulos permanecían en silencio para beber sus enseñanzas y si alguno dibujaba la sonrisa en sus labios, era porque no comprendía la profundidad del gran maestro. No era un orador, no se distinguió en la Tribuna Sagrada, pero supo preparar a los mentores de la verdad.*
>
> What can we say of Enrique Thomson, another Helenist and Hebrewist, with a patriarchal majesty, blond beard, blue eyes, and penetrating insight into the interpretation of the Old Testament. This master knew how to teach, and when he spoke his pupils remained silent in order to drink in his teachings, and if one of them chanced to smile, it was because he did not understand the profundity of the great master. He was not an orator, he did not distinguish himself in the Holy Tribunal, but he knew how to prepare guides of the truth.

In 1893, Dr. Thomson returned to the United States. Because of his expertise in teaching theology to Mexican students, he was offered the chair of theology at the newly-established College of the Southwest in Del Norte, Colorado. When that school closed for financial reasons in 1898, Thomson moved to Albuquerque and reopened his classes in conjunction with Menaul School in 1902. In 1905, he became the second pastor of Second Presbyterian Church in Albuquerque where he remained until 1907. During this time he also preached at The Presbyterian Church at Las Placitas and edited the Synod paper LA AURORA. Included among his students were Juan Baros, Victoriano Valdez, A.V. Lucero, Juan Quintana, Benedicto Sandoval and Melecio Trujillo. In 1907, Dr. Thomson resigned to accept an appointment as the American member of a committee of three named by the Bible Society to revise the Pratt translation of the Spanish Bible.[5]

JUAN QUINTANA
1904, 1909 - 1911, 1922 - 23

Reverend Juan Quintana, a man of short stature with a huge mustache, was born at Ranchos de Taos, New Mexico, on November 28, 1868. His family was poor, but they valued education so highly that they sent him to a local private school when he was nine years old. When he was twelve, his family moved to Las Animas, Colorado. There he entered public school, but as there were five children in the family and he was the oldest, he was soon forced to leave school to help with the work. The family returned to Taos in October 1886.

In 1883, while Quintana was still living in Las Animas, Colorado, a man came to his house selling Testaments. Quintana told him that he had no money to buy them, so the man gave him two Gospels, Matthew and Luke, for a piece of bacon. Quintana later recalled that:

> At that time I thought it was a law book, and I wanted to study to be a lawyer. When my neighbors and friends knew that I had a Bible, they thought that I would go crazy. But, the more I read it, the more I learned and understood. Through reading the Bible I found the road that showed me the true way of salvation, so that I could abandon the beliefs of the Roman Church.
>
> Once when I heard of a Protestant service I was curious and asked someone if they [the members of the congregation] would let me enter. When I reached the door, I hesitated, not knowing whether to enter or not. The preacher, Mr. Juan Domingo Mondragon, a very sincere

> man, came and led me in and gave me a seat. I stayed to the end of the service. From then I began to change. The conflict grew almost more severe than I could stand. It seemed almost impossible for me to determine which problem came from God, and which from the devil, and which from my own heart. I could understand and believe that I was a sinner, and believe, too, that I must be born again.

Juanita Manzanares, daughter of Higinio Manzanares, an early Protestant evangelist, was another important influence upon Quintana's life. They were married November 28, 1888, in Conejos, Colorado, by the Reverend Francis M. Gilchrist. Quintana later recalled:

> From that time on I began to live a new character and experienced the New Life. I asked God to teach me my duty. My relatives refused to lend me their wagons or horses to do my work. This I gave up for the love of Christ.

Quintana was baptized by the Reverend S.W. Curtis, December 19, 1888. In 1889, he opened a private school below Ranchos de Taos. He had 42 pupils and a salary of $15.00 a month. At the end of three months the directors gave him a certificate and raised his salary to $18.00. Quintana used this money to buy a lot and build a house, something that helped his standing in the community since he later wrote: "My neighbors, seeing that I owned a house, were glad to call me El Maestro."

Reverend John Whitlock took Quintana under his wing, tutoring him in the teachings of the Bible and the art of preaching. When the plaza of Embudo (now Dixon) asked for a mission school teacher, Quintana applied for the position. Two weeks later he received a commission from the Woman's Board of Home Missions of the Presbyterian Church USA in New York for three months of teaching at a salary of $75 for the three months. His wife taught another mission school nearby.

Reverend J.J. Gilchrist and his brother the Reverend Francis Gilchrist persuaded Quintana to continue his studies at Del Norte College. Following graduation he taught at Cañoncito, Arroyo

Seco, Chamita, and Córdova and assisted the Reverend Gabino Rendón in starting the Presbyterian Church in Chimayo. It was while thus engaged that Tomás Atencio and Victoriano Valdez were converted, later to become Presbyterian ministers themselves.

On May 20, 1897, Quintana was licensed to preach by the Presbytery of Santa Fe. In May 1904, he went to preach in Las Placitas while Mrs. Quintana taught the public school in the village. The family moved to Cerrillos in 1905. In May 1909, the Presbytery ordained him to the ministry and he returned to Las Placitas to take full charge of that church as well as the Spanish Presbyterian Church in Albuquerque and others in La Madera and Pajarito. In 1911, he was sent to Socorro for a year, and then to Cuba in 1912. In 1925, he received permission to retire.

In 1936, he and his family returned to Albuquerque where he served Second Presbyterian Church as the Adult Sunday School teacher and frequently filled the pulpit in the absence of the minister. In this so-called "retirement" he also worked part time at a local lumber mill, where he conducted noontime services. It is appropriate that his favorite hymn was *"Yo Quiero Trabajar por El Señor, "("I Want to Be a Worker")*.[6]

JOHN MORDY
1913 - 1917

Reverend John Mordy was appointed by the Rio Grande Presbytery to minister to Las Placitas in 1913. He was the first Sunday School missionary in New Mexico, beginning this work in 1906 after having been minister at Laguna Pueblo for a number of years. He worked in both the Spanish and English fields and had two Spanish-speaking young men as his helpers. He also had charge of the church in Pajarito, a few miles south of Albuquerque, and "an undefined area east of the Sandias." As he recorded in a note appended to the minutes of the May 1, 1913 Session of The Presbyterian Church at Las Placitas, *This rendered it impossible for him to visit the church more than once a month*. During his ministry in Las Placitas he oversaw the renovating of the little mission schoolhouse into a proper church, and the Session agreed, for the first time, to ask members to give a monthly contribution for the minister's salary. Mordy officiated at the burial of Juan Baros, and at the marriage the following September, of Juan's widow, Rumaldita, to widower José Librado Aron Gurulé.[7]

JOSEPH W. WINDER, JOHN D. HENRY, M.B.S. LEGARE 1911 - 1917

Joseph W. Winder, John D. "Uncle" Henry, and M.B.S. Legare all served Las Placitas as Sunday School Missionaries during the second decade of the twentieth century. The purpose of the Sunday School Missionary was to take a knowledge of the Gospel and Christian faith and services into areas where there was no organized church life. He was a pastor-at-large, working under the direction of his Presbytery to bring the non-Christian to Christ and to provide services of worship to unrelated Christians living in isolated communities and sometimes in cities where the church had not been able to keep up with the fast growing population. The missionaries' vital concern was for children and their training in Christian living, and for that purpose he established and maintained Sunday Schools, Daily Vacation Bible Schools, Camps and distributed the Bible and Christian literature. He was a counselor where there was a need in the vital relationships of life, and always sought to bring assurance and comfort to the afflicted, discouraged, needy, and suffering.

Winder came to New Mexico in 1911 and John D. Henry in 1912. In 1916, Winder reported that he had organized 13 Sunday Schools that year, with 58 teachers and officers, and 470 pupils. He had traveled 2,783 miles, visited 649 families, delivered 160 addresses and sermons, had 59 conversions in three Evangelistic meetings, and held 18 Workers' Conferences. In the early days Winder, like all of the Sunday School missionaries, traveled around the countryside on horseback, by walking, and occasionally by stage and train. When the automobile came into general use it was not unusual for a missionary to travel 20,000 miles or more a year. M.B.S. Legare was the only Sunday School missionary of the period to work full time among the Spanish-speaking people.[8]

VICTORIANO VALDEZ
1917 - 1922

Reverend Victoriano Valdez was born in Embudo, Territory of New Mexico (now Dixon) on January 3, 1875. He received his early education at the Embudo Presbyterian mission school under the tutelage of Catherine Kennedy, one of the first Plaza Mission teachers. She used him to interpret, and this job, added to his schooling, gave him a fluent command of English. At the age of 14 he purchased an English New Testament for which he paid two burro-loads of wood. The Gospel touched him so deeply with its message that he determined to dedicate his life to the ministry of the Word. He joined the Presbyterian Church at age 20, becoming another of many self-converts to the Protestant faith, and then, though he had no money for tuition and board, he enrolled in the College of the Southwest in Del Norte, Colorado. To pay his way he worked after school hours at the college as a janitor, and also chopped wood at homes wherever he found work. After four years at Del Norte, he followed Dr. H.C. Thomson to the Menaul School in Albuquerque. He finished the course and received his diploma in May 1906.

While at Menaul he did his "practice" preaching in Los Lentes and Pajarito under the Reverend José Ynés Perea. Upon completion of his theology studies, he was ordained by the Presbytery of Santa Fe and assigned to the Taos field in May 1906. On August 11 of that year he married Miss Lulu Perea, daughter of the Reverend José Ynés Perea's brother, Francisco. The young couple accepted their first assignment to the church of Ranchos de Taos, with preaching stations at Ranchito, Taos, Prado, and Petaca, braving intense persecution at the hands of non-Protestants. The Valdez's first two children, Alice and Elizabeth, were born in Taos. Elizabeth later became the wife of the Reverend Porfirio Romero.

Victoriano's next call came from the Presbyterian church in Chimayo, which had been organized by the two men who had influenced him to enter the ministry—the Reverends Gabino Rendón and Juan Quintana. The Chimayo church had a mission school in its charge similar to the one at which Victoriano had received his education as a young man. He was delighted to be able to "repay" the Presbyterian Church for the educational opportunities it had extended to him by providing the same opportunities to others. While at Chimayo he had charge of the churches at Truchas and Córdova, making the trips there by horse and buggy.

In 1917, after five years in Chimayo, Reverend Valdez was called to take charge of the Spanish Churches of Albuquerque and Las Placitas and the preaching stations of La Madera and Pajarito. In 1921, he answered the call of the church in Las Cruces. There he labored with a congregation composed almost entirely of transient Mexican laborers on their way to Colorado to the beet fields. Although he endeared himself to his congregation, neither he nor his family grew to like the region. When a vacancy at the Las Vegas church was announced in 1928 he applied and was promptly called to serve both that church and the preaching stations of Trementina and Cebolla. Reverend Valdez then served the Nacimiento Church in Cuba, New Mexico, as well as the surrounding preaching stations. His last parish was the church in Garcia, Colorado, and the nearby church in Costilla. He returned to Albuquerque to retire and was recruited by Reverend José I. Candelaria, a former Menaul student he had ordained as an elder in years past, to take charge of the Adult Spanish Bible Class at Second Presbyterian Church. Valdez served in that capacity for many years. He died in 1966 at the age of 91.[9]

ACORCINIO LUCERO
1922 - 1927

Reverend Acorcinio Lucero accepted the call from the Spanish Presbyterian Church in Los Martinez of Albuquerque in 1922 and served both that church and Placitas until 1927.

Reverend Lucero, born May 27, 1884, in Chacón, Territory of New Mexico, was one of 14 children of Andres Lucero and Jesucita Vásquez. Lucero attended the Chacón mission school, but fell far behind his classmates. Fortunately, his teacher realized that he was very bright and arranged for him to see an eye doctor in Albuquerque. The doctor discovered that he was extremely nearsighted. Thus at age 17, fitted with a pair of very thick lenses, he began primary class. With his brilliant mind and good retention, he rapidly caught up to his classmates. His thick lenses were his trademark for the rest of his life.

After graduating from the Chacón mission school, Lucero attended Menaul, becoming one of the six members of the first graduating class in 1906. While Lucero was at Menaul, his friend and classmate Gabino Rendón convinced him to enter the ministry. He then attended Tusculum University in Tennessee on a scholarship and graduated with honors from that institution in 1910. That same year he married a schoolmate, Myrtle Olive Painter. The couple had four children, the two youngest dying in infancy. The remaining son, Robert, became a Presbyterian minister.

Following graduation from Tusculum Lucero returned to Menaul to take preparatory classes under Dr. Henry Thomson. He then went to McCormick Seminary in Chicago. In 1913, following his graduation from McCormick, he was ordained and assumed the pastorate of the church at Raton, New Mexico. While there he championed the cause of prohibition and became so outspoken against the evils of "drinking" that the people of Union County persuaded him to run for State Senator on the Prohibition ticket. He won the election and served one term in the state legislature. Governor Lindsay appointed him to edit the "War News" during World War I. He also organized the United States Public School Service Reserve.

By this time his mother feared that he might leave the ministry. She confronted him with the question; "*¿Y qué vas hacer, servir a Diós o servir al Diablo?*" ("What are you going to do, serve God or the Devil?"). This question, he said, got him back into the ministry.

In 1920, during his next assignment in San Gabriel, California, his first wife, Myrtle, died. A year later he met and married Ester Molinar, a church social worker in the Los Angeles area. She bore him three children: Ernesto, Andres, and Paul. During these years he delivered a series of lectures on "The Mexican Missions of the Southwest" at Western Seminary in Pennsylvania. Paul L. Warnshuis, who was to be his successor at Second Presbyterian Church and Placitas Presbyterian Church, was a senior there at the time.

In 1922, Reverend Lucero and his family moved to Albuquerque. He served as pastor of the Spanish Presbyterian Church in Los Martinez and at Placitas Presbyterian Church until 1927. During this time he helped Mr. Donaldson at Menaul to organize and prepare Gospel teams to serve outlying preaching stations. Ester is remembered for her fine voice and her work with women's organizations, both Presbyterian and inter-denominational.

In later years Acorcinio Lucero served churches in San Bernardino and San Francisco, California; in Walsenburg, Colorado; San Antonio, Texas; Phoenix, Arizona; and Casa Blanca, California before finally retiring in Albuquerque. He died on May 12, 1961. Acorcinio Lucero's Christian spirit of dedication in serving his Lord and the Spanish people left its mark on all whom he met and served. His winning smile and infectious sense of humor paved the way for him to reach many with the truth of the Gospel. Both he and his wife were dearly loved.[10]

PAUL LIVINGSTONE WARNSHUIS
1927–1929

Reverend Paul Livingstone Warnshuis was born in Auburn, Pennsylvania to the Reverend and Mrs. Henry Warnshuis. Paul attended school in Auburn and graduated from the university there before entering the Western Seminary to prepare for the Presbyterian ministry. While enrolled in the seminary he attended lectures by Acorcinio Lucero on his work with the Spanish missions. This led him to spend one summer in Los Angeles helping organize Vacation Bible Schools. During the summer of 1921, he took the "Chili Line" railroad from Antonito, Colorado to Petaca, New Mexico, to assist the Reverend Tomás Atencio, pastor of the Spanish-speaking Presbyterian Church in that community. Warnshuis, who knew almost no Spanish when he arrived, had a crash course in Hispanic village culture. He lived with a local family, learned to ride the horse they provided for transportation, and gained a great appreciation for their simple lifestyle.

That summer proved to be a decisive moment for his career. He met longtime Presbyterian mission volunteer Maude Hart at a

Spanish Presbyterian Workers' Conference and through her influence became fascinated with the work being done in the mission schools, churches, and clinics in northern New Mexico. He also determined to learn to speak and write in Spanish.

His great fondness for the Spanish people that began that summer in Petaca led him to devote the rest of his life to their service. Upon graduation from Western in 1922, he accepted a Presbyterian Fellowship to continue his studies in Mexico, then he traveled to Chile to teach at *El Colegio Americana*. In 1927, he accepted a call to the Spanish Presbyterian Church in Martineztown in Albuquerque. He remained there for two years before being appointed assistant to the Director of the Board of National Missions of the Presbyterian Church USA. While pastor at Second Presbyterian Church and Placitas Presbyterian Church his energetic efforts earned him the nickname "Mr. Warnshoes."

Warnshuis had charge of all mission work among the Spanish-speaking people at the Board of National Missions from 1930 until his retirement in 1962, except for a brief time out to work on his doctorate in Chicago. In this capacity he was instrumental in starting the Interdenominational Council of Spanish Work in the United States, now known as COSAW (Council on Spanish American Work).

Warnshuis remained a faithful member of the Rio Grande Presbytery of the Synod of New Mexico until 1955, when his offices were transferred to New York. Until that time his close ties and dedication to New Mexico were evident by the fact that he rarely missed a meeting of the Rio Grande Presbytery even though it required him to travel all the way from Los Angeles.[11]

GEORGE P. SIMMONDS
1929 - 1935

Reverend George P. Simmonds was born in San Francisco, California, on September 3, 1890. He married his wife, Nancy, fondly called Nessie, in 1913, and both went into evangelistic services in Syracuse, N.Y. There George served as song leader and she as organist and pianist. Following Simmonds's ordination on January 10, 1915, the couple traveled to Ecuador where they stayed for seven years under the Christian Missionary Alliance of the Board of Foreign Missions of the Presbyterian Church USA (PCUSA). Simmonds's daughter, Elizabeth, was born while they were in Ecuador. The Simmondses returned to the United States in 1923, but they were barely settled when two explorers persuaded George to join them on an expedition to South America. They had heard of his knowledge of the region and ability to speak Spanish. The expedition took about six months to complete and crossed the Andes to the Amazon River along the border between Peru and Brazil. The following year Simmonds returned to South America with his family to work for the American Bible Society in Peru distributing Bibles and religious tracts. In 1929, they returned again to the United States.

In 1930, Reverend Simmonds accepted the call of the Board of National Missions of PCUSA to become the pastor of the Second Presbyterian Church in Albuquerque, the Las Placitas Presbyterian Church, and the Spanish Presbyterian Church in Santa Fe. As if this were not a big enough assignment, he frequently preached at First Presbyterian Church in Albuquerque when its pastor, Dr. Cavitt, was ill. Paul Warnshuis assigned Alfonso Esquibel, Porfirio Romero, and Manuel Sandoval, all students of the ministry, to assist him. Simmonds later started work in Alameda and served La Madera.

A man of enormous energy, Reverend Simmonds immediately set about adding additional space and modernizing the building of Second Presbyterian Church. He also applied for, and received, $2400 to build a new church facility at Placitas. Simmonds was known not only for the resourceful ways in which he managed to get financial help for these projects but also for the way he pitched in with the physical labor.

In his "spare time" Simmonds worked at a project that he had begun while still in Ecuador. That project, which was to fascinate him for the rest of his life, was the translation of hymns from English to Spanish. Eventually he had over 1500 titles published. His hymns appeared in Spanish language hymnals of many different church denominations and were published for use in Spanish churches in the United States and abroad.

About 1930, Simmonds attended a conference of the Council on Spanish American Work. It was made up of people from various denominations, all of whom worked among Spanish-speaking people. He was chosen to head up a Committee on Music and Worship, and held that position for more than a third of a century. Since no Spanish choir music was available at that time, he was asked to prepare some. He finally ended up with 54 pamphlets of *chorales* which are still in use today. With the money from the sale of the choral music, he edited and published a beautiful 448 page hymnal in 1964.

In 1935, "*Don* Simon," as he was affectionately called by his parishioners, moved to Santa Fe to accept the full-time pastorate of the First Presbyterian Church. This was the oldest Presbyterian church in the state and Simmonds's first "English" church since his days in New York. While there he facilitated the shared use of the church building with the Spanish-speaking Westminster Presbyterian Church congregation.

In 1939, he accepted the call of El Siloe Spanish Presbyterian Church in East Los Angeles and the directorship of the Clelland House of Neighborly Service for Spanish-speaking people. He was called back to Santa Fe in 1950, this time to Westminster Presbyterian Church, where he oversaw the building of a church building for the Spanish congregation in 1955.

Simmonds retired to Albuquerque in 1956 only to be called out of this short lived retirement six months later to organize a new Presbyterian church in Miami, Florida for Cuban refugees. Having done that, he again retired to Albuquerque only to be persuaded by the First Presbyterian Church to join their staff of ministers. In 1965, he retired again, this time to live in Pasadena, California. There he continued to supply pulpits and sing solos in churches of various denominations, happy to be able to spread the Word of the Gospel through his music. At the age of 98 he sang the National Anthem for the Dodgers in their Los Angeles stadium. After turning 100 he did a repeat performance at the Dodger Stadium to help the Dodgers celebrate their own centennial in 1990. He became a television celebrity singing the National Anthem for the Kings Ice Hockey Team and the Clippers Basketball Team. He died at the age of 101 on June 7, 1991.[12]

VICTOR MANUEL SANDOVAL
1936 - 1937

Victor Manuel Sandoval was born in Albuquerque to Petrita and Benedicto Sandoval. Victor's father was a Presbyterian minister. He attended Menaul School and received an excellent academic education, as well as considerable religious training and experience as a member of the Gospel Team that regularly visited the villages and conducted meetings. He graduated in 1932.

During his high school years and his first years in college Sandoval showed his aptitude for Christian work by helping Reverend George Simmonds in the Spanish Presbyterian Church in Albuquerque. He also assisted him in Placitas and, after Reverend Simmonds left for San Francisco, *Don* Manuel (as he was called) took full charge of the Placitas Presbyterian Church.

After graduating from the University of New Mexico in 1937, Sandoval followed his mentor, Reverend Simmonds, to San Francisco, where he worked as pastor's assistant in the Church of the Good Shepherd. He also had charge of a small Spanish mission and ministered to Spanish-speaking prisoners at San Quentin Prison. In September 1937, he entered the San Francisco Theological Seminary to complete his study in the ministry. [13] He was ordained at Second Presbyterian Church in Albuquerque and later served churches in Walsenburg and Trinidad, Colorado, and in California.

PORFIRIO ROMERO
1932 – 1935

Reverend Porfirio Romero was born at El Valle in Taos County, NM. His early education was in the school at El Valle, but after three years spent in the fifth grade because his teacher could not instruct him beyond that level, he transferred to the school at El Rito. While there an aunt enrolled him and his brother in the Menaul School without his parents' knowledge. However, when the papers admitting the boys to Menaul School arrived, his father, who was a very strong Catholic and *Mayordomo* of the local Penitente brotherhood, signed them in spite of intense pressure from the local Catholic priest. The Catholic church excommunicated Porfirio's father because of this action. The priest then went to work on Porfirio's mother, telling her that the Bible the boys were reading at Menaul contained Black Magic. She, like her husband, resisted this pressure because they so greatly desired to see their sons well educated. Eventually both parents, like their sons, became Presbyterians, and the father was ordained as an elder.

While at Menaul Porfirio and his brother joined Second Presbyterian Church. Porfirio graduated from Menaul and, while still living and earning his board and room at Menaul, attended classes at the University of New Mexico. He served as student pastor at Las Placitas during these years. Christine Gonzales recalled him as the "romantic preacher" because during that time he married Elizabeth Valdez, daughter of the Reverend Victoriano Valdez. Romero eventually went on to graduate from the McCormick Theological Seminary in Chicago. He served as pastor of the House of Neighborly Service in Brighton, Colorado, at Chacón in the Mora Valley, and at Dixon, and then he organized the Edgewood Spanish Church at San Antonio, Texas. Romero returned to New Mexico to be pastor of the Presbyterian churches at Ranchos de Taos and Truchas. Reverend Romero ended his ministry at Cuba in April 1974. Since then he has acted as interim pastor at Ranchos de Taos.[14]

JOSÉ INÉS CANDELARIA
1937 - 1952

Reverend José Inés Candelaria was born in 1894 to Fidelia Abeyta and Anastacio Candelaria in the northern New Mexico community of Rosa. He was the eldest of three sons and two daughters. When he was 12 his father died and the family was taken in by an uncle, Agustiniano Candelaria. José had promised his father on his deathbed that he would get an education. That summer his cousin Merejildo returned from studies at Menaul School. José was so inspired by his cousin's enthusiasm and the words of a hymn that his cousin sang over and over that at age 14 he determined to gain entrance to Menaul School. The words of the hymn were: "At the cross, at the cross where I first saw the light, and the burden of my heart rolled away. It was there by Faith I received my life, and now I am happy all the day."

José joined the Second Presbyterian Church in 1911 while a student at Menaul. In 1914, the Board of National Missions of the Presbyterian Church USA employed him at their preaching stations in Lemitar and Magdalena. After graduation from Menaul in 1916, he enrolled at the Presbyterian College in Marysville, Tennessee, only to have his college education interrupted a year later when he was drafted into the army. He served briefly in France and was discharged in 1919. He then returned to Menaul School to work as a Spanish teacher while attending classes at the University of New Mexico. In the summer of 1920, he married Adela Cháves, a Harwood student. The couple remained at Menaul until 1921 when Candelaria went to Dubuque University to complete his undergraduate work and begin his seminary studies. He graduated from Dubuque in 1922 and in October 1923, with his wife and two children, he answered the call to the Central Presbyterian Church in Denver to work at its Spanish Mission in Jerome Park. He completed his seminary studies at Iliff School of Theology in Denver and was ordained in 1926.

During his twelve years in Colorado Reverend Candelaria successfully organized and developed churches in Jerome Park, Brighton, Greeley, and Fort Collins. He was greatly in demand as a speaker and was frequently asked to talk about his work among the migrant workers. Dr. Warnshuis asked Reverend Candelaria to help organize the Interdenominational Council of Spanish-speaking in the United States and also to represent the Presbyterian Church at conferences and in seminars throughout the Southwest and in Mexico.

In 1935, Candelaria was called to the Second Presbyterian Church in Albuquerque. He served that church for over 26 years until his retirement in 1962. While there he organized and supervised new programs at the Martineztown House of Neighborly Service and pastored the Spanish churches in Santa Fe and Placitas. His 27 years of service included developing the membership at Second Presbyterian Church, bringing the church to self-supporting status, and adding a community center for Martineztown.

Besides his pastorate, Candelaria participated in the Albuquerque Ministerial Alliance, organized the Hispanic Ministerial Alliance, helped organize the Council on Spanish American Work (COSAW), served as Moderator of the Synod of New Mexico and the Rio Grande Presbytery, and worked on numerous committees. He persuaded KGGM radio to donate one half hour a week to the Spanish churches to air a Spanish message—a program that lasted for almost ten years.

Like several other ministers at Second Presbyterian Church, Reverend Candelaria had charge of four Presbyterian churches at the same time—Second Church, Alameda, Bernalillo, and Placitas. He was invited several times to give the invocation at the opening of the New Mexico Legislature and was made an honorary member of the staff of the Secretary of State. Always quick to give credit to the many who helped him through his ministry, he claimed to have many right arms. The first was his wife; the second was his aide Matilda Tapia.

Reverend Candelaria "retired" from active ministry on Easter Sunday, April 22, 1962. Nevertheless, he subsequently served as interim pastor at Northminster Presbyterian Church in Albuquerque, and at El Buen Pastor Church in San Francisco, California. José Candelaria died on June 10, 1977. In October 1983, his wife, Adela, joined him.[15]

ANTONIO JIMÉNEZ
1950 -1951

Reverend Antonio Jiménez, a Methodist evangelist from Las Cruces, arrived in June 1950 to assist Reverend Candelaria with the Placitas, Bernalillo and Alameda churches.

Jiménez was born into a traditional Catholic family on December 20, 1880, in Lampasos, near Monterrey, Mexico. He attained the equivalent of a fifth grade education in Mexico before coming to the United States at about the age of 14. He enrolled in Draughn's Business College in San Antonio, Texas, and in order to support himself and pay for his education, he worked as an apprentice barber and a delivery boy for a pharmacist. He graduated from Draughn's with diplomas in bookkeeping, business arithmetic, and penmanship.

Gifted with a great enthusiasm and the ability to sell anything to anyone, Jiménez worked for a number of years as a very successful insurance salesman. At one time during these years Teddy Roosevelt visited San Antonio during an election campaign. The story is told that Jiménez walked into a bar, and upon seeing the future president seated there, invited everyone for a drink. He then had a photograph taken of himself standing next to the President with the entire happy group hoisting their beer mugs. Jiménez treasured this photograph and kept it in his office. In later years the Methodist Bishop of Las Cruces took him to task for it, expressing his dismay that a man of the cloth would display a photograph of himself in the act of drinking beer. Jiménez answered that he kept it as a reminder—and proof—-of his conversion.

It was Jiménez's wife, Ofelia Cháves of the New Mexico Cháves clan, who brought about his conversion. Jiménez met her while she was a missionary teacher at the Methodist Howchen Settlement school in El Paso, Texas. She was obviously a strong influence on him. He not only adopted her Methodist faith, he decided to become a preacher. Unable because of his family responsibilities to go to a seminary, he took courses by correspondence and in night school and eventually completed most of the studies required for ordination. He began preaching at Hot Springs (now Truth or Consequences) in 1920, then three years later transferred to Las Cruces. As a "circuit riding" pastor, he covered all the neighboring villages in a three-county area, first by horse and buggy and later in a Model T Ford. When the Methodist Church could not pay him a salary during the Depression, he sold Watkins Products so as to continue his ministry, preaching to all the widely dispersed families on his sales route. He also preached regularly at the local prison, influencing several hardened criminals to take up the ministry. Shortly before 1940, he decided to become an evangelist.

Jiménez and Reverend Candelaria met through their wives, who were cousins, and it was Candelaria who persuaded Jiménez to come to preach at Placitas at a time when he felt the community was badly in need of a restoration of hope and faith. After serving the three-point field of Placitas, Bernalillo, and Alameda for a year and a half, he returned to Las Cruces to work as a Bible teacher for the Baptists—-a position he held until the year before his death at the age of 101. Jiménez and Ofelia had 13 children, ten of whom survived.[16]

KENNETH J. GREEN
1951 - 1955

Reverend Kenneth J. Green came to serve the Placitas, Bernalillo, and Alameda churches in 1951. He was born in Chesham, Bucks, England, on July 10, 1910, and attended the Regent Street Polytechnic in London and the All Nations Bible College. In 1935, he was commissioned by the Worldwide Evangelization Crusade in Bogota, where he served as missionary for fifteen years. Deciding to immigrate into the United States, Reverend Green accepted an assignment with the Board of National Missions of the Presbyterian Church USA to go to New Mexico. Placitas was his first post. He was ordained by the Presbyterian Church in Albuquerque in 1952.

For three years he successfully carried on the pastorate of the three small congregations. He resigned his position in 1955 because of his wife's health. He later served churches in Pomona and Los Angeles, California, worked for twelve years as a National Mission worker in Alaska, and finished his career as a pastor in Westmorland, California. Reverend Green has resided in Monte Vista Grove, California, since 1989.[17]

RODOLFO TORRES
1955 - 1957

Reverend Rodolfo Torres replaced Mr. Green and served the Placitas, Bernalillo, and Alameda congregations for two years. Born June 18, 1896, in Escobedo, Nuevo Leon, Mexico, Rodolfo Torres had a very early exposure to Presbyterianism when a teacher encouraged him to attend a Protestant mission school in his hometown. He later attended a seminary in Tampico. After graduation he was ordained and took a missionary position at McAllen, Texas, for four years. He then moved back to Mexico, where he took charge of the church of El Buen Pastor in Monterrey. During the twenty-eight years he served as its pastor, Torres built up the congregation to become the second largest Presbyterian church in Mexico.

Sometime during 1953 or early 1954, Reverend José I. Candelaria visited Monterrey and persuaded Reverend Torres to accept a call to come to New Mexico to serve the three small churches in Placitas, Bernalillo, and Alameda. Torres was suffering from poor health, and the idea of exchanging the responsibility of a big city church for three small rural churches appealed to him. The Torres family arrived in Bernalillo in August 1955 and settled into the Bernalillo manse. Torres served the three churches faithfully, although it was hardly the restful semi-retirement he had envisioned. He conducted three services every Sunday, preaching in Alameda in the morning, in Placitas in the afternoon, and in Bernalillo in the evening. His wife, Eloisa, who was an accomplished musician, played the piano or the organ and led the congregation in singing. He left in December 1957 to accept the call of two churches in Arizona, one in Miami and the other in Globe.[18]

HARRY WILLSON
1958 – 1966

Reverend Harry Willson came to New Mexico "sight unseen" directly from Princeton Theological Seminary in the spring of 1958. Prior to completing his seminary studies, Willson and his family spent a year in Spain in preparation for entering the field of Foreign Missions. During this time Willson became completely fluent in Spanish. He also developed an aversion to the dictatorial government of General Francisco Franco. After returning to the United States and graduating from Princeton, Willson accepted the invitation of Paul Warnshuis, director of the Spanish-Speaking Department of the Board of National Missions of the Presbyterian Church USA, to come to New Mexico. Warnshuis originally expected him to take charge of one of the Presbyterian "plaza" schools as well as its church, but he ended up assigning Willson to minister to the Placitas, Bernalillo, and Alameda churches. Warnshuis hoped that, through a yoked ministry, they could all three be made self-supporting. However, within a few months after Wilson's arrival, the Rio Grande Presbytery gave up the Bernalillo ministry.

Harry Willson served the Placitas and Alameda churches for eight years. In 1967, he left the ministry and for a while worked almost full time for the Civil Rights Movement. The Southern Christian Leadership Conference (SCLC) assigned him to direct the Atlanta Alliance for Peace, and in 1968 he was chairman of the Poor People's March on Washington. He now lives in Albuquerque's South Valley where he writes and publishes books. His wife is the former Adela Amador of Placitas.[19]

DAVID HAMMACK
1967 - 1970

Reverend David Hammack was born in San Diego in 1929. He came to New Mexico in 1956 with his wife and young family as an employee of the Board of National Missions to teach science at the Presbyterian Allison-James School in Santa Fe. When that school closed in 1959, he moved to Albuquerque to teach chemistry, mathematics, and physics at Menaul School. He also began a close association with St. Andrew United Presbyterian Church.

In 1964, Hammack left Menaul to attend the San Francisco Theological Seminary. He graduated in 1967. Hearing from his old friend and associate at Menaul School, Harry Willson, that Willson had just left the Placitas and Alameda Churches, Hammack sent them his resume. Shortly thereafter he answered their call and served both churches for three years, during which time he lived in the manse in Alameda.

Hammack left the Placitas and Alameda churches in September 1970. He remained in Albuquerque and started an electrical contracting business. He designed and installed the electrical system for the addition to the Las Placitas Presbyterian Church that was completed in 1984.[20]

FLOYD B. SOVEREIGN
1966, 1970 -1972

Reverend Floyd B. Sovereign was born in Buffalo, New York. He studied theology at Evangelical Seminary in Naperville, Illinois, at Colgate Rochester Divinity School, and Union Seminary in New York City. He met his wife, Marie, while both were students at Houghton College.

Sovereign's first pastorate was in Rochester, where he served three years before accepting the call of the Presbyterian Church in Brazil in 1947. There the couple worked for nine years in new church development and rural evangelism. Their final assignment was to the Presbyterian Theological Seminary in Campinas, Brazil, where Floyd served as dean and taught church history and where Marie taught English and for a time served as librarian.

The Sovereigns returned to the United States in 1963. They moved to Albuquerque where Floyd worked for eleven years as chaplain at Presbyterian Hospital and Marie as teacher of Portuguese at the University of New Mexico. During these years Sovereign served the Placitas Presbyterian Church as Temporary Supply for several periods while the church was between regular pastors. In 1974, the Sovereigns moved to Pompano Beach, Florida, where Floyd served as pastor until his retirement in 1984. They now make their home in Las Cruces.[21]

GEORGE JACOB ADAMS
1972–1980

Reverend George Adams was born in Taiku, Korea, August 6, 1907, the son of Presbyterian missionaries who hailed originally from the First Presbyterian Church of Topeka, Kansas. George attended school in Korea through his freshman year of high school. His parents took a year's furlough to the States, and he attended South Pasadena High School. Then, with his parents back in Korea, he lived with relatives in Topeka and graduated from Washburn Rural High School. He attended the Presbyterian College of Emporia for one year and graduated from Occidental College in Los Angeles in 1929. In 1930, he married Margaret Loraine Roberts, with whom he had four sons.

George next attended San Francisco Theological Seminary and graduated from there in 1932. He was ordained the following February by the San Francisco Presbytery, and he and his wife left almost immediately for Korea to work as missionaries for the Board of Foreign Missions of the Presbyterian Church USA. Before leaving for Korea they attended an outgoing missionary conference in New York, which gave them a good excuse for traveling to the Orient by way of Europe and the Holy Land.

George Adams spent the next nineteen years in Korea where George served 35 to 40 churches, visiting each one twice a year to conduct weddings, baptisms, and funerals and to catechize potential church members. He then transferred to Japan and served there for eleven years, seven of them in the Tokyo area and four on Kyushu, Japan's south island. In 1965, George married his second wife, Michiko Kashiwagi.

After a total of forty-five years spent in the Orient, Adams decided in 1971 to renew his ties with his native country. He asked a friend in Albuquerque to circulate his resume, and it came to the attention of the Placitas Presbyterian Church. Although the Placitas Church wanted him to come immediately, the Adams's had to postpone their arrival until their son, Kenneth Kei, was born. George Adams served the Placitas Presbyterian Church eight years. He resigned in June 1980, and he, Michiko, and Kenneth moved to Irving, Texas, where George expected to go into a well-deserved retirement. But duty called again, and one year later George took up the pulpit of the Trinity Presbyterian Church in Grand Prairie, Texas, a neighboring community to Irving. He retired again, on September 30, 1992. He and Michiko still reside in Irving, Texas.[22]

TOMÁS GONZALEZ
1970s-1995

Reverend Tomás Gonzalez has served the Placitas Presbyterian Church in one way or another ever since he was a member of the Menaul Gospel Team in the mid-1930s. Although he has never been its official pastor, he has filled in on countless occasions as guest preacher, and during the 1970s he often came out to give special services in Spanish for the older Spanish-speaking members of the congregation. After 1980, whenever Reverend Anderson was absent, Tomás Gonzalez was on call, and he served the congregation frequently with or in place of Jim in times of crisis. His gentle, caring stewardship deserves special recognition.

Tomás Gonzalez was born April 30, 1917, in Chacón, New Mexico. As a youth he attended the Chacón Presbyterian Mission School, continuing a tradition of Presbyterianism in his family. His maternal grandmother taught the adult Sunday School for many years at the Chacón Presbyterian Church. When Tomás joined the church at the age of nine, he told the Session that he wanted to be a minister. He credits this very early decision on the fact that, "the best person that ever came to our community was the Presbyterian minister. He was the best dressed, and very intelligent. He was a very good role model."

After graduating from the eighth grade in Chacón, Tomás's parents sent him to the Menaul School in Albuquerque, from which he graduated in 1935. He then enrolled in the University of New Mexico, but he continued to live at Menaul, working in the kitchen and serving as monitor in the dormitory. While at the University Tomás also got a job with the NYA (the National Youth Administration, a New Deal depression program for young people). In this job he did research for a history professor, traveling on Saturdays to Santa Fe to translate documents in the Spanish Archives. After he graduated from the University in 1940, he went to Louisville Presbyterian Seminary in Kentucky for two years, supporting himself by teaching conversational Spanish and preaching at various churches in the Louisville area. He finished his last year at the Iliff School of Theology in Denver while serving a little church in Brighton, Colorado.

Tomás served the Old Town church in Las Vegas for eleven years and then answered the call of a church in North Vernon, Indiana, where he stayed another ten years. On Sunday nights he also preached to a group of Cuban refugees at a church in Indianapolis. The climax of his ministry was receiving a call from Second Presbyterian Church in Albuquerque. He served that church until his retirement.[23]

JAMES R. ANDERSON
1980 - 1995

Reverend James R. Anderson was born April 15, 1929, in Saginaw, Michigan. He was adopted by a radiologist and his wife and grew up in a large family. His earliest memories are of participating in the life of the Presbyterian Church in Saginaw. As a young person he was a member of the Westminster Fellowship, an association that gave him his most intimate connections with the church. His pastor, Dr. Henry W. Fischer, frequently called on him to help with the Easter breakfast service, a service traditionally conducted by the youth of the church. Jim's youth group also traveled to other churches for hymn sings, and so he became acquainted with people from other religious backgrounds. While on these trips he heard some very effective preachers who laid out the responsibilities of Christian discipleship—sermons that moved him to make an interior commitment to be a minister, sure that it was the best and most proper way to be a Christian.

As Jim matured, his desire to be a minister came into conflict with an equally strong wish to follow in his father's footsteps and become a physician. Not surprisingly, his interest in medicine lay in the area of human service. Still, friends and teachers urged him to consider the ministry even after he had enrolled in a combined undergraduate/medical school curriculum at the Presbyterian college in Alma, Michigan.

After several years Jim came to terms with the fact that he wasn't cut out to be a doctor, though he still harbored idealistic dreams of becoming a medical missionary. He finished college with a double major in chemistry and biology and then went on to take a course in creative writing at Bayview College. The course was pivotal in raising his confidence in his creative abilities. Convinced at last that he should go to Seminary, he was taken under the care of the Presbytery. At his examination one of his examiners asked him: *"Would you say with Paul, 'Woe is me if I preached not the Gospel'?"* Jim answered thoughtfully that that had been his constant experience.

Jim graduated from the McCormick Seminary in Chicago in 1954 and was ordained when he was called to be an assistant at the church in Saginaw. He married for the first time while completing his seminary work. Assuming this financial responsibility required him to work one summer as a ditch digger for the Peoples' Gas, Light, and Coal Company of Chicago—back breaking labor that he has not forgotten.

He served at various other churches in Michigan, Indiana, and Ohio before deciding to enter graduate school at Michigan State to study pastoral counseling. While there he completed all requirements for the doctorate except the dissertation, in the meantime working at a number of jobs simultaneously. Eventually he landed in Laramie, Wyoming, where he served as an associate of the Presbyterian church and was employed by the University of Wyoming to train employment counselors throughout the state. In 1973, he came to Albuquerque where he organized the All Faiths Counseling Center. He also had a radio program with call-in counseling and served the First Presbyterian Church as interim youth minister. He married Mae Romero on September 2, 1978. In 1980, he came to Placitas as Interim Pastor, and on March 6, 1983 he was called to the full-time pastorate of Las Placitas Presbyterian Church. In November 1994, he announced that he would retire from this position on January 31, 1995.[24]

AFTERWORD

1995-2016

¡Adelante!

God's message to the people from Exodus 14:15 invoked by the Rev. James A. Menaul on the day of the founding of The Presbyterian Church at Las Placitas was *¡Adelante!* Faced with finding a way forward where there apparently was none, the people of God heeded the call to move onward. Surely the early founders of this congregation were familiar with that call—*¡Adelante!* They were now faced with responding in a new way. We are indebted to Suzanne Sims Forrest for gathering in this book the responses of generations of the faithful at Las Placitas Presbyterian Church (LPPC). Thanks to God's faithfulness, this story does not end with the first century of faith.

Placitas has continued to change over recent decades. The historic village of Placitas, where the Church was founded in 1894, remains. Descendants of the original families of the San Antonio de Las Huertas land grant still call this place home. Young children of these families continue to be baptized at LPPC. When their loved ones die, the sanctuary is again filled with voices in Spanish gathered to give Witness to *la Resurrección* and to join together in the celebration of a life lived in faith.

The hills, ridges, and mesas to the north and west of the village of Placitas have been populated over the years with homes inhabited largely by newcomers to the area. In the early 1950s, after pastoring this Church for more than 15 years, the Reverend José Inés Candelaria predicted that "while there was little hope that the Spanish population would increase" more Anglo families would continue to move in.

According to research done for this book, in 1940 there were three Anglo families in Placitas. In 1951, there were "at least ten Anglo-American families" here. In 2010, nearly 5,000 people called Placitas home. According to U.S. Census data, 75% percent of those residents were "white alone." Just under 21% were Hispanic.

In the midst of this demographic shift, the Church grew during the 1990s paralleling the population expansion of Placitas. The building addition, which had been dedicated in 1984, provided expanded space to extend the welcome of the original founding families to others. In 1996, the congregation called the Rev. Jane Harmes as their first female pastor.

Residents from the wider Placitas community and beyond joined the Church. Expanded facilities provided space for local groups to meet, including the Jardineros de Placitas, neighborhood homeowners' associations, and Alcoholics Anonymous. The acoustics of the new sanctuary offered an excellent venue for the concerts of the Placitas Artist Series. The walls of the fellowship hall became a gallery where works from local artists could accompany the music.

An Earthcare Covenant signed by the congregation in 1998 led to an Earthcare Fellowship that continues to provide worship and environmental education opportunities to the wider community. An evening Winter Solstice Poetry Reading to the light of a single candle in our darkened sanctuary has become a local favorite. A memorial garden including a columbarium just to the south and east of the Church along Paseo de San Antonio was designed and developed. Accompanied by the labor of many others, Church members Charles and Ila Little dedicated themselves to these efforts.

In the early 2000s, vital ministry led the congregation to perceive the need to grow again. Around this time, the Rev. Ken Cuthbertson became active in the life of LPPC. He later became a Parish Associate at the invitation of the Rev. Jane Harmes. The Max DeLara home and land adjoining the Church immediately to the east had previously been purchased. When the structure was deemed unsuitable for the congregation's needed growth, a building expansion was planned that ultimately included an extended fellowship hall, a large kitchen, new classroom, library, and childcare spaces, Church offices, and accessible restrooms. After much preliminary work and deliberation, a groundbreaking was held on August 27, 2004.

Nine months later on Pentecost Sunday, May 15, 2005, a dedication was held for the new expansion. A capacity crowd filled the Church. The Rev. Jaime Quiñones, a longstanding friend of the congregation from the Presbytery of Santa Fe, delivered the sermon that day. The congregation processed around the outside of the Church, ending up at the main doors to the new wing. Elder Vivian Gonzales DeLara, granddaughter of Juan Baros, along with former pastor the Rev. Jim Anderson cut the ribbon and opened the doors. The congregation of LPPC was then greeted inside by the choir from the Misión San Antonio, our Catholic neighbors, who were singing as they welcomed the Presbyterians into their new space.

Times have truly changed since the founding of this Church in 1894.

The new expansion provided the congregation with the opportunity to reclaim the 1930s sanctuary as "sacred space." Beginning on Ash Wednesday in 2006, worship once again was held there. The sanctuary that was built under the leadership of the Rev. George Simmonds is still used for an early Sunday morning worship service today. This sacred space, now called the Upper Room, is also regularly used for adult education classes, as well as church and community meetings.

The Rev. Jane Harmes retired in September 2007. Shortly thereafter, the Rev. Elizabeth Lyman came to serve in an interim capacity as the "Transitional Pastor." Under her leadership, the Casa Rosa Food Pantry was established to serve local residents in need. This effort, championed by volunteers from the congregation and the wider community, made excellent use of "the DeLara house" that had been originally purchased for other purposes. Casa Rosa has become a model food pantry in the state. It continues to be a vital outreach that weekly connects people across a wide spectrum of the Placitas community.

In 2008, the Church found itself facing financial difficulties. During his tenure in the 1970s, the LPPC Pastor Rev. George Adams had reported that despite the somewhat more affluent congregation, finances remained the most critical aspect of Church survival. The recession of the late 2000s that hit the U.S. and global economies did not leave the congregation unscathed. Challenging financial times, combined with a mortgage debt assumed for the most recent Church expansion, led some in the congregation to voice concern about the Church's capacity to continue employing a full time pastor.

In 2009, a Pastor Nominating Committee had been elected by the congregation to seek a new minister. In 2010, with the support of the Presbytery of Santa Fe, the Church's Session and Finance Committee recommended to the congregation that they seek a Designated Pastor, who would be elected to serve full time for a two-year limited term at the Presbytery's minimum allowed salary.

Rev. Lyman resigned in the summer of 2010, in part to alleviate the congregation's financial burden. The Rev. Steve Miller assumed the position of part-time Stated Supply until a new pastor could be called. In January 2011, the Rev. Drew Henry began under the above mentioned terms as the Designated Pastor of LPPC. Rev. Henry was the first bilingual pastor fully fluent in Spanish to serve the congregation of LPPC in over a generation. He came with a background and interest in stewardship, worship, church finances, and congregational redevelopment.

In their first two years together, the congregation and their new Pastor partnered to pay off the building expansion debt. Following generous gifts of members and former members, a "mortgage burning" ceremony was held on Pentecost Sunday in 2013; just eight years after the building expansion had been dedicated. A plaque was placed in the church's memorial garden to celebrate the retirement of the expansion loan. Now out of financial debt, the Church was free to dedicate more of its time, energy, and resources to the ministry and missions to which it is called.

LPPC continues to grow and evolve today. Worship, learning, and service remain at the heart of the congregation's life. An excellent music program and choir are highlights. The number of children and youth in the Church has grown. This is due, in no small part, thanks to excellent volunteer leadership in Christian Education from current members of the Church. At the urging of longtime members, an annual Vacation Bible School was reinitiated for children of the Church and the wider community. In 2015, the average weekly worship attendance was 120. Membership was near 170.

In the search for their most recent pastor, the congregation recommitted themselves to honoring their Hispanic heritage. Worship services now begin weekly *en español*. They regularly include readings, hymns, responses, communion liturgy, and prayers in Spanish. Although Rev. Henry was "not born speaking Spanish," he continues a long tradition of pastors of this congregation who have served the church as missionaries in South America. Paul Warnshuis worked in Chile. George Simmonds served in Ecuador and Peru. Kenneth Green had been a missionary in Colombia. Floyd Sovereign served the Church in Brazil. Drew Henry was a Presbyterian mission volunteer in Argentina.

Today descendants of the founding families continue to be an active part of LPPC. Though they are proportionally fewer in number now, their participation is equally as important. The number of non-Hispanic families in our congregation has grown, mirroring a similar growth in the wider community. LPPC is an inclusive, multicultural community that seeks to honor and respect our God-given diversity.

When I accepted the call to continue on as Pastor of LPPC in 2013, the term Designated was dropped from my title. In that same year, the Rev. Karl Gustafson joined the congregation as a second Parish Associate working in partnership with myself and the Rev. Ken Cuthbertson. I know all of us who serve here echo George Simmonds' conclusion of his *recuerdos* (memories) of this congregation. "The people of the Placitas Church loved their church and kept it always in tip-top condition. I feel honored to have been one of its ministers and part of its history."

Along with James Menaul, we continue to sound forth God's call—*¡Adelante!*

The Rev. Drew M. Henry
February, 2016

(I thank Ken Cuthbertson for writing some of the history of these past decades as well as the pastoral biographies that follow. I am also grateful to the congregation for encouraging me to write and to the Norbertine Community of the South Valley of Albuquerque for providing me a space in which to do so.)

Los Pastores de Las Placitas Presbyterian Church

Continued for 1995-2016

INTERIMS

During the year-and-a-half following the Rev. Jim Anderson's retirement in 1995, Las Placitas Presbyterian Church was served by two successive interim pastors, first the Rev. Art Opmeer, and then the Rev. Kathi Hunter.

JANE P. HARMES

1996–2007

The Rev. Jane P. Harmes was called to Las Placitas in the summer of 1996. She came from a pastorate in Troy, NY, to settle into her new New Mexico home in Ranchos de Placitas. Jane had served as a Director of Christian Education for many years before returning to seminary and being ordained in 1983 as a Minister of the Word and Sacrament in the Presbyterian Church USA. She is a graduate of Wesley Seminary in Washington, D.C.

Jane ("*La Pastora*") was LPPC's first installed female minister. She served here for 11 years. During her tenure, Rev. Harmes' strong, and sometimes outspoken, commitment to peace, social justice, and environmental issues was at times off-putting for some and an attraction for others. Pastor Jane was particularly interested in women's concerns, and for inclusivity of the LGBT (Lesbian, Gay, Bisexual, Transgender) community in both church and society.

Jane retired at the end of September 2007. As promised, after pronouncing the benediction she performed a cartwheel in the chancel on her final Sunday. Jane continued living in Placitas for a time, and eventually moved in early 2010 to Pilgrim Place, a church-related retirement community in Claremont, CA.

KENNETH L. CUTHBERTSON
2003–present

The Rev. Ken Cuthbertson began coming up to Placitas as an occasional pulpit supply in the early 2000's. In November 2003, Ken and his longtime lifepartner Doug Calderwood began regularly attending Las Placitas. Ken twice served as "Temporary Supply" Pastor, first during Jane Harmes' three month sabbatical in 2004, and again in the three-and-a-half months following Rev. Harmes' retirement in 2007. Ken served as a Parish Associate under Jane Harmes from 2005 until her retirement, and continued to function informally in that role during Rev. Elizabeth Lyman's tenure. In the summer of 2011, Pastor Drew Henry invited Ken to once again serve as a Parish Associate.

A Kansas native, Ken attended Gordon-Conwell Theological Seminary in Massachusetts (of which, he says, he is a very "a-typical" graduate). Ken did additional graduate work at the School of Religion at the University of Iowa and at San Francisco Theological Seminary. In March 2012, Ken and his now husband Doug were legally married at Niagara Falls, NY. Shortly after their return, the congregation offered them a blessing during Sunday worship. A reception was held in their honor afterwards at which a quilt handmade and signed by members of the Church was given to them as a wedding gift from the congregation.

ELIZABETH A. LYMAN
2008–2010

The Rev. Elizabeth Lyman came to Las Placitas Presbyterian Church (LPPC) in an interim capacity as "Transitional" Pastor in January 2008. She moved to Placitas from Tucson, Arizona. Prior to Tucson, she served with the Presbyterian Disaster Assistance in Louisiana following the devastation left in the wake of Hurricane Katrina. Elizabeth is a native of New Jersey and had previously served a pastorate in West Virginia.

In the spring of 2010, Rev. Lyman announced that she would be concluding her time at LPPC at the beginning of July. Shortly after leaving, Elizabeth was called to be the Pastor of Deep Run Presbyterian Church in Perkasie, Pennsylvania. She has since retired to Tucson, Arizona.

STEPHEN MILLER
2010

The Rev. Stephen Miller, a Minister of the Disciples of Christ denomination, was invited to serve as Temporary Supply as the congregation's search for a new Pastor continued. Rev. Miller had worked with a variety of Disciples, United Church of Christ, and Presbyterian congregations in the area as Interim Pastor over the years. Steve also had worked for the Presbytery of Santa Fe and the New Mexico Conference of Churches. From late July 2010 until January 2011, Steve served Las Placitas Presbyterian Church with energy, intelligence, imagination, love, and music. A member of the Celtic Coyotes band, Steve often included folk-style songs in his sermons and worship.

DREW M. HENRY
2011–present

The Rev. Drew Henry came to Las Placitas in January 2011. Drew is a native of Selma, Alabama. After graduating from Rhodes College, he served as a Presbyterian mission volunteer in Buenos Aires, Argentina. While in Argentina, Drew learned Spanish, met his wife Tamara, and completed his graduate theological studies at ISEDET *(Instituto Superior Evangélico de Estudios Teológicos).* Drew was ordained to the Ministry of Word and Sacrament in 2002 by the Presbytery of Shepherds and Lapsley in central Alabama. Before coming to Las Placitas, he served as an Associate Pastor of the First Presbyterian Church of Birmingham, Alabama.

Drew's ministry has led him to work with congregations that sit at the heart of the communities they serve. He is a lifelong Presbyterian who strives to take God more seriously than he takes the church or himself. Drew, Tamara and their two sons, Santiago and Paco, enjoy calling Placitas home. Since moving here, Drew has been an active member of the Presbytery of Santa Fe, as well as being very involved in the community of Placitas. He also serves on the board of the Menaul School in Albuquerque, maintaining that historic connection with the Placitas church.

KARL GUSTAFSON

2013–present

The Rev. Karl Gustafson joined Las Placitas Presbyterian Church as a Parish Associate after serving congregations in small-town southern Ohio, large-town West Virginia, rural Maine, and very urban Boston. Although he lived and served in all these different places, Karl has considered New Mexico his spiritual home since first visiting as a child.

Karl has always been drawn to the margins and the marginalized, challenged by the personal need to balance heart and mind, obligated to serve the call of justice, but would prefer to contemplate and create things of beauty. One of Karl's primary roles at Las Placitas has been to help the congregation explore ways to engage the arts in faith and worship.

JUBILADOS

In recent years, Las Placitas Presbyterian Church has been blessed to have a number of retired clergy as active participants in our worshipping community. While occupying no official role, they have been generous in sharing their time, energy, and experience—assisting in worship, pastoral care, and other key aspects of congregational life. These include:

The Rev. Joyce A. Thompson
The Rev. Georgiana Kugle
The Rev. Anne Hayes Egan
The Rev. Peter J. Frazier-Koontz

Sandia Holy Day

Words reprinted with permission of John Pitney

This song was written by John Pitney for LPPC's Earth Day Sabbath celebration in 1999. John is a Methodist minister, folk musician, community organizer, and sustainable food activist from Oregon. In the liner notes he writes: "Shortly before the event [Charles Little] called saying he'd had to get publicity out in a hurry and didn't have time to check with me, so he hoped it was alright. Reading to me over the phone I heard, "...and this wonderful day will premiere the song John has written just for the occasion, 'Sandia Holy Day.'" I hadn't heard I was writing a song! And with a title already!?!" Here are the results:

Chorus:

Sandia, Sandia, Sandia! El Día Santo, Sandia!
Sandia, Sandia! El Día Santo, Sandia!

1. Tilted and rifted above us Big Mountain you're standing
   Mantle uplifted with fossils of life once an ocean.
   Tho' flashflood and windstorm have worn you,
   Good friend, your devotion still
   Looks o'er us Sandia! Good Morning, Sandia!
   chorus

2. An orchid appears in a meadow and rare flies a falcon.
   Up an arroyo, swift foxes leap; owls sleep in pinions.
   Creator, the wolf and the bighorn have gone. Can we learn to share
   Dominions of beauty, preserving Sandia!
   chorus

3. For 10,000 years, Holy Mountain, you nested a people,
   Who, even conquested, have taught us to love *little places*.
   As progress encroaches, Great Spirit, create in us Common Good

To keep sacred spaces. Delightful! Sandia!
chorus

4. Our church folk like vigas from the pines of Las Huertas, uphold us:
Gurulé, Baros, Lucero, Escarcida, Salazar;
y DeLara, Gonzales, Arriola, Martinez these families are
A refuge, the future, our conscience, Sandia!
chorus

5. So when we sing and pray,
When we leave this Holy Day,
Our light will rise with watermelon sunset
Filling our eyes, and no regret…

Sandia, Sandia, Sandia! El Día Santo, Sandia!
Sandia, Sandia! El Día Santo, Sandia!

Photos—Post 1995

The Rev. Jane Harmes with her dog Ebony.

Below: Jane Harmes leading the annual "Worship in the Mountains" service at the Sandia Mountain Retreat Center.

The Memorial Garden was dedicated September 26, 1999. Envisioned under the leadership of Charles and Ila Little, it was designed by Bill Hays and Judith Phillips. This sacred space includes a columbarium, where ashes may be inurned, as well as many hardscape features and native plants which were donated in memory of loved ones.

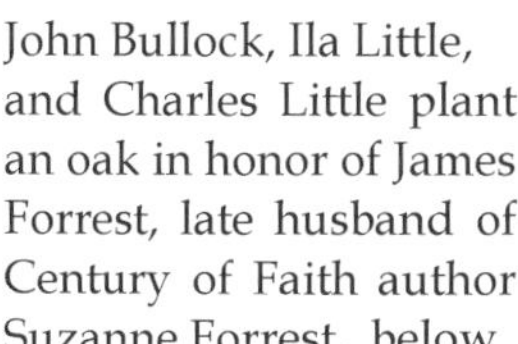

John Bullock, Ila Little, and Charles Little plant an oak in honor of James Forrest, late husband of Century of Faith author Suzanne Forrest, below.

Dedication of the oak in the Memorial Garden. L–R: Suzanne Forrest, Ila Little, Ilona de Borhegyi, Margaret Palumbo, Charles Little, and the Rev. Jane Harmes, 2005.

2005 saw a major addition to the Church.

Left: Ground breaking as Chloe Hoses turns the first shovel of dirt while Reverend Jane Harmes and others look on.

Above: Concrete is poured.

Left: General Contractor Drew Owens, Building Committee chair David Southwick, and elder Leland Bowen just after installation of the new LPPC cross on the exterior north wall.

Designed by Dorothy Bowen, the cross was built by David Southwick, with metal work by Leland Bowen.

Left: May 5, 2005, the Sanctuary is decorated for the dedication of the new addition.

Below: Members of the new building committee included Bud Brinkerhoff, Linda Bullock, Dorothy Bowen, Don Tubesing, Bill Stephenson, and chairman David Southwick.

Sally and Jack Curro visit with Wilda and Kendall Schlenker after the dedication service. Kendall served as general contractor for the 1984 addition.

The 2005 addition included a new kitchen, staffed by this happy crew. Phyllis Broom and Elsie DeLara, front, with Clara Stephenson, Bev Schippers, Joyce Mahnke, Wilda MacLauchlan, and Joan Dennis.

Below: The new space for the Mothers' Day Out (MDO) preschool program is organized and ready to go.

MDO director Debbie Stueber joins her munchkins in costume for a Halloween party.

The Rev. Kenneth L. Cuthbertson has served LPPC in these capacities since 2003.

- Sabbatical supply in 2004 while Jane Harmes was away.
- Parish associate 2005-2007.
- "temporary supply" Oct. 2007 – Jan. 2008.

He became Parish Associate again in late 2011 or early 2012, and continues in that role as of 2016.

Pastor Ken leads an Earth Vespers service in the Sandias to celebrate the Summer Solstice with the Earth Care Fellowship, 2007.

Shown here leading an Earth Day celebration, the Reverend Elizabeth Lyman was called to serve as Transitional Pastor in 2008.

One of the first programs to grow from Elizabeth's ministry was the Casa Rosa Food Pantry, which opened its doors on August 30, 2008, to serve Placitas residents in need every Saturday. The Pantry is housed in the home purchased from Max and Esther DeLara. Located just east of the church, the new property allowed LPPC to expand its parking as well.

Just to the east of this house the church supports the local art community by providing space for a large tent for artists in the annual Placitas Holiday Fine Arts and Crafts Show in November.

Pastor Elizabeth coaxes a village donkey to play his part as the Palm Sunday service begins, 2009.

Mission committee members Pat Thorpe and Joyce Hoses sell "Just Coffee" and other items during the Fellowship Hour.

Annual Christmas pageants attract angels, shepards, and wise men.

Above: Thomas Dickson, Annabella Mayorga, Rob Kaiser and Jackson Skinner.

Above: Jackson and Claire Skinner
.

Sally Gosnell watches as the children perform. Seated behind: Sarah Watkins and Rob Kaiser.

The Reverend Stephen Miller served as Interim Pastor from 2010 to 2011. Steve is shown here on his final day with us wearing the prayer shawl given to him in gratitude for his ministry.

The Rev. Drew Henry was called as Pastor in 2011. Drew is shown here with wife Tamara Hudson and their sons Santiago (Santi) and Francisco (Paco).

The youth ministry remains strong and active at LPPC.

Pastor Drew shares a moment with Thomas Dickson.

Dana Douglas adds her sweet voice to the choir.

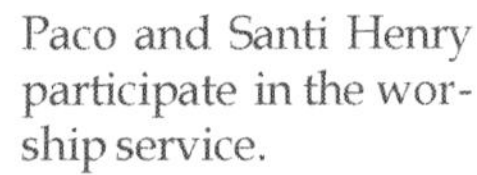

Paco and Santi Henry participate in the worship service.

The congregation worships both inside the sanctuary (above) and outside (below).

The Rev. Ken Cuthbertson (left) assists Pastor Drew as John Bullock leads the music during a communion service at the Sandia Mountain Retreat Center.

Vacation Bible School, July, 2013: children explore the wonderful world of mission, visiting five countries on their very own LPPC Airline! The theme was "God Calls Us Around the World."

"Captain" Jeff Dickson leads the 2013 Vacation Bible School adventure.

Church night at the Albuquerque Isotopes baseball game: Elizabeth Dickson hugs Thomas and Rob as Elsie DeLara looks on.

Drew Henry (left) and Ken Cuthbertson (right) celebrate the burning of the mortgage for the 2005 building on May 19, 2013.

TIMELINE HISTORY
Las Huertas and Las Placitas

In 1540-42	**Francisco Vasquez de Coronado led expedition north from Nuevo España claiming as Spanish** the land explorers would later name Nuevo México. Expedition spent winters of 1540-41 and 1541-42 in land just west of **an area they named Las Huertas—after the orchards they saw.**
July 7, 1540	**Coronado held** a feast of thanksgiving at Hawikuh (near present Zuni Pueblo in New Mexico)--**the First Thanksgiving in an area that would eventually be part of the United States of America.** [This was 79 years earlier than the "1st Official Thanksgiving" in the English colonies at Berkeley Plantation in Virginia on December 4, 1619 and 81 years earlier than the Pilgrims' Thanksgiving in 1621 in Massachusetts.]
1563 & 1581	**The area north of Nuevo España was given the name of Nuevo México** because Spanish explorers believed it contained wealthy native cultures similar to those of the **Méxica** (Aztec) empire. [This area was **NOT** named after the country of Mexico, which did not exist until 1821—over two centuries later.]
In 1598	**Juan de Oñate led a party of Spanish settlers** with first capital established along the Rio Grande at San Juan. They survived the first military skirmish between natives and Europeans in what would become the American West.
In 1610	**Nuevo México's capital moved south from San Juan to Santa Fe.**
ca. 1660	**Diego de Trujillo built home in the Las Huertas Valley, as probably the first settler, and mined silver and lead.**
In 1680	**Puebloans rebelled against Spaniards and drove them out.**
In 1692	**Diego de Vargas re-conquered Nuevo México for Spain.** Settlers mostly lived along the Rio Grande.

In 1765	**Juan Gutierres of Bernalillo petitioned King of Spain to grant Las Huertas land in perpetuity** to him and eight other family heads.
Dec. 1767	**Settlers at San Jose resubmitted their petition to have Las Huertas land granted to them**—now including 21 families.
Jan. 13, 1768	**Spanish Governor and Captain General Pedro Fermín de Mendinueta awarded the San Antonio de Las Huertas Land Grant to the 21 families**, who were required to build a settlement in the form of a fortified plaza. **The settlers named their village San Jose de Las Huertas.**
In 1795	**The Catholic faith had come to Nuevo México with the Spanish explorers and settlers, and Las Huertas was assigned to the San Felipe Pueblo Catholic Mission**, requiring villagers to make a 16-mile round trip to San Felipe for baptisms and marriages and for carrying their deceased loved ones for burials. The lack of a local priest continued to be a problem for settlers.
Fall, 1821	**After war with Spain, Nuevo España became independent as the First Mexican Empire---**extending north into land that would become the eventual US states of Texas, Arizona, New Mexico, Colorado, Utah, Nevada, and California.
After 1821	**The Santa Fe Trail, an ancient passageway, was used regularly by merchant traders from the Missouri River to Santa Fe**. Santa Fe was close to the end of the El Camino Real de Tierra Adentro, an historic Spanish trading route from Ciudad de México, capital of Nuevo España and then the First Mexican Empire. Later in 1825, the U.S. Government obtained the right-of-way for the Trail following a treaty with the Osage Indians.
1823	**The First Mexican Empire became the Republic of Mexico.**
1823	**Mexican Gov. Antonio Vizcarra ordered residents of isolated villages to move to areas along the Rio Grande**, due to the Spanish army no longer being

available to offer protection from raiding Apaches, Comanche, Navajos, and Utes. Las Huertas settlers had to abandon their homes.

In 1824 **The Republic of Mexico became the United Mexican States, but gradually the country was just known as Mexico.**

In 1828 **Gold was discovered in the Ortiz Mountains.**

Mid 1830s **Settlers began returning to the Las Huertas area,** but the springs had dried up near their old village of San Jose. **No longer constrained by Spanish laws to live within a defined area, other settlements were started.** Some moved a mile south to an area they named **San Antonio de Padua de Las Placitas** (Las Placitas marking the spot of several Indian ruins). For protection from roaming tribes and wild animals, they initially lived in an extended community house with each family having one room. Several other families moved four miles east and settled in an area called **Tejon.**

1830s-1840s **A spring-fed acequia system was established** to supply irrigation and domestic water to the villages.

In 1839 **Gold and copper deposits were discovered in the San Pedro Mountains.** Twenty Las Huertas settlers moved to an area on the far east side of the San Antonio de Las Huertas Land Grant and established **San Pedro Rancho**. A few years later they sold rights to this land and moved a short distance away to a place they called **La Madera**—connected to Las Placitas by a narrow passage.

By 1840 **The pass through the mountains became the southern extension of the Santa Fe Trail,** and Tejon became an important overnight stopping place between Albuquerque and Las Vegas (located 65 miles east of Santa Fe).

In 1840s Some families settled a half mile east of old San Jose and called this place **Tecolote**. As springs became more abundant, some families from

Algondones and Tejon moved a couple miles up Las Huertas canyon to a place that became known as **Ojo de la Casa**—the fifth separate community populated by descendants of the original San Antonio de Las Huertas Land Grant along with newer settlers.

1844 **A struggle for the land began between the Land Grant grantees and land speculators** (the latter interested only in obtaining mineral rights) that continued until the end of the 19th century.

1846-48 **The Mexican-American War. The US Provisional government of New Mexico was established** during the War. [New Mexico had varying boundaries, but was much larger than the current State of New Mexico.]

1848 **Mexico formally ceded the New Mexico region to the US** after the Treaty of Guadalupe Hidalgo; a temporary US wartime government continued until 1850.

1850 **The Territory of New Mexico was established**, which included current New Mexico, over half of current Arizona, and portions of current Colorado and southern Nevada.

1852 **What would become the State of New Mexico was formed into nine counties**, with the Placitas area being in Bernalillo County (named for the noble family of Gonzales-Bernal who settled the territory in the 17th century).

1860 **The Territory of New Mexico passed a law establishing a public or free compulsory school system**. Early school teachers had little or no training and few or no materials to help with teaching—especially in remote areas such as Las Placitas. In 1864 the first teacher was appointed for Las Placitas, but he was illiterate—as were many of the local residents.

1861-1864 **The Civil War saw three Las Placitas men fighting with the Union forces** to resist an invasion in 1861

	by a Confederate armed force from the State of Texas.
Early 1870s	**A burial ground in Las Placitas was finally consecrated by a priest** from Bernalillo. It became known as the Placitas or San Antonio Cemetery.
1891	**Congress created the United States Court of Private Land Claims**. The Las Huertas settlers were thus forced to test the legality of their title to their royal Spanish land grant of 1768.
1893-1900	**A Presbyterian Mission School in Las Placitas held classes for both children and adults**.
1901	**First post office opened** in Las Placitas.
1903	**Sandoval County** (named for the Sandoval Family who were prominent Spanish landowners) **was established** and included the Placitas area.
1907	**After many years of litigation, the U.S. Government finally patented the San Antonio de Las Huertas Land Grant (SADLHLG)—which originally may have covered hundreds of thousands of acres—as containing only 4763.59 acres** (of which the eastern one third was claimed by the grantees' lawyer as payment for his services).
1912	**New Mexico and Arizona** (the major parts of the Territory of New Mexico) **each received statehood, as the 47th and 48th states.**
1914-1918	**World War I occurred. The U.S. declared war on Germany on December 7, 1917, and six young men from Las Placitas served until the armistice on November 11, 1918.**
By 1920s	**Including "Las" before Placitas began to disappear from common usage.**
1926	**Route 66 was the designation given to the Chicago to Los Angeles section of the national program of highway and road development.** Route 66 crossed the middle of New Mexico from Texas on the east through Albuquerque to Arizona on the west [location somewhat similar to current I-40]. At Santa Rosa (NM) the original Route 66

	turned north to Las Vegas (NM), then northwest to Santa Fe, and then southwest to Albuquerque. This latter section was near the Las Huertas area and helped introduce outside influences to the remote mountain community.
1937	**The New Mexico Highway Commission required a Right of Way Easement to the Sandia Forest Project through Placitas**, splitting the properties of many owners, including the Presbyterian Church. The easement provided easier access to and from Placitas and was **later widened and paved as NM State Hwy 44**.
1938	**The first three telephones arrived in Placitas** with the first being at Frank Pierce's Placitas Trading Post, which was located in the village within the extensive house built by Juan Armijo in 1860. [While the telephone had been invented in 1876 and phone calls could be placed from the east coast to the west coast by 1915, telephone lines came to rural areas much slower.]
1939-1945	**World War II occurred, with the U.S. entering the war after the attack on Pearl Harbor on December 7, 1941**. **Several young men from Placitas served in WWII**, with one surviving the Bataan Death march and a Tokyo POW camp and three losing their lives. Service in other parts of the country and the world led to many Placitas residents seeking to live and work elsewhere after the war's end.
1940	**Three Anglo families resided in Placitas**.
Early 1950s	**Electricity gradually was brought to Placitas**. [The Rural Electrification Act had been passed by Congress in 1935, but it took time to get electrical lines erected in remote areas such as Placitas.]
1951	**Ten Anglo families resided in Placitas.**
In 1960s-70s	**Outside squatters arrived--leading to hippie communes sprouting** in the foothills around the Placitas area.
ca. 1973	**The Volunteer Fire Brigade was established, which led to the requirement of naming streets,**

	erecting street signs, and assigning house numbers in Placitas.
In 1970s	**Subdivisions began to be registered with Sandoval County** for development, thus starting an influx of gringo settlers.
1985	**Eastern half of NM State Hwy 44 was renamed as current NM State Hwy 165.**
2010	**Per U.S. Census data, 5,000 people were reported in Placitas, with 75% self-declared as white and just under 21% as Hispanic.**
Present Day	**Descendants of and heirs to the 1768 grantees are still members of the surviving San Antonio de Las Huertas Land Grant association.** There are **still members of the original spring-fed acequia system** established in the late 1830s and early 1840s to supply irrigation and domestic water to the Placitas village area, and these members are required to participate in the annual spring maintenance in order to continue to receive water.

Compiled by Sherrill Cloud
Contributing Editor

TIMELINE HISTORY
Las Placitas Presbyterian Church
(Originally organized as The Presbyterian Church at Las Placitas)

The Seeds of Presbyterianism in Las Placitas

1882	**Rev. José Ynés Perea, the nation's first ordained Hispanic Presbyterian minister, was invited by José L. A. Gurulé to meet with six Las Placitas villagers**, which led to frequent invitations for Presbyterian ministers to visit Las Placitas through the 1880s and 1890s.
1882-83	**A petition was submitted for a Presbyterian school teacher** by several Las Placitas villagers to The Board of Home Missions of the Presbyterian Church USA (PCUSA).
1882-1894	**Rev. José Ynés Perea** was the first Presbyterian pastor in Las Placitas.
1882-1901	**Rev. John Menaul** was the second Presbyterian pastor in Las Placitas.
1890-94	Epifanio Arreola preached regularly in Las Placitas as a Presbyterian evangelist.
1893	**A Presbyterian school teacher, Lavinia Thompson, was approved by PCUSA for Las Placitas** and brought by José L. A. Gurulé from the mission school in Peña Blanca where she had been working. She immediately began teaching in a small adobe building in Placitas.

Century of Faith: 1894-1994

1894	**The Presbyterian Church at Las Placitas** was organized by a vote of 95 Las Placitas adults at a meeting on February 25. Church services would be conducted in the adobe building used for the Mission school (after the central partition was removed from the building to make one large room). **The San Antonio de Las Huertas Land Grant Cemetery was established** soon thereafter.

1900	**The Presbyterian Mission School closed** after operating seven years.
1903-06	**Rev. Henry C. Thomson** served as Presbyterian pastor in Las Placitas.
1906-1914	**Rev. Juan Baros** served as Presbyterian pastor in Las Placitas, before and after other assignments, until his untimely death at age 44 from tuberculosis.
1909-11	**Rev. Juan Quintana** served as Presbyterian pastor in Las Placitas, in addition to having served one year in 1904.
1911-17	Joseph W. Winder, John D. Henry, and M.B.S. Legare served Las Placitas as Presbyterian Sunday School missionaries.
1913	**The one-room adobe building used for Church services was remodeled** by raising the walls three feet, adding an American-style sloped roof, enlarging the windows, and adding a bell tower—using the bell purchased in 1894 from the San Felipe Pueblo.
1913-17	**Rev. John Mordy** served as Presbyterian pastor in Las Placitas.
1914-18	**World War I occurred, with the U.S. declaring war on Germany on December 7, 1917.**
1917-22	**Rev. Victoriano Valdez** served as Presbyterian pastor in Las Placitas.
By 1920s	**Including "Las" before Placitas began to disappear from common usage.**
1920s	**The Sandia Conference Grounds** began to be used by Church members for various activities, such as a special Church service, a baptism, or a picnic.
1922-23	**Rev. Juan Quintana** again served as Presbyterian pastor in Placitas.
1922-27	**Rev. Acorcinio Lucero** served as Presbyterian pastor in Placitas.
1927-29	**Rev. Paul Livingstone Warnshuis** served as Presbyterian pastor in Placitas.
1929-1935	**Rev. George P. Simmonds** served as Presbyterian pastor in Placitas. From 1932-1935, Porfirio Romero

	served as a Presbyterian student pastor under Rev. Simmonds. Victor Manuel Sandoval served as a pastor's assistant to Rev. Simmonds and had full charge of the Church from 1936-37, the year after Rev. Simmonds left.
1930-32	**A new Church building was erected by Church members**, after they tore down the one-room adobe building where services had been held for 36 years.
1930s-1942	**Collection of folk tales and oral histories about Placitas and the Las Huertas area began with Lou Sage Batchen** (as part of the WPA Federal Writers Project) when she hired Max Delara and Christine Baros to compile and translate information provided by local residents.
1937-1952	**Rev. José Inéz Candelaria** served as Presbyterian pastor at Placitas.
By 1938	A fairly decent but unpaved road had been constructed by the WPA and enabled better access to and from Placitas village.
1939-45	**World War II occurred, with the U.S. entering the war after the attack on Pearl Harbor on December 7, 1941. Several young Placitas men, including Church members, served in the war. Christine Baros worked as a riveter** in San Antonio, TX.
April 2, 1943	**Tolling of the Church's bells signified the passing of José L. A. Gurulé**, the driving force behind bringing Presbyterianism to Placitas.
1945	**The Church building got its first plumbing** when members installed a water line to the Church basement.
1949	**The Church building acquired an oil heater** to replace the old wood stove.
1950-51	**Rev. Antonio Jiménez** was a Methodist evangelist who served the Presbyterian Church at Placitas for a year.
1951-55	**Rev. Kenneth J. Green** served as Presbyterian pastor at Placitas.
1953-54	In August 1953, **the Church building saw the installation of an electric motor to power new**

electric lights, which were finally installed in July 1954 to replace the gasoline lamps used until this point.

1955-57 **Rev. Rodolfo Torres** served as Presbyterian pastor at Placitas.

1958-1966 **Rev. Harry Willson** served as Presbyterian pastor at Placitas.

Jan. 1, 1963 **The Placitas and Alameda Presbyterian Churches became self-sustaining and were no longer dependent on financial aid from PCUSA**. Due to limited income, these two churches, which shared pastors, had been yoked in a shared financial relationship for about two decades, but that would cease in a few years.

1967-1970 **Rev. David Hammack** served as Presbyterian pastor at Placitas.

1972-1980 **Rev. George Adams** served as Presbyterian pastor at Placitas.

1980-1995 **Rev. James R. Anderson** served as Presbyterian pastor at Placitas.

July 1981 **The Church congregation voted to switch to natural gas** to save on fuel costs.

Nov. 17, 1981 **The passing of Barbarita Baros Luceros** signified the loss of the last surviving person who attended the Church's organizational meeting in 1894.

Sept. 30, 1984 **A large extension to the 1932 Church building was dedicated.** This added 5800 square feet to the 1932 Church's 2100 square feet and provided a new and larger sanctuary, a fellowship hall, a dedicated kitchen, and (for the first time) inside restrooms. **A large sign was erected outside the Church that proclaimed the name of Las Placitas Presbyterian Church (LPPC)**—a rearrangement of words in the original founding name and a return to the use of the area's historic name.

1984 **An old family organ was given** by the Proetts. **A new Yamaha upright piano was given** by Sally Curro in honor of her mother. By the late 1980s, Sally Curro's family replaced this upright piano

	with the **gift of a new Yamaha six-foot grand piano,** which has been used extensively since then in Church services and music concerts.
1985-present	**The newly-constructed Fellowship Hall provided meeting space for local groups** (such as Jardineros de Placitas and home owners associations).
1985-present	**Art exhibits began to be hung in the Fellowship Hall** after a group of artists in the Church began organizing these exhibits, which continue to present day.
1986-present	**The Placitas Artists Series was begun** in the new Sanctuary when the Church's Music Committee organized two benefit concerts for an injured child and found that **the acoustics of the new Sanctuary were ideal for music concerts**. The Placitas Artists Series eventually became an independent tax-exempt organization that has continued to hold its concerts at LPPC.
Aug. 1989	**Mothers' Day Out began** as a one-day-a week play group (later expanded to two and then three days a week) for young children and their moms in the basement of the 1932 Church. A playground was built outside the basement door.
Early 1990s	**Restoration of the Sandia Conference Grounds** was led by Rev. Anderson to update the camping facilities and build a modern kitchen building.

Afterword: 1995-2016

1995-96	**Rev. Art Opmeer** and **Rev. Kathi Hunter** served as successive Presbyterian "Interim" pastors at Placitas.
1996	**Rev. Jane P. Harmes** became the first installed female Presbyterian pastor at Placitas.
Late 1990s	**A new organ** was acquired by the Church.
Sept. 26, 1999	**Dedication of a Memorial Garden, including a columbarium**, which had been envisioned by Charles and Ila Little and designed by Bill Hayes and Judith Philips. Around this same time, **a**

	parking lot with handicapped access was added on the west side of the Church.
2003-present	**Rev. Ken Cuthbertson** has served as "Temporary Supply" Presbyterian pastor at Placitas in 2004 and 2007 and as "Parish Associate" from 2005 to present.
May 15, 2005	**A new expansion that added 4000 square feet to the Church was dedicated**, bringing the Church building's total size to 11,900 square feet. The expansion included an extended Fellowship Hall, a larger and code-compliant kitchen, new classroom, library, and childcare spaces, Church offices, and code compliant and accessible restrooms.
2005-present	**Mother's Day Out became a cooperative nursery school and day care center** serving families five-days-a-week throughout the year in dedicated space made possible by the 2005 expansion to the Church.
2008-2010	**Rev. Elizabeth Lyman** served as "Transitional" Presbyterian pastor at Placitas.
2008	**Casa Rosa Food Pantry was established** as an outreach mission of LPPC in a nearby house (owned by Max DeLara before being purchased by LPPC). The Pantry serves clients every Saturday morning in a grocery-store setting.
2010	**Rev. Stephen Miller** served as "Temporary Supply" Presbyterian pastor at Placitas.
2010-present	**Rev. Drew Henry** has served as Presbyterian pastor at Placitas.
2013-present	**Rev. Karl Gustafson** has served as a Presbyterian "Parish Associate" at Placitas.
2013	**A mortgage-burning ceremony was held** on Pentecost Sunday to reflect that LPPC no longer had financial debt.

Compiled by Sherrill Cloud
Contributing Editor

Abbreviations Used

CSWR	Center for Southwest Research, University of New Mexico.
HMM	HOME MISSION MONTHLY, Journal of the Board of Home Missions, Presbyterian Church USA.
LPPC	Las Placitas Presbyterian Church. [While the Church was established in 1894 with the title The Presbyterian Church at Las Placitas, the Church was generally referred to over the decades after WWI as the Placitas Presbyterian Church. With the large addition to the Church in 1984, an outside sign was erected proclaiming the name of Las Placitas Presbyterian Church, which thereafter became the official title.]
MHL	Menaul Historical Library, Menaul School, Albuquerque.
MNMHL	Museum of New Mexico History Library, Santa Fe.
NMSRCA	New Mexico State Records Center and Archives, Santa Fe.
PCUSA	Presbyterian Church USA
PLC	Records of U.S. Court of Private Land Claims.
SADLHLG	San Antonio de Las Huertas Land Grant
SG	Records of Surveyor-General of New Mexico

Endnotes

PROLOGUE

1. Unsigned and undated history of Las Placitas Church, probably compiled by Reverend George Simmonds from oral interview with José Gurulé, Placitas file, MHL; history of Las Placitas Church compiled from interview with José Gurulé by the Reverend José I. Candelaria, Placitas file, MHL. Alice Blake, History of Presbyterian Missions in Colorado and New Mexico 1837-1915, "The Las Vegas Field," 1936, MHL.

CHAPTER I

1. Frank C. Hibben, "Discoveries in Sandia Cave and Early Horizons in the Southwest," PROCEEDINGS OF THE AMERICAN PHILOSOPHICAL SOCIETY, 86: 247-254.
2. Fray Angelico Chavez, ORIGINS OF NEW MEXICO FAMILIES IN THE SPANISH COLONIAL PERIOD (Santa Fe, NM: William Gannon Publisher, 1975), pp. 107-08. Dan Scurlock, "Historic Irrigation Farming in the Las Huertas Valley, Sandoval County," THE SIGNPOST, June, 1994. There are remains of a pre-1680 house site, known as the Casa Acequia and listed in the National Register, on the north side of Las Huertas creek west of the ruins of the old San José de Las Huertas village. They consist of an eight-room, masonry-mud *estancia* (ranch) and relatively extensive ditch and field system. There is no way of knowing whether this was the Trujillo ranch, or whether his *estancia* was located further up the valley in the vicinity of the Montezuma Mine.
3. Chavez, ORIGINS, p. 296
4. Mark Simmons, NEW MEXICO (Albuquerque: University of New Mexico Press, 1988), p. 77.
5. The San Antonio de las Huertas Grant is indexed in: Albert James Diaz, A GUIDE TO THE MICROFILM OF PAPERS RELATING TO NEW MEXICO LAND GRANTS, (Albuquerque: University of New Mexico Press, 1960); documents relating to it are in Records of the Surveyor General Reel 26, File 88, and Court of Private Land Claims File 43, Case 90, New Mexico State Records Center and Archives, Santa Fe (hereinafter NMSRCA); and in the Thomas Benton Catron Papers, 1898-1901, Box 43, No. 269; Box 18, No. 90, Center for Southwest Research, Zimmerman Library, University of New Mexico, Albuquerque (hereinafter CSWR).
6. Lou Sage Batchen, "Out of Bondage," 7 May, 1941, unpublished manuscript in the New Mexico Federal Writer's Project Files, NMSRCA; J.J. Brody, and Anne Colberg, "A Spanish-American Homestead Near Placitas, New Mexico," EL PALACIO, 73(Summer, 1966): 11-20; Alan Ferg, "Historic Archaeology on the San Antonio de las Huertas Grant, Sandoval County, New Mexico" in Volume 2, Historic Resources, TESTING AND EXCAVATION REPORT, MAPCO's ROCKY MOUNTAIN LIQUID HYDROCARBONS PIPELINE, Woodward-Clyde Consultants, San Francisco, California, 1982.
7. Batchen, "Las Huertas," 8 October, 1938, NMSRCA.

8. One cannot be sure of the translation, but it was so recorded by Batchen, "Las Huertas," 8 October, 1938, NMSCRA.
9. Batchen, "Placitas,"13 August, 1938, "Las Huertas," 8 October 1938; "Tales of the Towns Settled by the Las Huertasans: Ojo de la Casa", 12 November, 1938; "Tales of the Towns Settled by the Las Huertasans: Ojo de la Casa (concluded)," 26 November, 1938; "Tales of the Towns Settled by the Las Huertasans: La Madera," 17 December, 1938; "Tales from the Towns Settled by the Las Huertasans: La Madera, Part II," 6 January, 1939; "Tales of the Towns Settled by the Las Huertasans: Tejón," 20 January, 1939, NMSRCA, MNMHL.

CHAPTER II

1. Andrew T. Smith, "The People of the San Antonio de Las Huertas Grant, New Mexico, 1767-1900" Colorado College, © Andrew T. Smith, 1973, p.10.
2. Suzanne Forrest, THE PRESERVATION OF THE VILLAGE: NEW MEXICO'S HISPANICS AND THE NEW DEAL (Albuquerque, University of New Mexico Press, 1989), p.123.
3. Max DeLara, taped interview, 23 January 1994.
4. Lou Sage Batchen, 14 Letters of Lou Sage Batchen, 1938-1942, WPA Federal Writers Project Collection, NMSRCA.
5. This biography of José Ynés Perea has been gathered from a number of sources, all of them found in the files of the Menaul Historical Library. The single most important is an unpublished manuscript by Mark Banker, "Missionary to his Own People: José Ynés Perea and Hispanic Presbyterians in New Mexico." Other sources are an unpublished account of the founding of the Las Placitas Presbyterian Church as told to Alice Blake in 1936 by José L.A. Gurulé and recorded in "History of Presbyterian Missions in Colorado and New Mexico;" a "Memorial Sketch of the Reverend José Ynés Perea—1837-1910" that appeared in LA AURORA, Vol. 11, Number 22, 15 November 1910, published in Las Vegas, New Mexico; and an account by Perea's grandniece, Elizabeth Valdez Romero, recorded by Jane Atkins Grainger, editor, in EL CENTENARIO DE LA PALABRA, copyright Menaul Historical Library of the Southwest, 1980, p.l0.
6. Batchen, "The Story of an Indian Raid," 29 January, 1941, NMSRCA.
7. The concept of *verguenza*, so important to Hispanic culture, goes far beyond the literal translation of the word, "shame." It is described and discussed in detail by Facundo Valdez, "Verguenza," in Paul Kutsche, ed., THE SURVIVAL OF THE SPANISH AMERICAN VILLAGES, (Colorado Springs, Colo.: Colorado College 1979), pp. 99-106.
8. Blake, "Presbyterian Missions," 47, MHL
9. Batchen, "The Fury of 1869," 4 June, 1941, "Antonia and Her Saints," 13 March 1942, NMSRCA. Batchen relates two versions of this story that are essentially the same, but in one the aunt is named "Petra" and in the other "Juana."
10. Batchen, "Dos Hombres Sabios de Las Placitas," 30 June, 1941, NMSRCA, MNMHL.

11. David J. Weber, THE MEXICAN FRONTIER, 1821-1846: THE AMERICAN SOUTHWEST UNDER MEXICO (Albuquerque: University of New Mexico Press, 1982), pp. 69-81; Howard R. Lamar, THE FAR SOUTHWEST. 1846-1912: A TERRITORIAL HISTORY (New York: Norton, 1970), pp. 18-19.
12. Batchen, "An Old Native Custom: The Cruel Moon," 9 April, 1941, NMSRCA, MNMHL.
13. Batchen, "The Story of an Indian Raid," 29 January 1941, MNMHL.
14. Batchen, "Life in the Old Houses (Part IV)," 30 May 1939, NMSRCA, MNMHL, Smith, "The People of the San Antonio de las Huertas Grant", 116-117.
15. Gerald McKevitt, S.J. "Italian Jesuits in New Mexico: A Report by Donato M. Gasparri, 1867-1869," NEW MEXICO HISTORICAL REVIEW, 67(1992):357-392. The Jesuits did eventually establish a college in Las Vegas in 1877 (see footnote 17). For a time the Jesuits also administered and staffed public schools in the Territory of New Mexico, a controversial action that, according to Dianna Everett, "The Public School Debate in New Mexico, 1850-1891," ARIZONA AND THE WEST 26 (Summer 1984), 134, "left behind legacy of bitterness that seriously retarded the growth of the public school system in New Mexico for many years."
16. Batchen, "Easter Tide," 18 June 1941, "Life in the Old Houses (Part IV)," 5 May, 1939, "The Story of an Indian Raid," 29 January 1941, MNMHL.
17. Gabino Rendón, HAND ON MY SHOULDER (New York: Board of National Missions, United Presbyterian Church (U.S.A.), copyright Edith Agnew, 1953) pp. 31-34, 77. Gabino Rendón, one of New Mexico's most influential early Hispanic Presbyterian ministers, seems to have had an equally inspiring brush with Father Gasparri. Rendón heard Gasparri preach in Las Vegas and considered him to be the most eloquent speaker he had ever heard. In 1877 the Jesuits opened a school in Las Vegas to counteract the "heretical influence" of Presbyterian missionary John Annin. Rendón's father took his son out of Annin's school and, in return for the promise of tuition, gave the priests a plot of land from the family land grant for their "college." This school later moved to Denver where it exists today as Regis University. Rendón considered Father Gasparri to be an excellent teacher. Despite this concentrated dose of Catholic teaching and theology, Rendón became a Protestant, and in 1893 he and his friend Manuel Madrid graduated from the ministerial training school at Del Norte, Colorado.

CHAPTER III

1. David J. Weber, ed., "All the Rights of Citizens," editor's introduction, FOREIGNERS IN THEIR NATIVE LAND (Albuquerque: University of New Mexico Press, 1982) pp. 190-191.
2. It appears that we may never know the original boundaries of the San Antonio de Las Huertas Grant. When Governor Fermin de Mendinueta made the grant on December 31, 1767, he promised to extend the eastern boundary beyond that requested from his predecessor, Governor Velez de Cachupin in 1765, because of the greater number of settlers and their probable increase, and because extending it to the north, south, and west would infringe on the lands of the San Felipe and Santa Ana Indians and the

3. Town of Bernalillo. The revised eastern boundary was set forth in the Act of Possession, which was delivered to the Las Huertas grantees on January 13, 1768. Unfortunately, the only known copy of this document is torn and illegible at every mention of the eastern boundary. Just when and how the document came to be so mutilated is an historical mystery that may never be solved.
4. Records of the Surveyor-General of New Mexico, San Pedro Grant No. 14; Miscellaneous Land Grant Records, Las Huertas Grant, M.A. Lovato vs J.S. Ramirez et al, 24 Feb., 1847; Santa Fe County District Court, Civil Case No.8, 1847, NMSRCA.
5. Since the actual grant documents were missing for both the San Pedro and Tejón Grants, Pelham approved them on no more evidence than Ramirez's sworn testimony that both had existed prior to American occupation. SG, 14, San Pedro Grant; NMSRCA. Victor Westphall, MERCEDES REALES: HISPANIC LAND GRANTS OF THE UPPER RIO GRANDE REGION (Albuquerque: University of New Mexico Press, 1983), pp. 81-83.
6. SG 14, San Pedro Grant; SG 16, Tejón Grant; District Court, Bernalillo County Civil Case No. 538, José Manuel Gallegos vs Maria Antonia Sandoval, administratrix of estate of José Serafin Ramirez, NMSRCA. Westphall, MERCEDES, pp. 93-95.
7. Batchen, "El Bandolero de Ojo de la Casa," 5 April, 1940; "The Terror of Ojo de la Casa," 15 March, 1940; "An Old Native Custom: El Indio Viejo," 19 May, 1940; "Out of Bondage," 7 May, 1941; "Legend of the Montezuma Mine," 26 November 1938; "Gold Fever in Ojo de la Casa," 26 November 1938; "The Year It Rained Tortillas," 13 February, 1942; "Life in the Old Houses, Part I: Josefa and Her Son," 24 February, 1939; "Life in the Old Houses, Part II: Life in the House that Juan Built," 17 March, 1939; "Life in the Old Houses, Part IV," 5 May 1939; "Life in the Old Houses, Part VII: Gabrielita and Placida," 30 June 1939, NMSRCA, MNMHL.
8. SG Reel 26, Las Huertas Grant, NMSRCA. Stories of the Placitas gold rush are in N. Howard Thorp, "San Antonio de Las Huertas Grant," 11 December, 1938, WPA Land Grant File 81, NMSRCA; and in Henry F. Hoyt, A FRONTIER DOCTOR (Boston and New York: Houghton Mifflin, 1929).
9. SG 26, Las Huertas Grant, NMSRCA.
10. SG 26, Las Huertas Grant, NMSRCA.
11. Batchen, "Placitas," 13 August, 1938, MNMHL.
12. Batchen, "Placitas," 13 August, 1938, MNMHL.
13. SG 16, Town of Tejón Grant, NMSRCA; Thomas Benton Catron Papers, File 305, Box 3, CSWR.
14. SG 26, Las Huertas Grant, NMSRCA.
15. Court of Private Land Claims, File 43, Case 90, Las Huertas Grant, NMSRCA; Catron Papers, File 301, Box 18, No. 90, Box 43, No. 269, CSWR. Westphall, MERCEDES, pp. 234, 249, 254-58.

CHAPTER IV

1. HMM, Vol. V, 1890-91: 9; Vol. VI, 1891-92: 84; Vol. VII, 1892-93: 12.
2. "History of the Las Placitas Presbyterian Church," MHL

3. R. Douglas Brackinridge and Francisco O. Garcia-Treto, IGLESIA PRESBITERIANA: A HISTORY OF PRESBYTERIANS AND MEXICAN-AMERICANS IN THE SOUTHWEST, 2nd ed. (San Antonio: Trinity University Press, 1987), pp. 46-47.
4. Brackinridge and Garcia-Treto, pp. 32-62; HOME MISSION MONTHLY, Vol. VII, 1892-93: 12.
5. Florinda DeLara, daughter of José Gurulé, interview, 26 July, 1992; Max DeLara, grandson of José Gurulé, taped interview, 23 January, 1994.
6. Reverend Tomás Gonzalez, taped interview, September, 1992.
7. Mark T. Banker, PRESBYTERIAN MISSIONS AND CULTURAL INTERACTION IN THE FAR SOUTHWEST, 1850-1950 (Chicago: University of Illinois Press, 1993), pp.88-90.
8. HMM, Vol VII (1892-1893): 8; Banker, PRESBYTERIAN MISSIONS, 31, 113.
9. Edith Agnew and Ruth Barber, "The Unique Presbyterian School System of New Mexico," JOURNAL OF PRESBYTERIAN HISTORY, 49 (Fall, 1970): 206-207.
10. HMM, Vol VII (1892-1893): 13; "Brief History of Presbyterian Church at Placitas," notation on back of photograph of first Placitas church in Placitas File, MHL; Florinda DeLara interview.
11. HMM, Vol.X (1895-1896): 17.
12. Alice Blake, "History of Presbyterian Missions in Colorado and New Mexico." 1936, p.48
13. HMM Vol. XIII (1898-1899): 15.

CHAPTER V

1. PLC, Case 90, file 93, Reel no. 43, CSWR.
2. Batchen, "Folklore," 17 September 1938, MNMHL.
3. Batchen, "Life in the Old Houses (Part I): The Story of Josefa and her Sons," 24 February 1939, NMSRCA, MNMHL.
4. Batchen, "Dos Hombres Sabios de Las Placitas," 30 September 1941, NMSRCA, MNMHL.
5. Batchen, "Life in the Old Houses (Part II): Life in the House that Juan Built," 17 March 1939, "Life in the Old Houses (Part IV): Story of Francisco Gonzales," 5 May 1939, NMSRCA, MNMHL.
6. Batchen, "The House that Juan Built."
7. Batchen, "Tales of the Towns Settled by the Las Huertasans: La Madera," 17 December 1938, NMSRCA.
8. Batchen, "Life in the Old Houses (Part VII), Gabrielita and Placida," 30 June 1939, NMSRCA, MNMHL.
9. Batchen, "Clotilde and Francisca (The Story of an Indian Raid)," 29 January 1941, MNMHL.
10. Batchen, "Juan of Tecolote (Part II)," 23 October 1940, MNMHL.

CHAPTER VI

1. Juan Baros file, MHL
2. THE BULLETIN, January, 1940, MHL; Minutes of the Session, Las Placitas Presbyterian Church; Recollections of Juan Baros by his daughter, Christina Gonzales, Juan Baros File, MHL

3. Minutes of the Session, LPPC.
4. Lauretta Dickey, ed., "Missionaries and School Teachers," PRESBYTERIAN CHURCH HISTORY, unpublished manuscript.
5. Brackenridge and Garcia-Treto, IGLESIA PRESBITERIANA, p. 48.
6. Batchen, "Placitas," 13 August, 1938, MNMHL.
7. Special thanks go to: Bert DeLara, who taped an interview with his mother, Florinda DeLara; to Willie Escarcida, who taped an interview with his aunt, Celia Longacre; and to Willie Escarcida and Amarante Lucero, who taped a conversation between themselves. Thanks also to those who shared their memories of early days in the Las Placitas Church and in the village in taped interviews with Suzanne Forrest: Rubén Cobos, Dulcilina Salce Curtis, Max DeLara, Willie Escarcida, Tomás Gonzalez, Tony Lucero, Norma Martinez, Reynaldo Salazar, Sam and Siria Salazar, Helen Sanchez, and David Tafoya.

CHAPTER VII

J.I. Candelaria, Sr., "History of the Placitas United Presbyterian Church"; 29 Sept., 1974, Placitas File, MHL.

1. Reynaldo Salazar, taped interview, 18 August, 1993.
2. Willie Escarcida and Amarante Lucero, taped conversation, 28 November, 1992.
3. Minutes of the Session, LPPC.
4. Christine Gonzales, "A Brief History," 30 Sept., 1984. Placitas File, MHL; Oral interview with George P. Simmonds made by Carolyn Atkins, 31 Dec., 1979, MHL.
5. Ruth K. Barber, "Mission Schools and Evangelism in the Spanish Speaking Field," File 85-12-A, MHL; Christina Gonzales, "Brief History."
6. Max DeLara, taped interview, 23 Jan., 1994
7. Reynaldo Salazar, Max DeLara, interviews.
8. Batchen, "Placitas."
9. J.I. Candelaria, "The Placitas Field," 1951, Placitas File; George Simmonds, Oral History; Minutes of the Meeting of the Council on Spanish-American Work, 13 Dec., 1952, Paul L. Warnshuis Report; Fiftieth Meeting, Dept. of Music and Worship, Council on Spanish-American Work, 13-15 Feb. 1962, Santa Fe, NM, File 85-12-D, MHL
10. Carlos Candelaria, taped interview, 22 July, 1993; J.I. Candelaria, "The Albuquerque and Placitas Fields", 1951, Placitas File, MHL.
11. Willie Escarcida, oral communication.
12. J.I. Candelaria, "Placitas Field," Carlos Candelaria, Matilda Tapia, oral communication, J.I. Candelaria "History of the Placitas United Presbyterian Church."
13. Minutes of the LPPC

CHAPTER VIII

1. Bill F. Gurulé, FLEETING SHADOWS AND FAINT ECHOES OF LAS HUERTAS, (New York: Carlton Press, 1987).
2. J.I. Candelaria, "The Albuquerque and Placitas Fields."
3. Minutes of the Session, LPPC.

4. Candelaria, "Albuquerque and Placitas."
5. Minutes of the Session, LPPC; Candelaria, "Albuquerque and Placitas."
6. Paul L. Warnshuis, Board of National Missions, Spanish speaking work in the Southwest, to Dear Fellow Worker, 25 Sept., 1947; "Memoirs of Mission in New Mexico," 1963, Warnshuis File, MHL.
7. Antonio Jiménez II, letter to Jim Anderson, Pastor, LPPC, 4 April 1994, and oral interview with Suzanne Forrest, 25 May, 1994; Minutes of Session.
8. Paul L. Warnshuis, "Memoirs of Mission in New Mexico."
9. Florinda DeLara, taped interview, 26 July, 1992.
10. Minutes of Session, LPPC.
11. Report on the Sixtieth Anniversary Service, Placitas Presbyterian Church, 7 February, 1954, Placitas File, MHL.
12. Florinda Delara tape.
13. Samuel Torres, son of Rodolfo Torres, interview, 31 May, 1994; historical notes written by Christina Gonzales, Placitas File, MHL; Minutes of the Session, LPPC.
14. Story of Two Churches," PRESBYTERIAN LIFE, 15 (Dec., 1962): 22-23, 41-42.
15. Harry Willson, taped interview, 17 March, 1993.
16. Willie Escarcida and Amarante Lucero; George Randle, interview, 12 October, 1992; Madeline Randle oral communication.
17. Willson tape, Escarcida and Lucero tape.
18. Willson tape, Minutes of Session of LPPC.
19. Minutes of Session, LPPC.

CHAPTER IX

1. John L. Sinclair, "Upstairs Albuquerque," NEW MEXICO MAGAZINE (March, 1967): 6-9
2. Dede Feldman, "Growth Perils Placitas, IMPACT, ALBUQUERQUE JOURNAL MAGAZINE (12 MAY, 1981); L.M. Crosse, "Tuapa, Farewell," THE SIGNPOST (May, 1993); Jack Weber, "Placitas Community, They Try to Practice Christianity," ALBUQUERQUE, Vol. VIII , 14 (4 Sept., 1969); Berry Hickman, "More Placitas Past-Another View," THE SIGNPOST (July, 1990); Laurie Macrae, interview (1 June, 1994); Lynn Montgomery, oral communication, 2 November, 1994.
3. Crosse, "Tuapa Farewell."
4. Feldman, "Growth Perils Placitas"; Bruce Campbell, "Historic Placitas Beset by Changes, Growth," ALBUQUERQUE JOURNAL (22July, 1973); Kay Matthews, "Heralding Spring with a Shovel," THE CHRISTIAN SCIENCE MONITOR, 12(March, 1992).
5. Minutes of the Session, LPPC; Feldman, "Growth Perils Placitas."
6. Vivian DeLara, "The tradition of Las Posadas de Placitas," The SIGNPOST (December, 1993).
7. Ibid.; Tony Lucero, taped interview, 5 June, 1992.
8. When not otherwise indicated, information for this chapter was gathered from interviews with George Adams, Jeanne Army, David Hammack, Laurie McCrae, George Randle, and Ruthie (Mrs. Howard) Schleeter, and from the Minutes of the Session of the LPPC.

CHAPTER X

1. Jim Anderson, taped interview, 25 June, 1993.
2. Anderson tape.
3. Minutes of the Session, LPPC.
4. Kendall and Wilda Schlenker, taped interview, 28 August, 1993; Minutes of the Session, LPPC.
5. Anderson tape, Minutes of Session, LPPC.
6. Minutes of Session, LPPC.
7. Schlenker tape.
8. Schlenker tape; Jeanne Army, taped interview, 8 March, 1993; Schleeter tape.
9. Schlenker tape; Minutes of the Session, LPPC.
10. Victoria Klemz, "Placitas Church Dedication—-A Day of Joy and Gratitude," SANDOVAL COUNTY SENTINEL (5 Oct., 1984); Minutes of the Session, LPPC.
11. Minutes of the Session, LPPC.
12. Sally Curro, "Memories of Music," Summer, 1992 and interview, 11 November, 1994.

CHAPTER XI

1. *See* endnote 5, Chapter II
2. Mark T. Banker, "Presbyterian Missionary Activity in the Southwest: The careers of John and James Menaul," JOURNAL OF THE WEST, vol. 23, (Jan. 1984): 55.
3. From the Epifanio Arreola file, MHL
4. From the Juan Baros file, MHL. Most of this information was supplied by his daughter, the much loved Christina Gonzales who was a pillar of the Las Placitas Presbyterian Church.
5. From the Henry S. Thomson file, MH
6. From THE BULLETIN, January, 1940, MHL, and from information compiled by the Second Presbyterian Church of Albuquerque.
7. Lauretta Dickey, ed., "Missionaries and Schoolteachers," BOOK OF PRESBYTERIAN HISTORY, 1984; Minutes of the Session, LPPC.
8. Lauretta Dickey, PRESBYTERIAN HISTORY; Minutes of the Session, LPPC.
9. THE BULLETIN (October 1937), p.4, MHL, and information provided by Rubén Valdez, Jr., his grandson, for The Second Presbyterian Church of Albuquerque
10. Information compiled by Second Church for its Centennial from interviews with Reverend Robert Lucero (son) and Mrs. Amalia Cruz (sister).
11. Paul Warnshuis file, MHL.
12. George Simmonds File, MHL; and notes compiled by Second Church.
13. THE BULLETIN, July and August, 1938, p.8, MHL.
14. Taped interview with Porfirio Romero and Elizabeth Romero at Ranchos de Taos by Jane Atkins Grainger, 15 Sept., 1974.
15. J.I. Candelaria File, MHL; Matilda Tapia and Rebecca Martinez, sisters, oral communication, Dec. 27, 1994.
16. Antonio Jiménez II, interview by Suzanne Forrest, 25 May, 1994.
17. Kenneth Green, letter to Suzanne Forrest, January, 1994.

18. Samuel Torres, interview by Suzanne Forrest, 31 May 1994.
19. Harry Willson, taped interview, 17 March, 1993.
20. David Hammack, interview, January, 1994.
21. Floyd Sovereign letter to Suzanne Forrest, January, 1994.
22. George Adams, interview, January 22, 1994.
23. Tomás Gonzales, taped interview, August 15, 1992.
24. Jim Anderson, taped interview, 25 June, 1993.

Subject Index

E

F

G

H

J

L

S

T

V

W

Made in the USA
Columbia, SC
15 February 2019